Praise for *Cause for Change*

"*Cause for Change* is well researched and clearly and colorfully w[ritten.] Derrick Feldmann provide a point-by-point action plan for nonprofits (and commercial businesses) to utilize the numbers, energy, dedication, and idealism of Millennials—America's next great generation—to change the nation and the world for the better in the decades ahead."

> —**Morley Winograd and Michael D. Hais,** authors, *Millennial Makeover: MySpace, You Tube, and the Future of American Politics* and *Millennial Momentum: How a New Generation Is Remaking America*

"*Cause for Change* is a timely and compelling book that offers a critical guide for anyone working in philanthropy today. As organizations grapple with how to engage the rising generation of Millennials, Saratovsky and Feldmann offer executive leaders a straightforward approach and a road map to success in the twenty-first century."

> —**Dottie Johnson,** president emeritus, Council of Michigan Foundations; trustee, W. K. Kellogg Foundation

"Millennials are at the nerve center of a growing movement of people who are passionate about their ability to make a positive impact on the world. Harnessing their talent, passion, and unique power is not just *a* priority for those in the social change business—it is *the* priority. Saratovsky and Feldmann have created an indispensable guide for leaders across all sectors who not only recognize but are ready to unleash the potential of a generation that is poised to change our communities and our world in the twenty-first century."

> —**Lynn Schusterman,** chair of the Charles and Lynn Schusterman Philanthropic Network

"The generational divide within organizations and between nonprofits and their communities is the biggest threat to the future success of most organizations. *Cause for Change* is a gem of a resource for leaders of organizations struggling to bridge the gap between older leadership and Millennials who think and operate in very different ways. Pick this book up, don't put it down, and put it into action!"

> —**Allison Fine,** coauthor, *The Networked Nonprofit*

"Saratovsky and Feldmann present a people-oriented approach to adapting organizations toward the needs and engagement of Millennials. Building on the model of relationship-based fundraising that successful development officers and nonprofit leaders have used for years, *Cause for Change* reveals ways to engage Millennials and maximize their unique circles of influence to make a meaningful difference in the world."

> —**Eugene R. Tempel,** founding dean, IU School of Philanthropy

"The Millennial generation is inheriting an extraordinary set of social and environmental problems. But more, it's inheriting the institutions, resources, and roles to solve them. Saratovsky and Feldmann offer an open hand for those trying to manage that inheritance. *Cause for Change* is not just a guide to understanding the sometimes curious behavior of Millennials but an actionable plan to engage them and capture their talents."

> —**Jacob Harold,** president and CEO, Guidestar

Cause for Change

THE WHY AND HOW OF NONPROFIT MILLENNIAL ENGAGEMENT

Kari Dunn Saratovsky
Derrick Feldmann

Foreword by
Jean Case

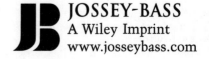

JOSSEY-BASS
A Wiley Imprint
www.josseybass.com

Published by Jossey-Bass
A Wiley Imprint
One Montgomery Street, Suite 1200, San Francisco, CA 94104-4594 www.josseybass.com

Cover design: JPuda
Cover image: ©Ciaran Griffin/Getty

Jossey-Bass books and products are available through most bookstores. To contact Jossey-Bass directly call our Customer Care Department within the U.S. at 800-956-7739, outside the U.S. at 317-572-3986, or fax 317-572-4002.

Wiley publishes in a variety of print and electronic formats and by print-on-demand. Some material included with standard print versions of this book may not be included in e-books or in print-on-demand. If this book refers to media such as a CD or DVD that is not included in the version you purchased, you may download this material at http://booksupport.wiley.com. For more information about Wiley products, visit www.wiley.com.

Library of Congress Cataloging-in-Publication Data

Saratovsky, Kari Dunn, 1979-
    Cause for change : the why and how of nonprofit millennial engagement / Kari Dunn Saratovsky, Derrick Feldmann.—First edition.
        pages cm
    Includes bibliographical references and index.
    ISBN 978-1-118-34826-0 (pbk.); ISBN 978-1-118-41680-8 (ebk);
    ISBN 978-1-118-42031-7 (ebk); ISBN 978-1-118-45400-8 (ebk)
        1. Generation Y—Employment. 2. Youth—Employment. 3. Nonprofit organizations.
    4. Intergenerational communication. 5. Personnel management. I. Feldmann, Derrick, 1978- II. Title.
    HD6270.S354   2013
    658.3'01—dc23
                                                                    2012046248

Printed in the United States of America
FIRST EDITION
PB Printing   10 9 8 7 6 5 4 3 2 1

To Bis and Elias, whose encouragement, love, and good humor

have anchored us through our writing—and always.

And to our "Generation Z" kids—Paige, Blair, and Liya—who are a

daily reminder that the world they inherit is

only as good as the one we leave them.

CONTENTS

List of Figures   ix

Foreword: The Next "Greatest Generation"   xi
  Jean Case, CEO, Case Foundation

Preface   xv

Acknowledgments   xix

About the Authors   xxi

ONE The Importance of the Next Generation
    and Why They Matter to You   1

TWO Developing Your Millennial Engagement Strategy   19

THREE Generation Connected   41

FOUR A Call to Action   67

FIVE Peer Influence   93

SIX The Millennial Donor   115

SEVEN Millennials in the Workplace   139

EIGHT Millennials as Nonprofit Leaders   165

Conclusion   191

Notes   195

Index   199

LIST OF FIGURES

CHAPTER ONE

Figure 1.1. Four Generations in the Workplace   5

CHAPTER TWO

Figure 2.1. The Virtuous Cycle of Engagement   23
Figure 2.2. The Millennial Engagement Platform: Introduction   32
Figure 2.3. The Millennial Engagement Platform: In Detail   38

CHAPTER THREE

Figure 3.1. How Do You Prefer to Learn About Nonprofits?   60
Figure 3.2. Generation Connected: Millennial Engagement Platform   64
Figure 3.3. Generation Connected: Five Key Takeaways   65

CHAPTER FOUR

Figure 4.1. The Future of Social Activism   71
Figure 4.2. Types of Volunteer Activities   76
Figure 4.3. The Volunteer Continuum   81
Figure 4.4. The KaBOOM! Website   84
Figure 4.5. Monterey County Rape Crisis Center Facebook Page   89
Figure 4.6. Call to Action: Millennial Engagement Platform   90
Figure 4.7. Call to Action: Five Key Takeaways   91

CHAPTER FIVE

Figure 5.1. Peer Influence   104

Figure 5.2. Peer Influence: Millennial Engagement Platform   112

Figure 5.3. Peer Influence: Five Key Takeaways   113

CHAPTER SIX

Figure 6.1. Millennials Raising Money for You   120

Figure 6.2. Donor Preferences for Method of Giving   129

Figure 6.3. Millennial Giving: Millennial Engagement Platform   137

Figure 6.4. Millennial Giving: Five Key Takeaways   138

CHAPTER SEVEN

Figure 7.1. Millennials in the Workplace: Millennial
    Engagement Platform   163

Figure 7.2. Millennials in the Workplace: Five Key Takeaways   164

CHAPTER EIGHT

Figure 8.1. Millennials as Nonprofit Leaders: Millennial
    Engagement Platform   188

Figure 8.2. Millennials as Nonprofit Leaders: Five Key Takeaways   189

FOREWORD: THE NEXT "GREATEST GENERATION"

Before transitioning to philanthropy, I spent nearly two decades helping to build a revolutionary new medium—interactive communications and the consumer Internet. Because these efforts were part of the broader burgeoning technology sector, there was a tendency to adopt an attitude of "If you build it, they will come." Having led marketing efforts at the earliest online startups, I knew that even though we were taking something new to the market, some of the old rules for understanding and segmenting marketing efforts definitely would apply if we were to achieve mainstream success. By the time we launched the AOL service in 1989, it was clear that we needed to understand our audience beyond just "anyone with a modem." We needed to know the characteristics of those who might find appeal in the service—and it became my job as chief of marketing to know the age group most heavily solicited by advertisers (which for many retail companies was and is eighteen to thirty-five, as these consumers are trendsetters and have a disproportionate influence on brand perception). To succeed at my job, I had to know exactly how to present an attractive, personalized appeal, what content influenced their decision to join, and what actions they would take once they were AOL members. I needed to know what issues they cared about, what times of day they were most likely to be in front of a computer screen, and whether they preferred to pay for things with cash or credit cards.

Now, as CEO of a philanthropic organization that invests in people and ideas that change the world, it has become even more important for me to know how market segments tick, especially twenty- and thirty-something Millennials, who are so-called "digital natives" and are idealistic about the future. But this time I have a different purpose. At the Case Foundation, our employee ranks consist largely of this important youth demographic. Many of our initiatives are about Millennials and created by Millennials. They have helped our organization dismantle silos, resist hierarchy, and embrace and buck trends as quickly as they come, and they've helped us make "having fun and being social" key organizational goals. They've also helped us stay true to our desire to seek solutions and partners irrespective of sector or pedigree. Millennials—both in our workplace and in the broader world—have helped us innovate and grow. So naturally, given our deep involvement with and appreciation of Millennials, other nonprofit leaders often ask me why I believe so much in this generation. My answer is simple: *we can't afford not to.*

Five years ago, *Cause for Change* coauthor Kari Saratovsky (Kari Dunn at the time) helped to lead the Case Foundation through the launch of an initiative examining the unique characteristics of what we termed "social citizens"— Millennials who were using new technologies and the unique characteristics of their generation to reshape activism and engagement. What we learned—and continue to see in our work in this space—is that this generation represents an epic shift in the way young people get involved, spend money, work together, and negotiate systems. They are transparent and collaborative; they don't care about hierarchy or silos; they want solutions; and they use a revolutionary set of interactive, instant, and personalized technologies to navigate the world.

One of the most important lessons we have learned in our studies of this generation is that although many try to generalize the characteristics that epitomize Millennials (collaborative, transparent, tech-savvy), Millennials continue to defy any one particular label. When Millennials think about changing the world around them, they don't think about it the way my generation (even in our twenties and thirties) thought about it. If government or nonprofits aren't moving fast or being effective, Millennials will channel their efforts through corporations or communities. And if corporations and communities aren't working, they'll use their dollars, followers, and friends to demand change or to support those institutions that are making change happen on their terms.

A decade of war sparked by a devastating attack on American soil, and a fragile economy have spurred Millennials to live in the moment and squeeze every last bit out of the here and now. These same experiences are also at the root of what makes this generation so incredibly special and unique. We know that bear markets have produced some of America's greatest innovations and most successful companies (IBM, FedEx, and Microsoft, to name a few), and I believe that the economic downturn that began in 2008, the lingering high unemployment rate despite the market recovery, and the unclear path forward, combined with unprecedented innovations in technology, have produced a generation that will create and mold dynamic new organizations, models, and approaches that will undoubtedly change the world. Add to this the remarkable number of those who have served our country and come home ready to roll up their sleeves in their communities, and the stage is set for something extraordinary to happen.

The generation that began about a hundred years ago—a generation defined by the Great Depression, two wars, an attack on our homeland, and a shift from farms to cities; that planted the seeds of the civil rights movement, launched scientific breakthroughs, and built great companies—has been called the "greatest generation." We believe that the Millennials are America's *next* greatest generation, and we had better make sure we know how to leverage, champion, and embrace them along their way.

At the Case Foundation, we've recently been thinking about two words quite a bit: *be fearless*. In this ever-changing world, if we want to be truly effective in solving social challenges, we must all take a fearless approach—we must take risks, be bold, and make failure matter. Bold young leaders are rising from the Millennial generation, which is collectively embracing this mantra. Millennials make big bets; they embrace experimentation; they don't let failures slow them down; collaboration beyond silos and sectors is second nature to them; and a spirit of urgency motivates everything they do. They are fearless.

Those of us charged with creating change have much to learn from this generation. We too must be fearless as we abandon ineffective traditions and norms to embrace the spirit of a generation that will forever rethink, retool, and redefine how giving back and doing good is done.

With nearly eighty million Millennials around the world who represent a combined $300 billion in purchasing power, their impact will be unparalleled. If you and your organization want to innovate and be innovative, it is important to recognize the value that Millennials bring to the table. And if you don't already know it, you will learn in this book that Millennials don't simply want to be served or asked to serve. They want a meaningful seat and voice at the table. They want to roll up their sleeves and have a role in developing solutions. If you're smart, you'll listen and make room for them as you or your organization go forward.

In a 1936 speech to the DNC, President Roosevelt told the gathered crowd: "There is a mysterious cycle in human events. To some generations much is given. Of other generations much is expected. This generation of Americans has a rendezvous with destiny." Today, Millennials have certainly been given much—a flatter, more diverse world with technologies that science fiction writers could have only dreamed of. At the same time, so much is expected of them—harnessing an ever-shifting global economy and keeping peace in times of rising conflict and obscure enemies. President Roosevelt's words ring true for this generation—they unquestionably have a rendezvous with destiny, and they have the tools, the character and characteristics, the passion and the purpose to transcend boundaries and transform challenges into opportunities . . . to become America's next greatest generation.

January 2013
Washington, DC

Jean Case
CEO
Case Foundation

PREFACE

Full disclosure: In 1979, when the majority of today's nonprofit executives were finishing college, starting their first jobs, and choosing career paths that would allow them to rise and ultimately sit at the helm of some of today's leading nonprofit organizations, the authors were in diapers, feasting on Cheerios, and happily watching *Sesame Street*. Thirty-three years later, as we sat down to write this book, each having spent more than a decade immersed in the public and nonprofit sectors, we were grateful to be able to watch our own children enjoy a very similar routine.

We don't typically offer up our age so quickly or so proudly. In fact, we usually qualify ourselves as "cuspers," as our birth dates fall on the cusp between Generation X and Generation Y. But we felt it was important to note this is a book about Millennials by Millennials for everyone seeking to better understand, well, Millennials.

Let's be clear: we're not here to defend our generation, nor are we cheerleaders for it. Like the generations that came before ours, we are pegged by generational generalities—oversimplified stereotypes that seek to place all eighty million of us in a nice little box with words like *coddled, narcissistic,* and *entitled* emblazoned on the sides. And although we can't deny that we have peers who fit these broad stereotypes, we also believe our generation is far too large and too complex to be constrained or defined by such labels.

The chapters that follow offer an honest assessment of the emerging trends we are witnessing across the nonprofit sector—and beyond—that we believe are being influenced in large part by our generation's eighty million members.

Here's how we see it: If the goal of our Baby Boomer parents was to beat the system, and the goal of Generation X was to defy the system, we'd say that the Millennial generation's intention is to do neither. We prefer building our own system, on our own terms, and we enthusiastically bring along others who share our vision and can help.

It's because of this approach that we think organizations can be opportunistic and use these qualities to their advantage when trying to engage the emerging generation of Millennials. Right now, the old way of working isn't exactly working. The problems are too vast, and organizations are not structured to react in ways that keep up with a generation who grew up in a twenty-four-hour news cycle.

There are already more than 1.8 million nonprofits out there competing for limited dollars, limited resources, and our limited attention spans. We see a struggle for survival coming between those organizations that can adapt and are willing to, versus those stuck in yesterday's reality. Because if Millennials can't shake things up from within, they will go at it alone—with an army of Facebook friends and Twitter followers rallying behind.

So rather than perpetuate the creation of new institutions that are in many ways duplicative and ineffective, what if we instead find new ways to get our institutions and the rising generation to mutually support one another? After all, although the world is flatter, faster, and more interconnected than ever before, individuals also have more power to achieve and to create change on their own terms than ever before, with a new ability to deliver their ideas to millions in an instant. We must work collectively and decisively in new ways if we are to affect our communities and society in the way we wish to.

Moreover, the problems that face our local and global communities call for exactly the values that Millennials believe in—collaboration, teamwork, openness, and transparency. We believe the rising generation has an opportunity to recreate our systems and institutions from the inside out. That's going to take a new way of thinking. It's going to take a new way of organizing. And it's going to take a new acceptance of approaches that may seem a bit overwhelming to traditional institutions—many of whom have been operating in much the same way since the mid-twentieth century.

That's why we've written this book. We believe the best way to bring others along with us is to help them understand who we (Millennials) are—what drives us, what motivates us, and what turns us off and makes us run the other way. As the data and feedback reveal, we are a generation primed to give it our all, but we also have certain expectations of organizations and institutions. And we will consider those factors when choosing to engage as a volunteer, employee, or donor.

The Millennial story is still unfolding, as ten thousand Millennials turn twenty-one years old each day. What follows are stories, woven together with new research, articles, and personal experiences, that help uncover how Millennials—our peers—are driving much of the change within institutions and beyond.

WHY SHOULD YOU READ THIS BOOK?

If you lead an organization, you should read this book from two vantage points. First, read it to learn *how* to engage Millennials. Gone are the days of questioning whether or not you should start a Millennial engagement program or wait to do something in the future. This generation is today's workforce, today's donor base, today's volunteers, and today's constituents. What better time than now to embrace it?

Second, read this book with an eye toward openness. Everything presented is based on the fundamental premise that your organization must be open to changing its current approach. Trying new ideas and methods is essential for succeeding with Millennials. This will challenge some traditional organizations, but it's a necessity if you want Millennials at the table with you solving today's social problems, rather than going at it on their own.

HOW *CAUSE FOR CHANGE* IS STRUCTURED

This book examines various strategies for engaging Millennials as constituents, volunteers, and donors, and focuses on how organizations can realign themselves to better respond to Millennials. The crux of *Cause for Change* is the Millennial Engagement Platform, an action-based rubric included in each chapter to help your organization create the infrastructure for a long-term Millennial engagement strategy.

After giving you a broad overview of the context and trends affecting the Millennial generation, we'll move through a series of specific behaviors and attributes. We'll examine how Millennials communicate, volunteer, take action, influence their peers, and choose to give their time and money.

We'll also look at how Millennials view their role in the workplace, and how their approach is reshaping nonprofit culture from within. Last, we'll profile Millennials who have emerged as dynamic leaders to create and manage movements in their communities, and we'll reveal how they are thinking and acting in today's rapidly changing nonprofit environment.

Overall, we have structured this book to take you through a process of developing your Millennial engagement plan. Your Cause for Change platform should be coupled together with your strategic, marketing, and development plans and used as a strategy document to help guide your organization through the generational transformation happening today. No one has all the answers about Millennials (not even the authors), but we can provide a solid launch pad for decision making and adaptation. The conversation doesn't have to end here, either; we encourage you to join us at www.causeforchangebook.com to share your stories and lessons learned.

Cause for Change highlights a movement and a cultural shift that requires more than just the will of one person. We encourage you to use this book collaboratively by taking each chapter and dissecting it, discussing it, and using it to create your own Millennial Engagement Platform. We hope you'll do this as a team with your peers, colleagues, and volunteer leaders. The best movements start with ideas created by one, strategies developed by a team, and the commitment of group of people.

Now let's get started—Millennials are waiting to be engaged.

January 2013

Kari Dunn Saratovsky
Houston, Texas

Derrick Feldmann
Indianapolis, Indiana

ACKNOWLEDGMENTS

As two Millennials growing up during a time when the term "social network" came to mean something that exists only online, we would be remiss if we didn't thank our extensive social networks. We mean those whom we've come to know both on- and offline, personally and professionally—all of whom have served as the inspiration and foundation for the ideas and concepts threaded throughout this book.

The beauty of the world we find ourselves in today is that we are in a constant state of learning with and from one another. We are amazed by the people we have encountered during the journey of writing this book. The generosity, candor, and creativity of both those we have known for many years and those we have come to know more recently have fueled us as well as these pages.

To be honest, writing a book was not exactly at the top of the bucket list for either of us. However, when our publisher, Alison Hankey, reached out shortly after the 2011 Millennial Donor Summit and told us that she could see the summit's program as the table of contents for a book on Millennial engagement, we quickly agreed and began writing. Thank you Alison, Dani Scoville, Mary Garrett, Kristi Hein, and the rest of the team at Jossey-Bass/Wiley for taking a chance on us and our ideas and for helping us see this book through.

Thanks to the dynamic team at Achieve (the creative fundraising agency of which Derrick is CEO)—Joanna Nixon, Justin Brady, and Lara Brainer-Banker—for their creative thinking, passion, and savvy design skills that helped bring the pages of this book to life. And our thanks to Julia Rocchi, whose patience and guidance (not to mention her editing prowess) played a critical role in early drafts of our manuscript.

A special thank-you to our friends and colleagues at the Case Foundation, who have advanced the Millennial movement in the nonprofit sector and beyond. Your willingness to be fearless and take a chance on Millennial engagement through programs like Social Citizens and your investment in the virtual MCON Summit are a model for philanthropy. In particular, we extend special recognition to Jean Case for her visionary leadership and to Emily Yu and Michael Smith for their consistent dedication to strengthening the Millennial voice within the social sector.

In addition, we want to thank everyone who provided their stories, thoughtful ideas, challenges, and achievements that we included throughout the book: Maya Enista Smith, Brian Elliot, Ryan Brady, Marty Posch, Michael Manness, Michael Brinker, Dvorit Mausner, Zach Maurin, Jonny Dorsey, Ben Rattray, David Smith, Erica Williams, Jeff Slobotski, Aaron Hurst, Jake Wood, Lana Volftsun, and Amy Sample Ward, among many others. Whether you know it or not, your stories and your willingness to open yourselves and your organizations up to us are greatly appreciated.

Special thanks to our friends and nonprofit colleagues who shared their opinions and lent an ear to the Cause for Change concept (as well as many of our other crazy ideas), including Alison Fine, Brian Reich, Cynthia Gibson, Peter Panepento, Beth Kanter, Ben Binswanger, Jennifer Hoos Rothberg, Michelle Nunn, Daniel Kaufman, Mike Berkowitz, Grant Garrison, Lisa Eisen, and Ted Grossnickle, among many others.

Lastly, we want to thank our most important social network—that of our closest family and friends. Although many of you still wonder what it is we do all day, we know that without your support, patience, and good humor this book would have never become a reality.

ABOUT THE AUTHORS

Kari Dunn Saratovsky is principal of KDS Strategies. She has spent her career working in both the government and nonprofit sectors building alliances, directing programs, and facilitating national efforts that advance social change. She established KDS Strategies to provide solutions to national and local organizations, with a focus on innovative program design, strategic communications, and social media strategy—all with a unique understanding of next-generation engagement.

Prior to establishing KDS Strategies, Kari served as vice president of social innovation at the Case Foundation and helped set the programmatic direction of the foundation as a member of its senior leadership. She also served as publisher of the highly regarded Social Citizens blog. Kari writes and speaks extensively on the rising generation of Millennials and how they are changing the nature of nonprofits and institutions.

Prior to her work in the philanthropic world, Kari was executive director of the President's Council on Service and Civic Participation, a presidential commission to support and expand volunteer service throughout the country and around the world. She also served as a senior advisor and White House liaison at the Corporation for National and Community Service. Kari is an avid volunteer and currently serves as chair of the board of Mobilize.org, board member for Repair the World, and advisor for startup Fuse Corps.

Derrick Feldmann is the CEO of Achieve, a creative fundraising agency. He is responsible for providing strategy to clients, overseeing the creative development of client work, and leading the full execution of fundraising efforts for clients. He leads the research team on the Millennial Impact Project (www.themillennialimpact.com)—an annual research initiative to understand how Millennials connect, involve, and give—and leads the planning team for the Millennial Engagement Summit (MCON).

When not working closely with Achieve clients, he is a speaker on the latest trends in fundraising, online engagement, and Millennial donors. Prior to founding Achieve, Derrick was responsible for national fundraising efforts at the LEAGUE and Learning to Give organizations. During his time at these organizations, he led successful expansion efforts into six new markets, acquired national TV partners for awareness campaigns, and saw an increase of 200 percent in fundraising efforts under his guidance.

Derrick is a graduate of Southeast Missouri State University. He received his graduate degree from the Center on Philanthropy at Indiana University. Derrick is a board member of the International Association of Fundraising Professionals and the Starfish Initiative. He also serves on the Editorial Board of the Nonprofit Board Report.

Cause for Change

chapter ONE

The Importance of the Next Generation and Why They Matter to You

> The world demands the qualities of youth. Not a time of
> life, but a state of mind.
>
> —Robert F. Kennedy

How do you define young alumni engagement?"

Derrick posed this question to the president of a mid-size university with more than fifteen thousand alumni between the ages of twenty and thirty-three. The president spoke for fifteen minutes, but her response came down to this: "We want our young alumni to be present. To be a part of the university community on and off campus—to be here and show pride, to be dedicated to their alma mater, and to assist us in making the institution better for the long term."

Great sound bites, to be sure, but they didn't really answer the question. This was the answer you might hear in the boardroom if a trustee asked about the importance of young alumni engagement. It's an answer we hear all too often from institutions that have probably not been proactive in their efforts to truly engage Millennials. Derrick wasn't satisfied. So he followed the president's answer with a much more direct question: "How do you *know* the university is connecting personally with young alumni?"

This was a critical moment. Not because Derrick was trying to trick the president of this very well-established institution, but because he was trying to understand the foundation for relationships that existed to engage their Millennial constituents. Derrick recognized this could go a number of different ways; this was the time when a leader could be honest with herself about the lack of engagement, or instead spend time talking about her alumni relations efforts that on the outside seemed to be working just fine but in reality were hiding the truth—that her institution had become more disconnected from their alumni than ever before.

Indeed, most leaders would have delved into lengthy monologues about how they are using email, social media, and other highly interactive social solutions because they know (or at least believe) that those methods are the silver bullet to engaging the next generation. But this president chose another route. She was smart and humble. She understood that the institution was not living up to its potential, and she knew they weren't taking full advantage of or institutionalizing the changes necessary to build toward a better future.

Her next comment helped Derrick understand the position that leaders in the nonprofit sector currently take about the Millennial generation. The president said, "Quite frankly, I don't know, and I don't think I should be expected to know the specific ways of engaging this generation.

"That is why you are here," she added, half-kidding. "Jokes aside, it is important. We cannot deny that these constituents and alumni will lead this university in the future. We cannot deny the job we have today as administrators to engage them now so the faculty and staff thirty years from now can reap the benefits of our hard work in making those personal connections.

"However, you are asking me to put aside capital needs, declines in state funding, growing demands from my trustees, and major donors with higher capacity to give—in order to spend time getting one young alumnus involved? I hope you can appreciate the delicate position I am in and the work I must do to lead this institution.

"So I ask you now: how can I spend my time and what can I do to engage this generation and help my staff and trustees understand the importance of personal connections so we can make this institution stand out and attract greater levels of young alumni engagement?"

Her statement captures the major reason why so many nonprofits fail to allocate the resources and spend the time necessary to engage Millennials. The leadership of organizations throughout this country conceptually understands why they need to engage Millennials; however, these concepts are not translating into action. Even though Millennials are the next generation of donors and constituents, leaders spend far more resources focused on maintaining their existing supporters rather than trying to cultivate new ones—so much so, that they cannot see beyond their current donor strategies and systems to a future where those supporters are no longer around.

This book is for the president of that university. It's for the CEO of a national nonprofit, and for the board of directors of a small community-based organization who will take a proactive approach to generational engagement rather than assuming a one-size-fits-all approach that works only for today's donors and not tomorrow's. It's for nonprofit managers who are trying to understand what drives and motivates Millennials to give, take action, and develop as leaders, so that in the future their organizations can be positioned for success. It's for the lead fundraiser and chief marketing officer who are trying to make tough decisions on a daily basis about how to engage the Millennial generation today.

Lastly, this book is for the organizational leader who is responsible for creating and championing a new movement internally to engage the next generation of constituents—the person who must tackle constant external and internal forces that impede progress in generational engagement, all in the name of return on investment (ROI).

WHO IS THIS MILLENNIAL YOU ARE TALKING ABOUT?

Let's face it: generations are complex, and dividing people into distinct categories based on birth year is an inexact science. Author Don Tapscott used the term "Net Generation" in 2008 to categorize the group born between 1977 and 1997; the trade magazine *Advertising Age* is credited with concocting the term "Gen Y" in a 1993 editorial.

William Strauss and Neil Howe first used the term "Millennial" in their book *Generations: The History of America's Future, 1584 to 2069*, published in 1991.[1] The authors didn't coin the term; rather, in a democratic fashion, they conducted a poll in which members of the generation themselves started to use the term to define their traits and characteristics. After publication, the term went on to gain widespread attention and general acceptance.

That said, not everyone who uses the label agrees on exactly when the generation began and ended. The Center for Information and Research on Civic Learning and Engagement (CIRCLE) uses the birth years 1984–2004, whereas the Pew Research

Center—which undertook a major study on the Millennial generation in 2009—uses birth years 1980–2001. The New Politics Institute and the Center for American Progress, on the other hand, suggest an earlier start, with the first Millennials born in 1978. Suffice it to say, there has been no shortage of labels to define the generation that we will refer to as Millennials throughout the book.

Putting names, labels, and years aside, we can all agree on the basic facts. As shown in Figure 1.1, the Millennial generation is the largest and most diverse generation yet, and right now they're in the middle of the "coming of age" phase of their lifecycle. The oldest members are in their early thirties; the youngest are going through their adolescence.

When Pew Research first set out to study the emerging generation in 2009, they already knew a few big things about the Millennials:

- They are the most ethnically and racially diverse cohort of youth in the nation's history. Among those ages thirteen to twenty-nine, 18.5 percent are Hispanic; 14.2 percent are black; 4.3 percent are Asian; 3.2 percent are mixed race or other; and 59.8 percent, a record low, are white.

- They are starting out as the most politically progressive age group in modern history. In the 2008 election, Millennials voted for Barack Obama over John McCain by 66 percent to 32 percent, whereas adults ages thirty and over split their votes 50 percent to 49 percent. In the four decades since the development of Election Day exit polling, this was the largest gap ever seen in a presidential election between the votes of those under and over age thirty.

- They are the first generation in human history who regard behaviors like tweeting and texting, along with websites like Facebook, YouTube, Google, and Wikipedia, not as astonishing innovations of the digital era but as everyday parts of their social lives and their search for understanding.

- They are the least religiously observant youths since survey research began charting religious behavior.

- They are more inclined to trust in institutions than were either of their two predecessor generations—the Gen X-ers (who are now ages thirty to forty-five) and Baby Boomers (now ages forty-six to sixty-four)—did when they were coming of age.

Because of this diversity, it is difficult to make sweeping generalities about every member within the ninety-two-million strong cohort. To fully understand the traits

Figure 1.1

Four Generations in the Workplace

Millennials 1980–2001	Gen X-ers 1965–1979	Baby Boomers 1946–1964	Traditionalists 1925–1945
Current U.S. Residents Census Bureau Estimate	*Current U.S. Residents Census Bureau Estimate*	*Current U.S. Residents Census Bureau Estimate*	*Current U.S. Residents Census Bureau Estimate*
92 million	62 million	78.3 million	38.6 million
Key Historical Events	*Key Historical Events*	*Key Historical Events*	*Key Historical Events*
• Columbine High School shootings • September 11 terrorist attacks • Enron and other corporate scandals • Wars in Afghanistan and Iraq • Hurricane Katrina	• AIDS epidemic • Space Shuttle *Challenger* catastrophe • Fall of the Berlin Wall • Oklahoma City bombing • Bill Clinton–Monica Lewinsky scandal	• Vietnam War • Assassinations of John and Robert Kennedy and Martin Luther king Jr. • First man on the moon • Kent State killings • Watergate	• Great Depression • Pearl Harbor • World War II • Korean War • Cold War Era • Cuban missile crisis
Traits	*Traits*	*Traits*	*Traits*
• Entitled • Optimistic • Civic minded • Close parental involvement • Values work-life balance • Impatient • Multitasking • Team oriented	• Self-reliant • Adaptable • Cynical • Distrusts authority • Resourceful • Entrepreneurial • Technology savvy	• Workaholic • Idealistic • Competitive • Loyal • Materialistic • Seeks personal fulfillment • Values titles and the corner office	• Patriotic • Dependable • Conformist • Respects authority • Rigid • Socially and financially conservative • Solid work ethic

Source: Ron Alsop, *The Trophy Kids Grow Up: How the Millennial Generation Is Shaking Up the Workplace* (Jossey Bass, 2008).

and characteristics of Millennials, one must also examine the environment in which they have grown up.

The vast majority of Millennials were born during a time when radical advances in technology were taking place. Those on the older end of the Millennial spectrum couldn't wait to boot up their Apple II and learn about history through computer games like *Oregon Trail*. By the time these older Millennials were in junior high and high school, the high-pitched, static-y sound emanating from their computers in the early days of dial-up was music to their ears, as were three simple words: "You've got mail."

For younger members of the Millennial generation, the idea of having to dial up to access the Internet is a foreign concept. Technology simply was always present. These individuals are in fact "digital natives." Although certain technological advances did occur in their lifetime, this generation has consistently been surrounded by a world in which technology was seamlessly interwoven with their daily lives. This is why we are seeing the generation adapt to technology more quickly than older generations—and why organizations must begin to get ahead of the game when it comes to these digital solutions, as we will discuss in the chapters that follow.

Although it's easy to point to technological advancements as the defining element of the Millennial generation, their understanding of and connection to cultural and world affairs is also remarkable. They are global citizens. What's more, they've grown up with high levels of tolerance; they support gay marriage, take racial and gender equality as givens, and have a generally open and positive attitude toward immigration. (After all, more than 40 percent of the Millennial generation are themselves minorities.)

Although not all will be able to remember when the Berlin Wall fell or when the Space Shuttle *Challenger* exploded shortly after takeoff, they did grow up when the tensions in the Middle East were high, the terrorism witnessed in the United States on September 11, 2001, remained an ongoing threat, and natural disasters like Hurricane Katrina and the earthquake in Haiti helped further define the ways they give and involve themselves in nonprofit work, as well as their ideologies and behaviors toward community change.

That's not to say these events didn't also impact other generations; they did. But the point in Millennials' lives when these events took place—their formative years—means they had a different result. Each took place at a time when Millennials were old enough to be aware and young enough to be shaped by their impact, to the point of becoming drivers of social and cultural change. We will examine how this generation has been a catalyst for change and what their impact has been on society through these recent events as well as their tendencies for everything from purchasing behaviors to use of technology.

Millennials also grew up with another important aspect when it comes to serving their communities: formal requirements that upon graduating from high school they will have completed a certain amount of hours of service to their community before walking the stage. Long-term, immersive, intensive service programs such as AmeriCorps and Peace Corps were heavily marketed and promoted to Millennials from the time they were in grade school. Given that structures for both long-term and episodic volunteering have always been present for them, Millennials' emphasis on community service and their interest in changing the world is not surprising. We'll explore this in greater detail in Chapter Four.

A Historic Election

The 2008 election not only marked the election of America's first African American president, but also saw the political emergence of a new, large, and dynamic generation. Millennial experts Michael Hais and Morley Winograd predict that this event will contribute to the realignment of American politics over the course of the next forty years.[2]

Their unified support for the first-term senator from Illinois, combined with high voter turnout rates, made the Millennial generation a decisive force in Obama's victory. Young voters accounted for about seven million of Obama's almost nine-million-vote margin over John McCain. What made the Obama campaign so successful with Millennials? Beyond the candidate's youthful energy and relevance to younger demographics, the campaign had several key ingredients that can be translated across nonprofits and other institutions developing engagement strategies and campaigns.

Messaging

"Together we can make a difference." This sentence was the spark of a joining movement fueled by Millennials. Barack Obama's team created messaging and a platform that forged a personal connection with Millennials who were seeking to join a movement for change. Phrases like "Yes we can" and the simplicity of words like *hope* and *change* resonated with a generation keenly interested in helping create a new government based on openness and support—ideals ingrained in the Millennial makeup.

(Continued)

Digital Media

The campaign's online organizing team—led by Chris Hughes (cofounder of Facebook and a Millennial himself) and the team at Blue State Digital, the agency of record for the campaign—also capitalized on one important aspect to send those important messages: digital media. Because the majority of Millennials could hardly remember a world without the Internet, the Obama team created strategies that brought together the likes of social media, informal communications, and ongoing impulsivity to inspire Millennials to give in the moment. The creation of the platform My.BarackObama.com was optimized for Millennial appeal. The campaign understood the Millennial generation's desire to interact with brands, so they positioned their candidate as a brand all on his own. The Obama campaign was able to further capitalize on this by creating a platform focused on the pronoun "my," thus giving ownership to a generation eager to find and use their voice to connect with others who shared their passion and commitment.

The site also showed a shift in customer relationship management (CRM) to a *customer-managed* relationship, in which young people could be in control of their relationship with the candidate. They were able to customize and personalize their pages, engage in discussions, post photos, and use many other interactive elements. The digital strategy team came up with other unique techniques and gimmicks, even tweeting from the @barackobama twitter account that Obama would announce "the VP candidate sometime between now & the Convention by txt msg & email."

Conversation Creation

The communications team was able to take their message, wrap it in conversational dialogue, and help every single Millennial understand that Obama was going to help them personally achieve their dreams. That ability to speak directly to Millennials created a new wave of online activists inspiring each other to join the movement on behalf of Obama. Millennials were given peer online messages that would help them communicate quickly, to the point, and informally with their friends, leading to the viral campaigning that made the Obama election effort so memorable in social media history.

What's more, Millennials were not just encouraging their peers to go out and vote; they were also shifting the conversation for their parents and grandparents as well. Efforts sprang up outside the official campaign, such as The Great Schlep (a reference to the Yiddish word for a long, arduous journey)—conceived of by Ari Wallach and Mik Moore to mobilize Jewish Millennials to head down to visit their grandparents in Florida, educate them about Obama, and in turn swing the Florida vote in his favor. The campaign reached out to others as well: "Don't have grandparents in Florida? Not Jewish? No problem! You can still become a Schlepper and make change happen in 2008, simply by talking to your relatives about Obama."[3]

GENERATIONAL GENERALITIES—BRING 'EM ON!

Just like all generations that have come before, the Millennial generation has attracted plenty of stereotypes. Some are fitting; others may not accurately define the whole group. Though much has been written on this generation's defining traits, we thought it was important to focus on a few key characteristics that will help your organization better understand how to engage with this complicated and constantly evolving demographic and ultimately convert them into supporters and champions for your cause. We devote more attention to each of them in the chapters that follow, but offer the following to set the stage.

Digitally Connected

Millennials have grown up in the age of the twenty-four-hour news cycle, giving them access to news and world events at the touch of a button. They are connected to technology and in particular through social media platforms that help them stay connected to their networks of family and friends—often through real-time updates, tweets, and texts that offer a glimpse into the current status of their lives. Although this concept of being digitally connected at all times is somewhat foreign to those in older demographics and may even come off as self-absorbed or out of touch with reality, it is simply a mode of expression for the majority of today's young people.

However, even with Millennials' wide adoption of these tools, we know that digital engagement with friends and family does not always translate to engagement with nonprofit causes. That's why an organization's use of digital and social media tactics will require additional support and engagement beyond simple posts and mass messages. For nonprofits seeking to engage Millennials in peer strategies for volunteerism and giving, potential opportunity exists through digital connections, but they can be challenging if the organization expects virality or the message lacks the necessary components to inspire conversation.

Creative

Millennials are creative when it comes to design and thinking. They enjoy spending time bringing creativity to a project or problem, and they revel in the chance to create a new way to present information, communicate an issue, or tell friends about a new brand or product. In fact, the emergence of new approaches to creativity and design thinking has led to the development of entire undergraduate and graduate school programs focused on the topic. The concepts of effective design—generally associated with successful consumer goods such as clothing, cars, furniture, and product packaging—can also be used to creatively address social problems by applying new approaches and techniques. Nonprofits can take this creative approach to help individuals in a given community understand how to actively engage in the cause's work.

Solution-Centered

Millennials want to create and develop new solutions to social issues, and utilize their networks for creative problem solving. As they have watched government and the private sector fail in solving some of the most pressing issues of our time, Millennials are standing at the ready and in many cases developing their own unique approaches to social problems. We'll share the stories of Millennials who are doing so by leveraging what makes their generation unique: collaborative styles of leadership, comfort and ease of use with technology, and transparency, to name a few traits. Millennials are keen to understand issues' complexities and then work toward addressing them. And regardless of how big a challenge may be, they are excited to be a part of a solution rather than sit on the sidelines.

This is where nonprofits can really work closely with Millennials through problem-solving and solution-based approaches. Harnessing the energy and excitement may be difficult, but creating those tangible milestones is important. We see this happen often in fundraising practices when organizations provide tangible gifting opportunities (for example, $10 will buy a net in Africa to help prevent the spread of malaria for one family). This model helps Millennials get involved in clear, easy, and impulsive ways.

Self-Organized

Millennials bring together other Millennials. They respond to friend requests, family calls for assistance, and peers in need. Through informal networks and groups, Millennials can come together and create a movement for change or even a small interest group. We'll refer to these activators as "free agents," a term adopted by social media mavens Beth Kanter and Allison Fine in their book *The Networked Nonprofit* to describe the individuals working behind the scenes or on social media platforms to help spread messages and build connections between an organization and its potential supporters.[4]

Self-organizing allows for small groups to help the organizations they care about in an informal setting that is not governed or programmed by the organization. The challenge is to let self-organization happen without impeding the dynamics of the group in the interest of your cause. This natural networking and connected trait of Millennials should be encouraged by organizations. Those who open themselves up to the idea of working with self-organizers and are able to get it right have an opportunity to be a resource for smaller groups so they can have a deeper impact on the cause.

Open and Transparent

Millennials thrive on knowing exactly where they stand in their relationships at all times. Whether in the workplace or with friends and family, their relationships are transparent and open, and they relish the opportunity for feedback on how they are doing.

What's more, Millennials want and even expect to be able to access information quickly and seamlessly, and this access includes the ability to pick up the phone to directly address a decision maker or person of authority. This transparent behavior translates to their community involvement. They want to know where the money is going, how it is going to be spent, and what specific stories of impact the nonprofit can share. Nonprofits that lack transparent behavior will have a hard time engaging Millennials who seek open relationships with the organizations they choose to support with time and financial resources.

Nonprofits can achieve such transparency in the form of information, data, stats, and updates on the health and current capacity of the organization. Online transparency can also be created in social media networks such as Facebook where authentic conversations can inspire trust and relationship building. Organizations must think about their offline transparency as well, which includes discussing the true state of affairs at special events, discussing the needs of the organization at volunteer activities, and helping donors understand where their dollars can go.

Although this generation has many other traits, the ones we just highlighted represent the most dominant aspects of the Millennial generation as they engage with nonprofit organizations. When we think about Millennials and their interests in changing the world, we must capitalize on the traits that make them unique and can best help the causes they want to support.

SELF-ORGANIZING CAME LONG BEFORE THE INTERNET

Although the concept of self-organizing may seem to have taken shape during the twenty-first century with the rise of the Internet and the explosion of radical new social technologies that have allowed individuals (many of whom we will profile in the chapters that follow) to build their own social movements, we need to go all the way back to the early nineteenth century to appreciate its origins.

At that time, the burgeoning of loose associations led people to come together in more deliberate ways. Citizens began self-organizing into structured institutions and associations that are now largely referred to, as a group, as the nonprofit sector. It was common for a committed group of caring citizens who shared an interest in helping one another deal with a cause, a problem in the community, or an issue affecting their families to get together and support each other through time and financial resources. These informal groups later formed larger, more formalized structures to do their work in the community. Staff began to take the roles of volunteers, specialists performed marketing, and fundraising became the sole function of certain employees.

Perhaps the easiest and most traditional way of thinking about the nonprofit sector is as one of three concentric circles like that of a Venn diagram, the other two circles being government and the private sector. Each overlapping circle has its own distinct programmatic functions, its own tax structures, and its own way of operating. However, in recent years we have seen the lines on that diagram blur. There are no longer hard and fast rules dictating that "doing good" and solving social problems can happen only through the structure and confines of nonprofit organizations.

When you think about it, today's nonprofits are able to create complex structures for earned revenue, governments are investing large sums of money in entrepreneurship and social innovation, and businesses care about their environmental footprint and have created entire departments focused on corporate social responsibility. Each example shows how the once distinct three-sector structure is blending.

Alexis de Tocqueville, a famous early observer of nonprofits, wrote in his book *Democracy in America:* "If men are to remain civilized or to become so, the art of associating together must grow and improve in the same ratio in which the equality of conditions increased."[5] We've watched over the past several decades as the nonprofit sector has experienced phenomenal growth in nearly every imaginable and measurable way. As the sector is becoming bigger, more diverse, and more organized, it's also come under higher levels of scrutiny. Sector leaders are becoming more professional, more confident, and more involved in public policy than in previous decades. Likewise, we've watched as government support of nonprofits has made them more top-down and bureaucratic.

In 2011, nonprofit organizations provided some 10.7 million American workers with employment, making it the third largest sector of our economy, just behind retail trade (14.5 million) and manufacturing (11.5 million). And even during the recent recession years, nonprofits have created jobs while the rest of the economy has shed them. The Johns Hopkins Nonprofit Economic Data Project shows that in the past three decades alone, nonprofits have grown to account for a substantial part of the U.S. economy and by some estimates for as much as 10 percent of the Gross Domestic Product (GDP).

That's the good news. The not-so-good news? With the rapid growth of nonprofits and the creation of hundreds of thousands of individual organizations competing for the limited dollars of funders and the limited attention spans of individuals, it's becoming more and more difficult to keep up and maintain these organizations, each of whom have their own staffs, missions, and operating costs. Although we know that institutions are necessary to focus efforts, provide institutional memory for communities, and champion issues for the underserved and underrepresented, they will need to look, feel, and operate quite differently from what they are accustomed to in order to authentically engage the voice, support, and eventually the dollars of Millennials.

WHY ORGANIZATIONS NEED TO ADAPT NOW

As nonprofit organizations began to grow, thrive, and receive major funding from both the government and private foundations over the course of the twentieth century, they also began formalizing their processes and taking on more hierarchical structures. Nonprofits were becoming more businesslike and institutional—just as individuals were becoming more wary of institutions.

Today these organizations are working to gain broad community support. They are building lasting change in the communities they serve through various forms of human and financial capital. Still, fundamental to their existence and growth is the role of individuals in the community—the key ingredient for community transformation.

As the individual becomes more central and important to the work of nonprofits, nonprofits must better understand and appreciate the complexity and changing nature of their constituents. The shifting demographics of constituents and donors are already beginning to have a major impact on the ability of nonprofits to attract, retain, and inspire the engagement of the next generation.

But these changes may not be entirely what you expect. Ignore the generation now, and you do so at your own peril. Making the choice now to engage with Millennials means you are taking the necessary steps to begin securing the future of your organization. Otherwise, you'll need to catch up in the years to come.

Although Millennials are friending, following, tweeting, and texting more than any other constituent base, new and emerging social technology is only part of the equation. As we'll discuss in the chapters that follow, what drives Millennials even more than technology and social media are the personal relationships and human connections they forge along the way. It's up to an organization to realign in a way that enables connected and fosters real-time, authentic relationships.

Organizations also need to understand and appreciate the demands being placed on the Millennial generation, all of whom are coming of age during a difficult period for our country and our world. Today's rising generation is faced with mounting levels of school debt and the realities of finding a job in a down economy. With so many external factors affecting their daily lives, it should come as little surprise that they may not place your cause or social issue at the top of their priority list. Even so, that doesn't mean you should turn away. Instead, find unique ways to engage them on their terms; by investing them in your issue now, you can help shape how they respond in the future.

There's also a financial reason your organization should focus on the Millennial generation: they have $300 billion in spending power, and of that, $62.7 billion is considered discretionary. Moreover, Millennials are the beneficiaries of a $41 trillion transfer of wealth from older generations.

All this means that Millennials are looking for areas and opportunities to spend their dollars, whether that be a new product or a social cause. This means a real opportunity to take advantage of resources potentially available to your organization. This cohort of twenty-somethings will be leading, guiding, and deciding the fates of organizations in the decades to come, and their spending decisions will benefit those organizations that have done the best job securing their familial and individual interests now.

Dvorit Mausner, a Millennial generational fundraiser for the Penn Fund at the University of Pennsylvania, put it this way when she addressed her volunteer leadership:

> If there is an expectation that this generation of alumni will be supporters, active alumni in sharing our need to raise financial

resources, and bring in other alumni to support our next capital campaign, engaging the young alumni of the Millennial generation is not an option but a necessity. We should not expect that young alumni, in their efforts to become involved with the institution, should start their relationship by giving first. We should expect that we would need to spend time with them in advance of our campaigns to help them understand the results of giving to the Penn Fund and how their contributions truly make a difference to our institution. Again, we must do that now, otherwise we will suffer in future campaigns.[6]

IS THERE A TRADEOFF?

The challenges facing nonprofit leaders in this current economic climate are astounding, and leaders of social causes are being called on to lead in very uncertain times. They need to build their constituency base, expand their financial contributions, and create an infrastructure for long-term sustainability—a combination of requirements that calls for leaders experienced in both constituent engagement and business operations.

However, should you build those long-term sustainable solutions at the cost of engaging a new generation of activists, supporters, and leaders? Not at all. Organizations that have focused less of their time on including this generation are impeding their own efforts to make that sustainable future a reality.

Indeed, when creating any new strategy or goal, organizations should incorporate into their thinking early on the concept that Millennials are part of the solution and execution rather than the product in itself. Consider the for-profit example of Facebook, which follows a "social by design" mantra to keep social engagement at the core of all its solutions, marketing efforts, and communication strategies. This means that as we move forward and toward a more people-centric Web, successful businesses will effectively leverage social connections and place great value on the ability and ease of sharing and amplifying a message.

With this in mind, perhaps nonprofits should consider a "Millennials by design" focus, incorporating Millennial traits, thinking, and work into their strategies from the beginning. During planning meetings, creative sessions, and other forms of strategic decision making, organizations should involve

Millennial thinking and engagement in getting the end results. In short, they should move beyond simple constituent engagement and surround the concepts of strategy with Millennial actions.

It is not either/or, but rather and. How do you fundraise for an organization *and* engage Millennials as advocates to help it succeed? How do you increase the effectiveness of your program outreach *and* involve Millennials in developing the program? How do you get some of the smartest leaders in the community to join you in re-envisioning your institution *and* include the voice of the Millennial generation in those discussions?

ARE YOU READY?

You may be ready. In fact, we hope that's why you're reading this book. But not every organization is ready to focus on Millennial engagement. If your organization needs to raise short-term cash quick, then spend your time and effort creating a new business model. If you lack a presence online, if you don't have the human capital necessary to pick up the phone and discuss the organization with new constituents, or if you devote less than 5 percent of your time to stewardship and cultivation of constituents, then Millennial engagement programs are probably not your best fit right now.

What organizations need to do first and foremost is show that they are open. This is not about being open-minded, although that is important. It is about opening your organization up to a generation eager to involve themselves in creating solutions to the challenges you face. It is about engaging in transparent behaviors with your community to help constituents, donors, and volunteers understand how you operate, how you generate money, and how you have the impact you do with their help. It is about being open to others' working on your behalf and about releasing the control that has prevented your organization from creating a true personal connection with an outside constituent. The Millennial generation feeds on openness. If you are not willing to be open, a Millennial engagement program is not for you.

THE MILLENNIAL ENGAGEMENT PLATFORM

There is an answer to the university president's question about how to engage Millennials. It resides in a new Millennial Engagement Platform designed specifically for this generation, consisting of the following cultural and operational components that organizations need in order to build an effective engagement program:

- *Leadership Inviting:* Provide access to organizational leaders and enable Millennials to take an active role in the development of their own leadership skills.
- *Tangible Transparency:* Exercise transparency in all that you do, and provide Millennials with the ability to access information, from how your organization affects the community to how you make and spend money.
- *Social Connectivity:* Develop engagement platforms that use distribution, connections, and messaging that are social in nature and allow for greater discourse and discussion both on- and offline.
- *Solution-Inspired Environment:* Create an environment in which Millennials can build solutions to challenges, own those solutions, and then execute strategies that fulfill those solutions. Millennials draw inspiration from creative design and solution-oriented thinking, not from already completed plans that they are expected to merely follow.

This type of platform requires cross-departmental institutional involvement. Throughout the book, we will explore how to implement such a platform in an organization. This type of engagement also requires ongoing resources and time devoted to make it successful. Without either of the two (resources and time), almost all Millennial engagement programs are destined for failure.

THE SILVER BULLET

We all want the silver bullet, but then we are reminded there's no such thing. Today's Millennials are constantly evolving, and with these changes comes competition between local and national issues and platforms vying for their attention. Though many organizations have tried to replicate a strong strategy from one organization and apply it to another, there is no "one size fits all" solution. And for every young professional group that has launched from a nonprofit, another one now sits as a binder on the shelf labeled, "Nice ideas that didn't work."

Although we won't claim to deliver you the silver bullet, we do have some guiding principles that can help you get closer to developing a strategy that resonates. It's a concept we like to use with organizations in conjunction with the just-described components of the Millennial Engagement Platform. It's how you

BUILD the Millennial platform, and we will walk you through it in more detail in Chapter Two:

Be unified as an organization in working with this generation.

Understand the complexities of this generation's environment.

Identify those seeking to make a difference.

Lead through engagement rather than participation.

Determine what Millennial success looks like to your organization.

In this book we will explore each of the Millennial engagement components and incorporate the concept of BUILD. We will show examples of great Millennial engagement programs and hear directly from Millennials and leaders of organizations working together for change in their community. We will discuss the role of technology, networks, and social capital—all strong influences of this generation. By the end you will understand how you can create your own platform and build a program to reach a generation yearning for social change.

Change will not happen overnight, but building awareness and opening yourself and your organization up to these new approaches is a necessary first step in creating institutions better prepared and equipped to compete for the Millennial generation's attention and passion. Your organization's future leadership expects you to act, and they are depending on your success navigating the new and evolving world of Millennials. We hope to make your journey a little easier.

chapter TWO

Developing Your Millennial Engagement Strategy

It seems like we can't get Millennials engaged in our organization. They are just not interested. And if we do get them to come to something, they never come back."

Sound familiar? This is a reaction we commonly hear from organizations who have tried to engage Millennials through a variety of techniques—volunteering, giving programs, or special events—with unsuccessful results. We believe this statement is an artificial roadblock created by organizations. We often find that many organizations are relying on outdated concepts of loyalty and engagement and therefore are failing to recognize, embrace, and encourage the loyalty and engagement that already exists or could easily be generated with this generation.

Simply put, loyalty and engagement look different today than they did just a few years ago. Take our friend Joe, who considers himself a loyal donor and constituent to the well-known environmental organizations he supports. Joe reads their emails, visits their websites, follows them on a variety of social media channels, and even volunteers when he has the time and when good opportunities arise. If we were to give Joe a quiz on the organization's activities, he could without a doubt score at least a "B." What's more, he's confident enough that he could tell others about the organization's work, give a quick pitch, and even ask for money.

When he reads articles that highlight the organization, he'll post them to his Facebook wall. He's purchased water bottles, T-shirts, and stickers for himself and his family to let everyone know of his support and to encourage action for the cause. Joe has participated in live chats with this organization and has liked and reposted content he thought was important for his personal and professional network to know. Would you say Joe is involved and engaged in this organization?

Well, let's compare Joe's level of engagement with that of another constituent.

Another donor to the same organization, Susan, has reliably responded to the end-of-year appeal for support. She has historically given at least $1,000 but recently gave $5,000 because of a special need. Because of the size of her recent gift, she received a phone call from the organization. Susan is not an email subscriber and thinks the technology stuff is for Joe's generation. When staff talks with her about the current happenings of the organization, she will often comment that she is not up to date on their work but believes "good things are happening." If she had to take the same quiz on the organization's work that Joe took, she probably would get a "D."

Who is more engaged with the organization? Depends on who you ask. The seasoned fundraiser, board member, and executive staff leader would probably consider the $5,000 donor more engaged. To the online marketing manager, webmaster, and communications staff, Joe would be more engaged. You can see the perplexing situation.

All the activity, knowledge, and behind-the-scenes evangelizing does not register with most organizations because they're too busy organizing and measuring in-person or capacity-based activities. They might dismiss participation like Joe's and not acknowledge it as a statement of involvement or see it as part of a more comprehensive approach.

This conundrum often is most visible in higher education. Just about every university strategic plan includes a theme or concept for "bringing alumni back to campus." Unfortunately, this is a skewed view of alumni engagement, especially for recent graduates. Think for a minute: When was the last time you went back to campus or participated in an alumni event? Been a while? So, does that mean you are not a loyal alumnus? Nope.

What your absence from campus probably means is, in this time-crunched world in which we live, you are reserving in-person engagement for those organizations that you feel must have or truly deserve a portion of your limited time. Do you ever follow your university in the news? Ever watch your alma mater's teams defeat your rivals? Ever visit the school's website to find alumni updates? You seem pretty loyal and engaged to me. Nonetheless, until you participate in person, your alma mater might consider you unengaged and uncaring.

Today's new nonprofit constituents are engaged in more new ways than ever before.

- *Today's Millennial constituents* have new technology tools like social media to support and leverage their thoughts and ideas.
- *Today's Millennial constituents* don't have formal titles such as "ambassador" or "class president." The constituents are not listed in an annual report or on the website.
- *Today's Millennial constituents* work behind the scenes, on social media platforms, and in local coffee shops to spread messages and build connections between the organization and potential constituents.
- *Today's Millennial constituents* work on behalf of the organization for many reasons, including their deep understanding of the nonprofit's needs, their personal interest, and their ability to get involved in crafting a project or solution. Give the Millennials a specific challenge and let them spread and communicate it through their networks.
- *Today's Millennial constituents* want to spread messages for you that are not manufactured in an office. They want to tell friends and family about the importance of the cause. Give these individuals a concept wrapped in a story to share, and it will be across the Web before the day is over.
- *Today's Millennial constituents* are going to use multiple channels and expect that the organization's website will continue the story and support the interest they create from their networks. Give these individuals specific links for their networks to take action, and their friends will jump because they heard it from a peer and not someone with a fancy title.
- *Today's Millennial constituents* are ready to spread messages beyond donation requests. They are excited about clear opportunities to involve others and will expect specific calls to action to engage their network. Give these individuals graduated levels of engagement or volunteerism for their networks to plug into, and success will follow.

How can organizations address this kind of loyalty and engagement? By changing their culture to reflect the differences of involvement, especially with Millennials. This generation gets informed, involved, and engaged without necessarily being onsite, and it's up to organizations to discover and leverage these behaviors to expand their own capacity.

When creating any engagement strategy with Millennials, we must embrace the notion that how we define engagement will vary; a one-size-fits-all approach is nearly impossible and will actually meet the needs of only a small segment of your audience. What works for Baby Boomers or Generation X applies to Millennials to a certain extent, but it still may not completely relate to or meet the expectations of the majority of the Millennial generation.

DEFINING INDIVIDUAL MILLENNIAL LEVELS OF ENGAGEMENT: A VIRTUOUS CYCLE

Before we begin discussing the strategies that support the Millennial Engagement Platform, it is important to understand how Millennials get involved with organizations. This will help your organization track, benchmark, and build stronger relational activities with Millennials as they participate in your programming.

Each level of engagement is built on the other and increases as the individual moves from relatively little information or understanding of an organization's work to an advanced relationship and connection with it. It's the idea of moving Millennials from a consumer mind-set to enabling them as creators of ideas, experiences, and solutions for an organization. Ultimately, Millennials will be able to create experiences in a self-initiated way for themselves and for their friends, while being supported in a new way by organizations.

The path is not a smooth one, and it's not necessarily a linear one, but it represents a new perspective on engagement. We like to think of it as a virtuous cycle of engagement whereby we move individuals through a path of discovery to become content consumers, then activists for a cause, and then ultimately influencers who encourage their own social networks to jump into the virtuous cycle all over again (see Figure 2.1).

First, a note: As with any audience segmentation, there are always outliers who outperform, are overinvolved, and bypass the typical levels we see with Millennials. These individuals represent a potential Millennial leader seeking more advanced levels of engagement than some of their Millennial peers do—levels that require more interactive forms of relationship. (We'll discuss this Millennial leader in Chapter Eight.)

Each of the levels discussed in this section is defined by the Millennial's individual interaction, participation, and level of interest in the organization. When you're looking to create a Millennial Engagement Platform, it's important

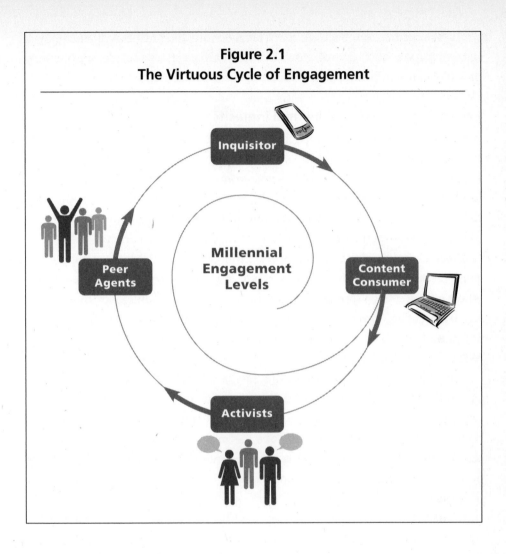

Figure 2.1
The Virtuous Cycle of Engagement

Inquisitor

Millennial Engagement Levels

Content Consumer

Peer Agents

Activists

to begin classifying Millennials and developing the community, support, and resources to bring each individual through your engagement program.

Often this starts with inviting Millennial constituents into the process very early on, perhaps before the process even exists. We know that individuals tend to engage and affiliate with organizations when they see others who "look like them" are involved. If you are to captivate the Millennial audience and keep them coming back, you need strategies that involve them and help them see themselves as a part of the organizational shift, not just as recipients of a new approach.

As an organization, begin to track and identify your Millennial constituents in the engagement levels we'll now describe. Each category provides an overview of Millennial action and participation in your organization's activities.

Engagement Level 1: Millennial Inquisitor

At this level, Millennials are exposed to a communication message either directly from the organization, from a peer, or through the media. There are many factors that go into how the message is received, from the construct of the message itself to the individual receiving it or even the method of delivery. Whatever the case, the goal should be for the Millennial to want to learn more and for the organization to capitalize on the impulsive nature of the Millennial generation.

Research indicates that Millennials are inherently impulsive about supporting causes and engaging with nonprofits. And let's face it, doing good is becoming a whole lot easier (and trendier, for that matter): we can "drink good" by enjoying fair trade coffee; "shop good" through products that give back, such as TOMS Shoes; and even "drive good" through car-sharing platforms such as Zipcar that reduce our carbon footprint.

But when doing good becomes this easy, are people still connecting it to the causes they are supporting? Here the real question of how to convert a new generation of organizational champions into loyal and passionate advocates and donors comes into play. If we can take the mind-set of the inquisitive or conscious consumer and translate this behavior into deeper engagement, then this becomes more than a trend for "good"; it has the potential to drive a deeper kind of engagement and social change.

In light of this potential, it's important that organizations spend time to simplify their messages and create clear and present calls to action. What's more, based on what Millennials read and their ability to quickly understand a given message, they will use technology—largely mobile devices, including tablets and phones—to consume and find even more information.

Of course, not all content and certainly not all websites are created equal. Organizations must spend time and resources to ensure that their organization's content comes through multiple devices and search platforms. And if the content is not optimized for these delivery platforms, organizations risk losing potential champions and supporters as frustration takes over. (We'll discuss this further in Chapter Three.)

Engagement Level 2: Millennial Content Consumer

At this level, Millennials have moved beyond general interest to content consumption. You've got them interested enough to poke around on your site, and now they crave a few key things: information, knowledge, and expertise. Typically we see Millennials either turn to a search engine like Google or simply go directly to the organization's website. Once on the website, the individual has a natural tendency to seek out the "About Us" section in an attempt to learn about the mission, people, and establishment of the organization—essentially, what the organization does and who the people are that make their work possible.

Above all, Millennials are trying to find an opportunity. This may be in the form of opportunities to volunteer, attend an event, or seek an active role as a leader. Creative visual representation and dynamic content through websites will determine whether or not they move to deeper participatory levels of engagement.

This critical point is also where the biggest drop-off occurs with Millennials if they fail to see the ways to involve themselves in an organization. They spend time culling through websites and use search engines to help them navigate, but are unsuccessful in seeing how they or their peers (friends and social networks) could do something to help the organization advance its mission or meet community needs.

Website optimization is crucial here. If you receive a message from a friend to visit a website, view a video, or connect on social media, you usually go. However, your personal experience once you are there will determine whether you take the time to engage in the organization or not.

It goes beyond just sending a link out to constituents. The highest conversion rates come from organizations using peer influence and agents to help spread a message and send all potential constituents to a webpage with specific and clear calls to action. Such sites usually use large graphics, include buttons for action, and are optimized for mobile devices.

Engagement Level 3: Millennial Activist

At this stage, individuals have gone through the discovery phase and engaged with an organization's content enough to find an active role that resonates with them and their personal goals for engagement. Now it's time for them to start taking action.

We typically see four major roles of activism: cause champion, volunteer, content creator, and financial supporter.

- *Cause Champion.* Millennials have a built-in messaging platform through their online social networks, and they are not afraid to spread messages and feature the great content or unique opportunities that an organization has to offer. This includes social media likes and reposts as well as other forms of online approval and support for a message. The focus at this point is much more on raising awareness; expectations about participation are low. Instead, it's an opportunity to introduce a message, a concept, or a cause to a new group of people.
- *Volunteer.* Millennials are likely to begin their engagement with organizations through short-term, episodic volunteer opportunities. These activities are likely to include offline actions like agreeing to attend an upcoming event and bringing a few friends along. Or it may be lending their professional skills through marketing and communications efforts, or "getting their hands dirty" through direct on-the-ground service opportunities with beneficiaries. Short-term volunteering usually includes two to five hours of volunteer work onsite. Although interest may be there for longer-term and ongoing participation in structured volunteer programs, initial participation is typically focused on lighter-touch, one-time activities—all the more reason for organizations to create well-managed, highly engaging opportunities to keep their volunteers coming back (and bringing their friends) because of the positive experiences they enjoy.
- *Content Creator.* The next step in the cycle of Millennial activism is enabling individuals to move from being content consumers and content "reposers" to providing their own content in the form of blog posts, comments, videos, and photos. Organizations must also be open to allowing Millennial supporters to develop their own programming. In some cases, they may be organizing meet-ups and happy hours that bring together their social networks to support an organization. Again, we know that Millennials tend to be more likely to affiliate and engage with organizations that "look like them." So provide support to Millennial content creators by providing peer Millennial staff time and resources to their self-organizing activities.
- *Financial Supporter.* Millennials will provide financial support to an organization based on its ability to clearly articulate how the funds are being used and how their support will matter. Rather than focus on the size of the gift,

organizations should view any contribution as an exploratory opportunity for the Millennial. Moreover, Millennials who open up their wallets and give to an organization are more likely to ask their friends. This trend is redefining philanthropy and moving it beyond rich people writing checks. Millennials have proven the model of democratizing philanthropy by pooling their resources in support of causes they care about.

Engagement Level 4: Millennial Peer Agents and Influencers

At this level, Millennials are engaged at the highest point and are actively seeking the involvement of their peers. Beyond just telling their friends and family through social media and other means, they are more persuasive in their efforts. They focus on how each individual in their closest networks can really get involved and be an active agent in the organization. From asking peers for money to getting volunteers or petition signers, this form of influence is genuine and intentional. Furthermore, it's a unique opportunity for organizations to interact directly with Millennials and bring them even closer to the organization.

At each level of engagement, as you increase in intensity, the number of Millennials at that level gets smaller. This is natural with this constituent base; given all of the forces competing for their limited time and limited dollars, they also tend to move from organization to organization as different causes and interests are presented to them. It's important for organizations to understand what messages, individuals, and tools facilitate the movement between each level to gain perspective on the motivation behind the individual's engagement.

In addition, the organization will want to capture the reasons for departure from each level. Simple survey mechanisms, such as text polls, as well as more intensive forms of feedback, such as focus groups, can help determine why the Millennial decided to leave.

Each level requires a strategy to help acquire and advance the individual to the next stage. This strategy should be built on a comprehensive approach of engagement—the Millennial Engagement Platform.

DEFINING PEER- AND GROUP-BASED MILLENNIAL ENGAGEMENT

As Millennial individuals take leading roles with an organization, it is important to understand how their peers (friends and families) get involved. As just described, Millennial Activists and Influencers will spread messages through their network. Based on the message read, the website visited, or the image viewed, peers will decide to either take action or passively say no. Assuming they say yes, peers get involved in the following ways.

Group Engagement 1: Self-Organized Group Engagement

At this level of engagement, Millennial Activists or Influencers begin to organize activities and events that benefit the nonprofit or cause they care about. These events and activities may include bringing some of the individuals in their network together to discuss the organization more broadly, participating in micro-volunteering actions as a small group, or spreading messages about the cause. This self-organized group does not have a close connection with the organization yet, given that the Millennial Activist or Influencer has done the heavy lifting thus far to garner excitement about the cause. At this engagement level, the organization can become a facilitator of information and help when called on, but should not manage the small group's activities.

Group Engagement 2: Event-Based Engagement

At this level, small groups led by the Millennial Activists or Influencers are now engaged in the organization's events as a cohort of the larger audience. This could include participation at a volunteer event or activity or a special event on awareness, or other ways that get the small groups to join others interested in the cause.

Moving to event participation means that the small group of friends has decided to join a larger group while also continuing to be involved together. The Millennial Activist or Influencer tends to still be the organizer and communicator to the small group when it comes to the organization's events. The fundraiser, marketer, and/or special events coordinator of the nonprofit organization will want to create a stronger relationship with the Millennial Activist or Influencer to ensure that proper messaging is communicated about the event and the small group's participation.

Event-based engagement is an episodic, short-term level of involvement. If the small group doesn't like what the organization has developed, it may decide to keep operating for the cause but not participate at a more committed level. Or, depending on how poor the experience was, some group might decide to start a new organization or entity entirely. Again, first impressions for the small group and Millennial Activist or Influencer count in this scenario.

Group Engagement 3: Young Professional Group Engagement

In this last level, the small group, still led by the Millennial Activist or Influencer, decides to become a part of a more formalized program, such as a young professional group hosted and organized by the nonprofit organization. If your organization does not have such a group, this level of group engagement would include any program developed by the organization for the sole purposes of connecting with and educating Millennials on the cause.

Participation here means the small group is increasing their involvement through formal programming led, managed, and facilitated by the nonprofit. Young professional groups provide a more structured way for small groups to get involved, and they result in broader awareness, involvement, and leadership potential for small group members and the Millennial Activist or Influencer.

This graduated level of engagement must take into account the need to keep peers connected. Remember, peer engagement is key for some Millennials to get involved with nonprofits. If your volunteer and constituent engagement programs focus on only individual tracks of involvement, they will not have much success with Millennials.

Also keep in mind that though an organization should help Millennial small groups and peer networks to move up the levels of engagement, it should not assume they want to be a part of the formal young professional structure (see sidebar, "Young Professional Groups as an Engagement Strategy"). Keep the young professional group optional, not required. Some will be satisfied with a communication relationship through social media and participating in one-time activities with their peers.

Young Professional Groups as an Engagement Strategy

The success of young professional groups can vary from organization to organization depending on their structure and staff support. Therefore it's important to thoroughly weigh the benefits of launching one before determining that this is the solution to your Millennial engagement program.

If you walk into a hip bar in any metropolitan area after work, there's a chance that you'll be greeted by a table draped with a banner bearing the logo of a local nonprofit. Over the music pulsing in the background, two young staffers will welcome you and offer you a nametag. On behalf of the

(Continued)

nonprofit's Young Professionals Group, they'll thank you for coming, encourage you to enjoy yourself, and offer you information about the organization.

This scenario has become increasingly common, and not altogether welcome. During a recent conversation with an executive director, he expressed concern about such groups. "More than ten organizations in the city have some sort of young donor group with an affinity to the organization," he said. "They're all competing with each other for attention."

It's true: The concept of the young professionals group (a.k.a. *young donors society* or *young donors group*) has spread faster than a funny video on YouTube. But do these groups work? We have a famous answer for this question (and many others): It depends.

Let's first look at the positives:

- **Right idea.** By establishing such a group, a nonprofit takes one step in the right direction, demonstrating that it recognizes the need to involve the next generation.

- **Front-line experience.** Group volunteerism and similar activities give the young professionals an opportunity to affect the community through organized service options.

- **Creative fundraising.** These groups raise support for the organization, often in creative and nontraditional ways. It's fun to see some of the ideas, such as fund-raising competitions, that emerge within the group and among their peers.

- **Energy boosts.** Millennial nonprofit employees can get excited about the organization's leaders who show interest in working with younger constituents. These internal leaders get excited to help develop activities and events to draw more young professionals closer to the organization.

Now let's consider some of the negatives:

- **Poor substitutes.** These groups too often act as substitutes for real relationships. A young professional group is an opportunity to create new relationships, but real engagement goes beyond that. As donors and constituents, young people expect a call, a conversation, and a personally meaningful engagement opportunity in addition to event participation.

- **Social, social, social.** Trust me—we like parties as much as anyone. But social activities can't provide real Millennial engagement. It's demeaning and disrespectful to assume that the key to engaging young professionals is throwing a party in a bar.

- **Benefits versus philanthropy.** There's a difference between a young professional group and a dues-paying society. If you pay dues, you expect a personal benefit; with philanthropy, however, you expect to give for the benefit of the community or the beneficiary of services. If young professional groups are established with dues expectations—even if the contribution is to the organization—the donor will expect some sort of personal benefit. As a result, once a young professional feels that the value of the relationship has diminished, he or she will leave. On the other hand, if his or her personal philanthropic interest and engagement are high, that person will stick around.

Now, if you're a young professional and a member of such a group, ask yourself the following:

- Outside of the group, have you ever had a conversation with the executive director or a board member of the organization—a personal conversation about your interest and the potential engagement you want to have?

- Does the organization provide more than social activities in order to enrich your passion or interest and meet your engagement needs?

- Does the organization come to you personally to talk about direction, new program initiatives, or challenges?

- Does the organization have a board with leaders like you—individuals who represent the next generation and are able to make decisions that interest you?

If you answered no to any of these questions, the organization may not be as sophisticated with its next-generation program as it thinks.

THE MILLENNIAL ENGAGEMENT PLATFORM

As introduced in Chapter One, the Millennial Engagement Platform (see Figure 2.2) outlines the following cultural and operational components that organizations need to build appropriate programs and levels for this cohort.

- Leadership Inviting
- Tangible Transparency
- Social Connectivity
- Solution-Inspired Environment

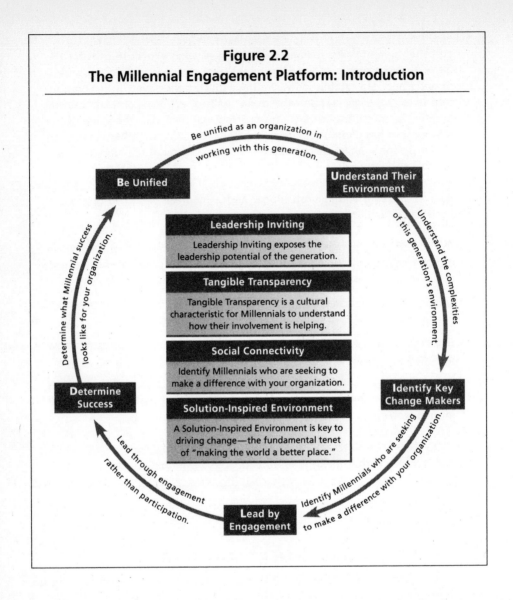

Figure 2.2
The Millennial Engagement Platform: Introduction

Be unified as an organization in working with this generation.

Be Unified

Understand Their Environment

Understand the complexities of this generation's environment.

Determine what Millennial success looks like for your organization.

Leadership Inviting

Leadership Inviting exposes the leadership potential of the generation.

Tangible Transparency

Tangible Transparency is a cultural characteristic for Millennials to understand how their involvement is helping.

Social Connectivity

Identify Millennials who are seeking to make a difference with your organization.

Solution-Inspired Environment

A Solution-Inspired Environment is key to driving change—the fundamental tenet of "making the world a better place."

Determine Success

Identify Key Change Makers

Identify Millennials who are seeking to make a difference with your organization.

Lead through engagement rather than participation.

Lead by Engagement

- *Leadership Inviting* is key to drawing out the leadership potential of the generation. The organization's leaders need to invite Millennials in and connect them with decision makers. Providing such access to a constituent will set an organization apart from its peers. In addition, organizations should provide leadership opportunities and encourage Millennials to take an active role in making decisions for the future.

- *Tangible Transparency* is a cultural characteristic necessary for Millennials to understand the scope and progress of the cause. In this area, organizations must provide tangible information for Millennials to understand how the cause affects the community, makes money, spends that money, and involves people at all levels. Without tangible transparent operations, Millennials will be overwhelmed with vague prose and messaging, ultimately leading to inaction.
- *Social Connectivity* is necessary for the platform to build and expand. The platform for engagement must use distribution, connections, and messaging that is social in nature to allow discourse and discussion. If the organization doesn't allow social connections, online and offline, there is no viability to the outreach to gain broader interest from Millennials.
- *Solution-Inspired* is an attribute that drives the change necessary to tackle local issues. Creating an environment in which Millennials can create solutions to challenges, own those solutions, and execute strategies for them will draw attention and create viability in the Millennial community. Millennials draw inspiration from creative design and solution-oriented thinking, not from already completed plans that they are expected to merely follow.

IMPLEMENTING THE MILLENNIAL ENGAGEMENT PLATFORM

So how do you position the Millennial platform—and by extension, your organization—for success? As we said in Chapter One, you BUILD it. This type of platform requires cross-departmental institutional involvement. It also requires ongoing resources and time devoted to make it successful. Without either of the two (resources and time), almost all Millennial engagement programs are destined for failure.

- *Be unified as an organization about working with the generation.* Get every level interested in what this generation can provide. Most will gravitate to the financial opportunities, but that's the wrong framework to lead with. Instead, all leaders, both volunteer and paid, must understand and agree that engaging Millennials is a long-term investment and crucial to fostering the future leaders and volunteers of the organization.
- *Understand the complexities of this generation's environment.* Beyond understanding why you should work with Millennials, appreciate the environment

this generation is currently in and the environment in which they have grown up. In large part, they do not remember the days without a mobile phone, the ability to watch shows on demand, or the myriad other technologies that have simplified life and changed traditional processes. Take the time to understand their environment; then you can create a role within that environment to engage them.

- *Identify those seeking to make a difference.* For every non-caring or uninterested Millennial, we can also identify a Boomer or Gen X-er who exhibits the same qualities. You must find those who want to work with you and make that change. Create calls to action that ask for Millennial leaders to identify themselves through solution- and idea-generation activities. Consider asking close supporters to also identify Millennials in the community who want to take their participation to the next level. This peer identification is a great brainstorming activity for your existing Millennial supporters and volunteers.

- *Lead through engagement rather than participation.* Focus on conversational and relationship engagement. If you are going for pure numbers at your event, you may have short-term wins, but that doesn't get at the heart of the platform. True engagement comes from attendees returning and telling friends about your message. As an organization you can create new levels of engagement that focus on getting to know Millennials and their interests. Engagement means you understand how they want to communicate, participate, lead, and challenge the organization to be better.

- *Determine your own Millennial success.* Before you begin, create a standard for Millennial success and engagement, then institutionalize it. Some organizations do really well with Millennial engagement because they have defined what it means for their cause and how they want Millennials to be involved. They identify a starting point, a goal, and the steps they'll take to get there. Help the organization you serve to understand those benchmarks and rally around them for short- and long-term success.

CREATING A MILLENNIAL ENGAGEMENT STRATEGY FOR THE PLATFORM

The first step in developing a Millennial engagement strategy is to ensure that it falls within the overall strategic plan or direction of the organization. Review the current strategic plan; assess where initiating a Millennial engagement strategy will coincide with the defined goals and help draw the generation into achieving them. Your organization does not have to set Millennial-specific benchmarks outside existing ones; rather, you can view it as an opportunity to involve Millennials in your current program and operational needs.

When selecting a targeted engagement strategy, consider these questions:

- How will we as an organization determine whether a Millennial constituent is engaged, based on the levels presented in this chapter?
- What is the current engagement of other constituents of the organization?
- Are there particular challenges and opportunities that Millennials can work closely on with existing human resources to reach our goals?
- Based on the organization's current volunteer work, leadership opportunities, and activist roles, what is missing to create specific, actionable steps at each level of Millennial engagement?
- What opportunities and outside influences may enable the organization to engage more Millennials than what is currently being done?

Millennial Engagement Questionnaire

Once your organization has identified the particular strategies and defined the particular approaches, you must determine your infrastructure needs. The following are discussion questions for each platform element:

Human Resources
- What are the skills and expertise needed to execute and meet the Millennial goals defined?
- Do your current staff and/or volunteer force have the necessary skills and expertise?
- If they do, how will their current role change, if at all?
- If they don't, how will you attain the leadership needed to meet the goal (hire, outsource, volunteers)?

(Continued)

Volunteer Resources

- How will you engage your volunteer leadership in the inclusive nature of the Millennial strategy?

- Do they have the skills needed to assist in executing and delivery?

- If not, how will you help the staff or volunteers get the skills needed?

Financial Resources

- Do any of the strategies require a financial investment?

- Do you currently have money budgeted for the new strategies?

- If not, how will you get the resources to execute the tactics?

Technology

- Will any technology be needed to reach the defined goals?

- If so, can the organization's existing technology platforms support the new strategy?

- If not, what are the needs and the potential vendors to approach?

Communication Instruments

- Will the organization need to develop new print or online collateral brand, themes, or materials for the new strategies?

- Will the current print and online materials be affected by the new strategy? Will they need to be replaced?

- Are there any other communication instruments needed to meet the goals?

Before embarking on a strategy, analyze what potential challenges might prevent success. Think beyond internal issues—consider challenges that may affect Millennials' ability to be involved. These simple questions can help guide your thinking:

- Is there an issue affecting the community you serve that has taken precedence recently that could affect the Millennials' work?

- How do Millennials perceive the organization?

- Are there any other major issues affecting the local community that could have an impact on the Millennial engagement strategy?

Lastly, note any internal issues that may prohibit success—for example, program offerings that could affect the strategy, or lack of staff time. Discuss solutions to help you overcome the potential roadblocks. It helps to create a new committee internally to work on the Millennial engagement strategy. This committee should consist of marketing, development, and program personnel able to devote the resources necessary to be successful.

Use the Millennial Engagement Platform at the end of each chapter as a guide for your organization to develop your own specific Millennial program. Spend the time to align your efforts with the Millennial engagement levels. Create the strategies based on the four major components and the BUILD strategy matrix. Externally communicate the various opportunities to take a Millennial constituent from interest and communication to participation at graduated degrees. No matter your cause, make your platform a remarkable opportunity for this generation.

THE MILLENNIAL ENGAGEMENT PLATFORM: A SUMMARY

The Millennial Engagement Platform is designed to help you organize and create a new program for Millennial involvement with your organization. The platform consists of four major tenets: leadership inviting, tangible transparency, social connectivity, and solutions-inspired. Every Millennial strategy, tactic, and work plan should contain these core components. Before designing any program, the organization should spend time to discuss internally how these components will be present and not compromised.

In addition to the components of the Millennial Engagement Platform, the key strategies should encompass elements of BUILD (see Figure 2.3). The BUILD strategies help guide a Millennial engagement program. When your organization is in strategic creative development, you should spend time to ensure that every strategy qualifies under at least one of the BUILD approaches. If a Millennial strategy you have developed does not fall within the BUILD structure, reconsider the approach altogether. This could mean the difference between a long-term, fruitful Millennial engagement program and a short-lived tactic that fizzles away with time.

Figure 2.3
The Millennial Engagement Platform: In Detail

Leadership Inviting

Leadership Inviting exposes the leadership potential of the generation. Millennials crave the opportunity to connect with organizational leaders and the ability to directly influence the decision-making process now and in the future. But in order to succeed at it, organizational leaders must invite this opportunity and make a deliberate choice to be accessible. Providing that access to leadership for a constituent will distinguish an organization from its peers.

Tangible Transparency

Organizations that provide the most tangible information, from how their cause affects the community to how they make and spend money, have a positive effect on the ongoing support they receive from Millennials.

Social Connectivity

Social Connectivity is the connection Millennials have to their peers, family members, and professional networks. Social connectivity is a form of network engagement through various platforms that allow for greater discourse and discussion both online and offline. If the organization or the issue area is not established to allow for social connections, both online and offline, the outreach has no viability to gain broader interest from Millennials.

Solution-Inspired

Solution-Inspired is core to driving change. Creating an environment where Millennials can create solutions to challenges, own them, and execute them will draw attention and viability within the Millennial community. Millennials draw inspiration from creative design and solution thinking, not from completed plans where only following is expected.

BUILD a Better Environment by Engaging Millennials

Be Unified

Be unified as an organization in working with this generation. Help all leaders, both volunteer and paid, understand and agree on the need to engage Millennials.

Understand Their Environment

Understand the complexities of this generation's environment. Appreciate the environment this generation is currently in, what they experienced growing up, and how the rapid advancements of technology and culture have shaped their involvement with organizations.

Identify Key Change Makers

Identify Millennials who are seeking to make a difference with your organization. This could be staff, board members, volunteers, and donors. Don't be distracted by stories of Millennials who don't care. These are "outliers" and every generation has them. You must find those who want to work with you and make change happen.

Lead by Engagement

Lead through engagement rather than participation. Focus on conversational and relationship involvement with your organization. Engagement means you understand how Millennials want to communicate, participate, lead, and challenge the organization to be better.

Determine Success

Determine what Millennial success looks like for your organization. Create foundational standards or benchmarks. Create realistic and incremental goals that will not hinder ongoing deployment of Millennial programming.

A SPECIAL NOTE TO THE EXECUTIVE LEADER

Change is hard for any institution, especially when so many programs and approaches are rooted in tradition. Thus the hardest part of institutionalizing this platform is changing your organizational culture to be ready to accept the Millennial generation as the next leaders, constituents, volunteers, and donors.

Spend the time with volunteer and paid leadership to guide them through the platform. Help your leadership understand the major tenets that will guide the decision-making process for your Millennial strategies. In addition, use and distribute the Millennial Engagement Platform summaries at the end of each chapter for the staff and board to review in advance of any discussion about Millennial engagement. These will be your guide for helping staff and board understand the direction, strategy, and reason for implementing particular approaches.

chapter THREE

Generation Connected

Imagine a world with no Facebook, no Twitter, and no texting.

Imagine a world where the only information I could learn about you or your organization was limited to what might be listed in the White Pages.

You don't need to go back in time very far to remember when this was reality. Yet for the Millennial generation—or what some are now referring to as "Generation C," given that they are constantly connected, communicating, content-centric, computerized, and community-oriented—those days are a distant memory, if remembered at all.

One of the paradoxes of technology adoption is that it is fundamentally a human endeavor. People are what makes technology matter; in fact, we'd argue that technology is more about a mind-set and the strength of relationships than it is about the latest app or new gadget. The real value of social media comes down to people, relationships, and the meaningful actions between them. And for Millennials, there is nothing more important than the cultivation of meaningful relationships, be it online or off.

Still, one of the greatest myths about social media is that social networks facilitate conversations about your organization that would not otherwise take place if you weren't present. But social media didn't invent conversations or opinions; the control you think you've lost by opening up to online engagement is actually control you've gained. Once you discover what people say and don't say, how they connect and what they share, suddenly you have created a blueprint for social media engagement. The question you have to answer is, "What do I want people to say, understand, and do?"

Innovations in new media are radically changing the way we operate, produce, and consume information, but our organizations and institutions are not adapting quickly enough or in the most strategic ways to accommodate for this new reality. Creating the means to do things better, faster, and cheaper is irrelevant if organizations don't simultaneously embrace new approaches and thinking about online engagement. So how do we move organizations from being users of social media to actually being "social organizations"? And what does today's social organization look like, in light of the fact that technology is the backbone of so much of how Millennials function?

There is no silver bullet for developing a social media strategy that best suits a particular organization. Every situation varies depending on the nature of the organization's work and intended outcomes. The good news is that as we watch social media infiltrate and become a strategy at more nonprofit organizations, the conversation has shifted away from *why* or *should* we do it, to *where* and *how* we should.

Plenty has been written about these concepts by people far better positioned than we are to provide insight into social media strategies. So rather than go deeply into any single theory, we thought it best to provide some of the best examples of innovative and effective campaigns, fueled by new social technology, that have moved Millennials to take action on issues they care about. In addition, based on a series of focus groups on this very topic, we will provide examples of how Millennials want and expect to be engaged through social media.

It boils down to this: New media is a necessary utility for functioning in the twenty-first century, but how it is best leveraged is an evolving process for most nonprofits and businesses alike. Organizations have to make it easy for Millennials (and everyone, for that matter) to find them, and once the Millennials arrive, nonprofits need to give them what they want, how they want it, and on their terms.

It is our hope that readers will walk away from this chapter having developed:

- An appreciation for the increasing role that social media are playing in the social change sector, and how organizations can make more informed decisions that benefit them and their constituents

- A new understanding and appreciation of popular social media and technology platforms and tools, and how Millennials wish to be reached by these tools

- An understanding of how the Millennial Generation's expectations of social media are affecting all generations

DON'T DISMISS THE SLACKTIVIST

Many refer to online activists simply as "slacktivists," arguing they take easy social actions like signing a petition, liking a Facebook page, or changing their social media avatars or profiles to support a cause or campaign—and then go no further. Yet we believe that these so-called slacktivists get a bad rap only because they *appear* to have made no real commitment or meaningful contribution to social change.

The merits and impact of slacktivism have been hotly debated. Dan Morrison, the founder of Citizen Effect, wrote: "The idea emerged because social media tools gave slackers with a heart an opportunity to get involved on their own terms. It is a mistake to think that slacktivists are just lazy. Some are too busy or uncomfortable getting involved with a cause in a public manner. Texting, tweeting, and social media gave them the ability to give during the limited time they had or provided the social cover they needed to get involved. So I think we should ask not what the slacktivist can do for us, but what we can do for the slacktivist."[1]

Today we can volunteer online, donate money online, participate in online discussions and forums, ask questions in live-streamed events, and shop (and boycott) online; soon we could be voting online. Obviously people still want offline interaction and opportunities, but it might not always be that way. Just as we are seeing the U.S. Postal Service possibly phase out just a couple of decades after email first became popular, many offline opportunities might eventually be phased out as well.

Meaningful action is already taking place online. So instead of putting our effort toward converting online connections to offline ones, why not put our effort toward getting people comfortable with staying online and getting highly engaged in communities there? Aren't we moving toward a time when our goal, instead, will be to move people up the online scale of engagement?

Case in point: The *Dynamics of Cause Engagement* study by Georgetown University's Center for Social Impact Communication and Ogilvy Worldwide shows slacktivists are actually *more* likely to take meaningful actions both off and online.[2] In this 2010 national survey, people who frequently engaged in activities to promote social causes were

- As likely as non–social media promoters to donate
- Twice as likely to volunteer their time
- Twice as likely to take part in events like charity walks
- More than twice as likely to buy products or services from companies that supported the cause

- Three times as likely to solicit donations on behalf of their cause
- More than four times as likely to encourage others to sign a petition or contact political representatives

When we think about civic engagement, we typically think of any effort that helps a community solve a problem. Volunteering, donating money, discussing community issues, staying informed, and connecting with civic or religious groups can all now happen online. And as the communities of Millennials and generations after us are decreasingly defined by location, much of our civic participation in those communities might move online as well.

So, how about if your organization were to embrace one-click actions such as adding a pink ribbon to your Twitter profile picture, voting on a nonprofit to increase its chances of winning a grant, or buying a virtual gift as low-level civic participation in global communities, rather than condemn it as slacktivism? You don't hear people criticize efforts to raise awareness offline—like passing out flyers, putting campaign signs in yards, or wearing LIVESTRONG wristbands—in the same way. Is it really that different?

SOCIAL MARKETING CAMPAIGNS: BEYOND THE COLORED WRISTBAND

Most social marketing campaigns involve creative marketing messages, product sales, and directed giving to an organization or issue area. So it probably won't surprise you to see Millennials as huge champions of social good campaigns that support top brands and their favorite causes and social interests.

They're in good company: The number of consumers who say they would switch from one brand to another if the other brand was associated with a good cause has climbed to 87 percent, a dramatic increase in recent years, according to a Cone Cause Evolution Study.[3] What's more, a newly released College Explorer study from Alloy Media reported that nearly 95 percent of students say they are less likely to ignore an ad if it promotes a brand's partnership with a cause.

Although what may be two of the hottest social marketing campaigns of the Millennial generation revolved around the colors yellow and red—Lance Armstrong's LIVESTRONG wristbands for cancer research, and RED merchandise available from Millennial-focused brands that supported the Global Fund to Fight AIDS, Tuberculosis and Malaria (the Global Fund or GFATM)—cause marketing campaigns have evolved immensely and a new concept of conscious consumerism has been born.

Take, for example, Pepsi's decision to forgo spending on Super Bowl ads and instead channel that money into the Pepsi Refresh program—an online platform and marketing campaign that solicited the best ideas from consumers and in return donated up to $20 million in grants to good causes and "great ideas" throughout the year. Interaction with the campaign's website significantly increased brand attributes—including favorability, intent, and trust, along with intent to purchase—among Millennials, a key cohort for Pepsi. With an average of 20,000 comments posted per month and over 183,000 ideas in the system, the Pepsi Refresh program was able to interact with the community on a larger scale than the company had achieved in other, earlier social campaigns.

Another example is that of the Ford Motor Company, who for three months provided twelve nonprofit organizations in the greater Los Angeles area with their own 2012 Ford Focus, a team of filmmakers, and a platform for financial empowerment through their People's Fleet program. Ford recognized that this is a generation that is inspired not only to do things differently but also to create a new road for ideas that were previously thought impossible. In an effort to further this movement, they gave nonprofits an opportunity to tell their story on a robust online platform through videos. Here's the catch—fundamentally, the videos that were made were car ads, but they never ran on TV and never explicitly discussed the car, its make or model, features or price. The people the Ford marketers hope to reach don't watch TV and aren't just concerned with the car's features—they want to know that the company has a social conscience.

In both cases, by doing meaningful work for others, brands have seen they can become relevant, likable, and sharable. And the sooner they do that, the larger their communities can become over time. What Pepsi and Ford have done is this: in addition to supporting and bringing attention to some important nonprofit organizations, they have issued a wake-up call to other brands that a new way of doing business can ultimately lead to a more sustainable world that is also profitable for brands—a good thing, since Millennials have continued to embrace socially conscious brands over others, often despite price.

GOING VIRAL

Web-powered activism is nothing new to Millennials. But to date, a cause has not spread as quickly or reached as many people as did the viral video "Kony

2012." Created by the California-based nonprofit Invisible Children to tell the story of Lord's Resistance Army head and indicted war criminal Joseph Kony, the video was seen by eighty million people within five days of its release—a major step toward creating global awareness of his crimes.[4]

As a result of the campaign, 40 percent of all Millennials said they had "heard a lot" about the video one week after its release—twice the percentage of those in any other generation, according to a Pew Research survey. One of the keys for the success of "Kony 2012" in gaining Millennials' awareness was the seamless way the video provided action steps, empowering young people to find a way to have their opinions heard and take action using tools embedded in their everyday lives.

Even so, not everyone was as impressed as the Millennials. Some were skeptical as stories began to unfold about the nonprofit's motives, executive salaries, and lack of transparency around what the funding was used for. What's more, as the campaign really swung into full steam, with millions of new viewers every day, experts on the trouble in Uganda began weighing in on the topic and questioned the validity of some of the facts in the video.

Despite these reactions, Millennials—who place their faith, in large part, on the wisdom of the crowd and have little interest in being lectured by experts who have not themselves been able to resolve the world's problems—were not dissuaded by the pushback. The video's tagline had stated its mission—to "make Joseph Kony famous"—but the larger goal was to help capture Kony and bring him to trial for his actions against humanity. The Millennials stood by this broader mission and continued to participate.

Millennials are hungry for social interaction, and viral marketing allows them to share in this phenomenon with friends and peers. It plays to their desires for exclusivity as they strive to be the first to share these campaigns, forgetting that they're doing the heavy lifting on behalf of a brand or service.

In this respect, viral marketing has come to play a big part in word-of-mouth marketing (WOMM). Still, it's not the whole story: A recent study from the Temkin Group shows that word-of-mouth feedback is more likely to occur via email, phone calls, in-person, or directly to the company as opposed to on social media.[5]

When Temkin studied the behaviors of ten thousand individuals after a good or bad interaction with a product, the following responses ranked highest: "I told my friends via email, phone, or in-person" and "I did not tell anyone about the experience." Facebook and Twitter came in fourth and sixth as the most likely venues for people to share their experiences. (Fifth were social review sites like

Yelp and TripAdvisor.) So if your organization is banking solely on Facebook and Twitter for WOMM, you've hampered your strategy right out of the gate.

Overall, organizations need to ensure that content is compelling and shareable, but they should also go a step further. Give customers different ways of sharing their experiences. Give easy access to a customer service team or build in experiences that foster online chatter, such as inviting everyone to use their mobile phones to rate their experience after they donate or volunteer. Remember, it's in your best interest to consider how you can empower your constituents to talk about you. We'll explore this concept in greater detail when we focus on the power of peer influence in Chapter Five.

Consumer Feedback—Love It or Hate It

Had a bad meal? Post your review on Yelp. Did the hotel room have a cockroach? Take a photo and post your issue on TripAdvisor. With the rise of mobile devices and the platforms to compile customer feedback, consumers are in the driver's seat now and providing instantaneous feedback that companies have come to both love and hate.

Posting a complaint or writing praise online in social media forums or websites such as TripAdvisor is a very strong Millennial habit that is based on peer and community influence. The goal of the feedback is to influence others to either purchase a product or service or choose to stay away. Over the course of the past five years, as the tools have become more mainstream, the wisdom of the crowd often rules. It is now very common for Millennials as well as those across all generations to check restaurant or hotel reviews before even stepping into a store or lobby.

So what is the power of consumer feedback sites? There is no question that thousands of small businesses have been discovered and put on the map because of consumer input. And in a study conducted by researcher Michael Luca at the Harvard Business School, who looked at the impact of Yelp ratings on Seattle-based restaurants, some interesting conclusions were drawn. Yelp had rated 70 percent of all operational restaurants in 2009, where as the city's largest newspaper has only reviewed 5 percent of them. Here's what Luca discovered: "A one-star increase in Yelp rating leads to a 5–9 percent increase in revenue." Meaning that when consumers have information they trust—in this case, from a random sample of the public—it influences decisions. He also found that online consumer ratings do not affect ratings with chain affiliations—rather, the biggest impact is on independent restaurants, which some might argue is helping to level the playing field.

(Continued)

Although similar rankings have not penetrated the nonprofit space in the same way, sites like Great Nonprofits are beginning to make some headway and enabling volunteers, donors, and activists to rate their experiences with nonprofit organizations. The question is whether or not the impact will be the same allowing for smaller 501(c)3's to gain the attention of a mass audience.

FROM ONE, MANY

Sometimes a movement can start in an even simpler way. Meet Molly Katchpole. Molly was a twenty-two-year-old nanny working two jobs in the fall of 2011. In college Molly received her degree in art and architectural history—hardly subjects that would give her the knowledge and tools needed for effective community organizing. Yet in the fall of 2011 she self-organized a movement that challenged Bank of America's decision to impose a $5 monthly banking fee simply for the privilege of using its debit cards.

Molly's quest reverberated across the entire banking industry. She started a petition asking Bank of America to drop the new fee, and more than three hundred thousand people joined together with her and against the banking giant. Molly and her story also garnered national media exposure, driving customers to leave Bank of America and inspiring dozens of people to start copycat campaigns targeting their banks.[6]

What's remarkable is that Molly kick-started the movement with only the tools she had at her disposal: her laptop, her mobile phone, and a growing social action site called Change.org. Later, *New York Times* columnist Nick Kristof would name Change.org the "go to site for web uprisings"—a claim not too far off the mark, with more than two million new users signing up each month to take action.[7]

Molly's petition was just one example of the site's activist power. In 2011–2012 alone, Change.org social media campaigns have stalled the Stop Internet Piracy Act legislation; helped convince the Susan G. Komen for the Cure foundation to reverse its decision to cut funding for Planned Parenthood; lobbied Secretary of State Hillary Clinton to support Saudi Arabian women's right to drive; and even leveraged the social media prowess of a fourth-grade class to get Universal Studios to redesign its *The Lorax* website before the movie's world premiere.[8]

Organizations must note the growth of these sites and movements. There is a new breed of activists around, and they are armed with not only the passion and conviction to topple dictators and challenge institutions but also the technological tools and know-how to do so.

Ten years ago companies like Bank of America could make decisions about their operations without worrying much about their customers organizing a revolt against them. A customer like Katchpole could have instead reacted quietly by switching banks and sharing her frustration with a few of her close friends or colleagues. But there would have been no way for her to channel the emotions of hundreds of thousands of other affected customers to mount a coordinated response. The power shift is already starting to have a deep impact. Now social media gives individuals the ability to connect, respond, and take action, and such immediate connection and access have radically changed the way that organizations—including our country's largest corporations and nonprofits—respond.

Recognizing the potential for promoting social good online, social networks have started rolling out initiatives catering to a new generation of change makers. YouTube gives registered nonprofits benefits like "Donate Now" buttons and overlays that allow people to take action by clicking directly on a link embedded in their videos. Facebook has partnered with the nonprofit Causes to enable nonprofits to collect donations without ever leaving the website, and in fact has raised more than $40 million for more than twenty-seven thousand nonprofits since its inception in 2007.

THE PINK RIBBON REVOLT

If Molly's story isn't reason enough for nonprofits to take note, then perhaps what happened to the darling of the cancer organizations, Susan G. Komen for the Cure, will be. When news broke in early 2012 that Susan G. Komen for the Cure had decided to pull its funding to support Planned Parenthood, it sparked outrage unlike any we've seen toward a nonprofit organization in recent years. And because the campaign was fueled by a combination of passionate women armed with modern technology, there was little room for Komen to hide behind its decision.

But putting politics aside, even while assessing all the steps and missteps Komen made in coming to a decision that is in many ways still reverberating against the positive image Komen built over its thirty years, it also demonstrated one thing that Komen did right: the organization had built a network of activists bound together by more than the color pink.

Komen donors, walkers and runners, volunteers, and activists shared a collective identity built on education, empowerment, and interconnectedness. This robust network of mothers, sisters, fathers, and sons, bound together by everything from pink yogurt carton tops to pink NFL football cleats, didn't need Komen at its center. The issue that drove people to support Komen is the same one that would drive them elsewhere to support and fund research that would help bring an end to this deadly disease.

Petitions and expressions of outrage felt good to this community, but it didn't seem like enough tangible action to make it clear to Komen that their decision was outrageous. It was only a matter of days before a group of women (who are each social media mavens in their own right) set up the online Wiki #takebackthepink, an awareness campaign to show people that, even as they might wish to walk away from Komen, they should not walk away from the quest for a cure.[9]

Take Back the Pink turned attention away from the negative and instead used the energy of the masses, and online activists in particular, to focus on the positive. The campaign explained, "We are interested in leading people to the many paths that will bring an eradication of cancer while educating on the importance of organizational transparency and integrity."[10] The campaign offered other outlets to support the fight against a disease that kills more than forty thousand women in the United States each year.

The key organizers of the effort—Lucy Bernholz, Allison Fine, Beth Kanter, Stephanie Rudat, Amy Sample Ward, and Lisa Colton—shared their reflections and key takeaways via a series of blog posts, much of which they encouraged us to share herein. For those looking to truly understand what it takes to get a social media campaign off the ground, here is how Take Back the Pink unfolded over a matter of days:

- Allison Fine started an open conversation on Facebook. Out of that conversation came the idea for an online fundraising effort to support Planned Parenthood using Causes on Facebook, called, "Komen Kan Kiss My Mammogram." She circulated the link by email and on Facebook and quickly gained more than 2,000 supporters who collectively raised around $5,000.[11]
- On that same Facebook thread, Deanna Zandt reported creating a Tumblr blog called *Planned Parenthood Saved Me*.[12] The site would enable hundreds of

people to tell personal stories of how their lives were improved or saved because of the health screening services at Planned Parenthood.

- Later that day, Beth Kanter created a Pinterest website with the same name, capturing the growing number of images expressing anger at and displeasure with Komen. She also posted on her blog about the anti-Komen activities that had taken place over the previous twenty-four hours.[13]

- Then an interesting exchange took place on an open Facebook thread between the president and founder of the nonprofit consulting firm CauseWired, Tom Watson, and Lucy Bernholz.[14] The conversation shifted to how to catch the attention of the Super Bowl's enormous audience. Given the potent combination of the game's status as the largest media event of the year, the controversy around Komen (a long-time NFL partner), and social media (it was *reported* afterward that 11.5 million tweets were sent during the game), the group thought it would be fertile ground for a protest of some kind.

- An idea developed: to capitalize on this perfect storm and make a loud statement about the need to take politics out of women's health issues by "jumping" the Komen hashtag on Twitter. The effort aimed to capture just a small sliver of people paying attention to Komen on Super Sunday—self-identified by their use of the Komen hashtag #supercure—to broaden the conversation about breast cancer and women's health beyond Komen. And they did just that, garnering thousands of social media impressions over the next few days.[15]

Although Stephanie Rudat and Amy Sample Ward, two of the six key voices behind the Take Back the Pink effort, were indeed Millennials, the effort showed that simply leveraging the passion, disagreement, and outrage of a core group of former supporters could rally them to support the broader cause they so loved. The bond they shared was ignited in each post, like, and tweet. And most significant, the fuel to the outrage fire was provided not by conversation in person, but rather online in a heated and networked manner.

THE DIGITAL EXPERIENCE MILLENNIALS WANT AND EXPECT

Successful causes like Katchpole's or the Pink Ribbon Revolt were organized quickly and transparently—a necessary combination for Millennials. Although rapid advancements in technology have made us more connected, the jury is out on how effectively these connections are playing out in our institutions and nonprofit organizations. We all see the potential of social media to reach new constituents and expose more people to our work, but organizations are also drowning in the effort to develop the best tactics as they try to grasp concepts like *return on investment, influencers,* and *authentic engagement.*

Rather than digging too deeply into those specific tactics, we thought it more important to share some of the ways in which Millennials expect to be communicated with via social media. Without a doubt, there's a heightened expectation of immediacy among Millennials to gain information as quickly as possible and with a set of clear and actionable ways to get involved.

With their constant connectivity comes a regular flow of information via Twitter streams, texts, Facebook posts, and more—all making it much more difficult for organizations to gain, let alone keep, this generation's attention. With this in mind, organizations must start thinking about a shift in messaging by keeping both the visuals and the content fresh, simple, and to the point.

KEEPING IT HUMAN

It should come as no surprise that people want and even expect to connect in real time to real people, not to logos or to avatars. They want the opportunity to engage in real conversations that include an honest and transparent back-and-forth, not one-way communications. The channels Millennials use to find information and share their lives are highly personal, and the way they are interacting with technology is incredibly purposeful. The key, therefore, is actually quite simple: Organizations must get smarter about humanizing their interaction with constituents.

Being human is hard for some organizations that have grown in a formal model of marketing and public relations wherein the right sound bite ruled. It is ironic that the humanistic side of our work, the pinnacle of the nonprofit work we do to help people, is so hard to convey to people in social settings online. Instead, we opt for formal discussions and stock photos in an environment in which the people that follow us want us to be real with them.

Today, those rules are being broken for honest and authentic conversations around a cause. Today's organizations shouldn't be afraid to invite hard conversations about the beneficiaries they serve and the difficulties of maintaining programs when the need outpaces the resources coming in. This is a time when we can help each other and not be afraid that the prose we write will reflect badly.

The average Millennial updates her Facebook or other online social status an average of three times a day. She is visiting sites with a clear purpose and is not interested in being interrupted by extraneous information irrelevant to the task at hand. That said, she will respond when a friend or family member reaches out and makes an ask. Remember, Millennials have ways of filtering out just as much as they allow in; this is why it's incumbent upon organizations to get a sense of how this generation most want to be reached.

Let's take a look at the highly innovative WaterForward campaign launched by charity: water last year. The concept behind WaterForward is simple: What if the nearly one billion worldwide users of social media collectively came together and chipped in a few dollars to help solve the problem of clean water access for the nearly one billion people around the world who don't have it?

The site, which is based on the idea of paying it forward, comprises an online book of all the faces of people who are helping bring clean water to those who don't have it. The catch is, you can't actually add yourself to the book. Instead, when you donate you are purchasing a place in the book for a friend, family member, or colleague. That person then receives a notice that you've "bought them" a spot in the book, and it asks them to pay it forward. The beauty of the campaign is that you can track your impact, see whether your friends have donated, and understand the reach and networked impact of your donation—all aspects that resonate deeply with Millennial donors and activists.

Although the WaterForward campaign hadn't quite reached one billion people at the time we went to print, more than thirty thousand people's names had been added to the "book," representing more than $310,000. And what really sets the campaign apart is the organization's ability to bring in new donors, which is another way to measure success beyond just dollars raised.

The way that charity: water went about using gaming mechanics—to not simply ask friends to donate, but to honor them by including them and then ask them to pay it forward—created a high-touch campaign with low-touch action. charity: water continues to break new ground as an innovator in the online fundraising space and chart new territory for online engagement.

Organization Spotlight: Building Tomorrow

Building Tomorrow (BT) "empowers young people to invest their resources, time and talents in providing students in sub-Saharan Africa with access to an education."

Organization Overview:

- Three staff in the United States and seven in Uganda
- Twenty-five college chapters engaging hundreds of Millennial volunteers
- A ten-member Young Professional Council
- A high priority of engaging Millennials
- Budget of $251,000–$500,000

Inspiring Millennials to Share Causes Through Online Interaction

In February 2011, Building Tomorrow launched an online outreach tool called CalculateIt.org. The website's first page provides minimal information about Building Tomorrow or what their mission might be. Instead, it asks a simple question—how much did your first through seventh grade education cost? The calculated cost of your elementary school education is compared directly with the cost of providing access to education for children in Uganda. The numbers are startling, and the call to action is directly there—donate, fundraise, share, get involved, do something. The next page, however, is all about the mission and further connecting with the visitor.

"As an engagement tool, this website was designed to pull in Millennials and others to take the first step in learning about why we do what we do," said Liz Braden, a representative from Building Tomorrow. "Overall, our website has been one of the most effective ways to directly engage young professionals and college students—showing them their ability to make a difference and the ways that they can engage in our work."

Key to Building Tomorrow's success is understanding the importance of Millennials' ability to share issues that move them.

Braden continues, "In working with a wide network of Millennials, both college students and young professionals, our biggest asset is 'word of mouth' or rather today, seeing it on your friend's Facebook wall. The action steps on our site are to 'tell someone' with social media sharing links and 'do something' with fundraising and donating links. The 'tell someone' links include the exact numbers of that individual's cost of education and what it could provide in Uganda—again making it personal, individualized, and easily sharable."

When designing the site, Building Tomorrow purposely avoided language that pointed out the disparity between the Western visitor and Uganda. They let the visuals and stats speak for themselves, giving Millennials a chance to have their own reaction. "We simply wanted the moment of 'Wow, how can this be?' with the hope that Millennials and others would click on 'fundraise, donate, tell someone' to take that next step into 'what can I do to change this?'" said Braden.

THE SEARCH IS ON

Millions of corporate and philanthropic dollars have been invested in platforms that aggregate giving and volunteering data and then connect individuals to opportunities. However, the surprising truth is that Millennials aren't rushing to use these platforms to find information and take action. Instead, they are turning to that tried-and-true resource, Google.

In other words, if I am a young person who wants to volunteer for an environmental organization, I would simply Google "volunteering opportunities, environment, [my location]." All of a sudden, thousands of opportunities are generated. The trick then is to cull through the data to find relevant and updated information.

This power of search means organizations need to put new and increased emphasis on how their organizations show up in searches—specifically, Google searches. If we think about the first branding opportunity any organization has with Millennials, it's in the two-sentence descriptions you see when you search for causes online. Millennials are getting first impressions based on how an organization describes itself, what they can do when they come to the website, and, more important, how they can get involved. A bad first impression can end a relationship before it even begins. We must not ignore this important branding step in the Millennial investigation to get involved in issue areas they care about.

But don't stop there. Make sure you pay attention to what potential donors find when they actually arrive at your site. Search engines troll for content, and this information is typically found on pages hidden behind the homepage. Most organizations assume that when donors come to their site, they come through the front door—the homepage—every time. This is not true. A search result may bring visitors to a page about a story three pages deep in the website hierarchy. Because of this, you need to ensure that every page of your site is optimized for great design, information, and actionable ways to get involved immediately.

MARKET SEGMENTATION

It's important to segment the Millennial market in a way that defines what they are doing as well as the benefit they are seeking so you're able to personalize your message or product just for them. Do what you can to collect this important demographic's emails on the front end so you can later craft relevant messages and offer compelling opportunities to take action.

As you begin to acquire email addresses, make an effort to separate them into different groups based on their age cohort, using an email campaign management program such as Constant Contact, MailChimp, or Emma. When you have sorted them, you can begin to analyze their viewing trends, clickthroughs on content, and open rates much more easily than by looking at your email base as a whole.

For six months, send the same exact newsletter content to all groups, including the Millennial email list you've established. After six months, review your Millennial readership and analyze what they are actually doing with your content. Once you understand what resonates with your audience, the opportunity to move them to action grows much greater and their engagement with your content becomes much deeper.

THE FEEDBACK LOOP

Real-time feedback now allows for deep and detailed insight into consumers and constituents, and organizations should take advantage of it. Build genuine understanding and give up on the illusion of control. After all, in a networked world, organizations can no longer control what people think—much less what they say about the organization. Rather than sit silently and worry about what's being said, it's best to jump into the conversation.

Listen and respond to the feedback you receive and then use it to improve the value of your message. You may be surprised to find that this approach with Millennials will attract Gen X and Baby Boomers as well. People want control, and if you give them tools that enable them to take more control, and you make it easy for them to engage, they will pay you back in attention, support, promotion, and maybe even dollars.

What does a feedback loop look like? If you really want to get results from social media, it begins with creating a process. The process is based on setting a goal and then aligning the resources and activities that you think will help you accomplish that goal. Remember, it's not just about increasing the number of Twitter followers or Facebook fans (although it's easy to use that as a default, because the information is readily available for you and your competitors to see). Never compare your fan and follower count to anyone else's; instead, focus on the business outcomes of the account.

For nonprofits, this may be converting followers to donors, fostering a greater number of people talking about your services, improving customer service, or even generating ideas for future programming or events. Monitoring analytics, engagement, and collaboration are all part of an effective feedback loop that will strengthen your ability to connect with constituents across all demographics.

THE FUTURE IS MOBILE

The rapid evolution of mobile technology is fundamentally changing the relationship between information, time, and space. Information is now portable, participatory, and personal. To give you some context, more people will buy an iPhone today than will give birth to a baby—378,000 phones versus 371,000 babies. With this growth in mind, organizations must ask themselves what their email, website, and donation forms look like on a constituent's mobile device.

More than three-quarters of respondents to the Millennial Impact Report produced by Achieve, a creative fundraising agency, and its partner, the strategic fundraising consultancy Johnson Grossnickle and Associates (JGA), said they own a smartphone—and another 7 percent expected to get one in 2012.[16] They're doing more than tweeting and texting on their mobile devices, though. They're using their smartphones as mobile computers—in other words, as a way to access email, gather web-based information, and connect with peers. The majority of those connections have been for the purpose of reading emails or e-newsletters (67 percent) or getting updates from an organization (51 percent).

We know that Millennials want to act quickly and connect easily, so it makes sense that the smartphone figures prominently in their interactions with nonprofit organizations. Eighty percent of responding smartphone owners said they have in some way connected with a nonprofit via smartphone, with one-third of respondents saying they have used their smartphones to share news or updates about a nonprofit organization.

Although text giving has attracted a lot of attention in recent years, little more than half of the respondents said they would consider using their smartphones to make a donation to a nonprofit, and only 15 percent have done so (mostly through text giving). Of those who said they have not used their smartphones to make donations, most cited one of two reasons: they've never been asked (47 percent), or they have concerns about security (43 percent). Concern with security was later discussed in focus groups conducted by Achieve and JGA with Millennials in advance of the Millennial Impact Report, and it was discovered that social media privacy issues prevalent with Facebook were a factor in deciding whether or not to give through such platforms.

Nonprofits should note there are limits to the appeals of technology. In focus groups, many Millennials made it clear they do not want to receive texts or calls on their smartphones from nonprofit organizations because they consider texting and calling to be personal forms of communication. And although 37 percent of respondents said they would be interested in using their smartphones (via Facebook) to check in at a nonprofit event, 54 percent said they'd rather just check in at the event registration or welcome desk.

Organizations like the Met Opera and Best Friends Humane Society use their mobile websites to help Millennials sign up for the next performance or a volunteer activity. They have learned to reduce the amount of content in emails for easy reading on mobile devices, and their mobile-friendly websites have specific buttons for contact information, volunteer opportunities, giving, and events—the key pieces of information Millennials need when on the go with friends and peers.

Overall, organizations who use mobile well capitalize on opportunities to combine an individual's immediate need with the ability to help. All organizations that are contemplating their mobile strategies should consider moving beyond mobile as a simple giving opportunity and instead looking at it as a way to make an impact in a variety of areas.

Before You Go Mobile

As we now know that Millennials use smartphones for learning about organizations, reading email, sharing information, and (possibly) making donations, nonprofits must design their websites and communications materials for viewing on mobile devices. In addition, they must be sure that information can be shared easily and that all smartphone actions are clear and easy to execute.

Nonprofits, take note: Even if you offer the most accessible mobile sites, you will fail to attract smartphone giving unless you make clear requests. Take some time to learn how Millennials like to use their smartphones and interact with your organization on them; then design your offerings accordingly.

Here are some steps to consider:

1. Start by defining your audience. Figure out what you want them to do and what your organization's mobile goal is. Think beyond donating; what services can you offer? How can individuals engage with the content you're making available?

2. Don't start with the development of apps unless you have a really good reason. Instead, spend your time and resources to ensure that you have a mobile-friendly website that allows for easy browsing and a good user experience on a mobile device.

3. Assess the resources you will commit and the anticipated return on investment. Don't spend lots of money on development until you know you have an audience that will engage and help enhance the experience.

4. Recognize that marketing your mobile app takes resources. Ensure that your outreach and engagement systems are ready for the introduction of a new mobile program.

5. Provide mechanisms for feedback. Trust the wisdom of the crowd. Recognize that your users want the best possible experience and that sometimes you can provide it by heeding their advice and suggestions.

6. Find mechanisms to use mobile as a way to build lists and collect mobile phone numbers. Start with small experiments that are low-risk, and see what resonates with your audience. Then, depending on the interest and uptake, move on to bigger engagement opportunities with mobile.

MULTICHANNEL APPROACH

As has been mentioned, too often organizations look to new media and technology as the solution rather than a tool for deepening engagement. Although mobile use is on the rise among Millennials in particular, don't assume you can connect with them only via their phones. Ignoring traditional channels for engagement can result in missed opportunities. That's why we encourage organizations to take an integrated multichannel approach to engaging with prospective donors or volunteers.

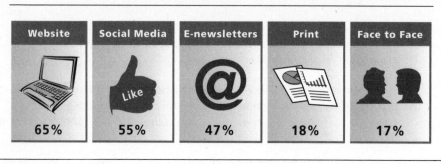

Figure 3.1
How Do You Prefer to Learn About Nonprofits?

Website	Social Media	E-newsletters	Print	Face to Face
65%	55%	47%	18%	17%

In any approach you choose, it's important that your brand message, tone, and manner are consistent. That way, if people first see your communication on a Facebook page and then get an email from you, they know right away that it's your organization and then know how to respond.

In the 2012 Millennial Impact Report, when asked how they prefer to learn about nonprofits, the majority chose websites (65 percent). Surprisingly, 35 percent (combined) said they prefer print and face-to-face contact in addition to social media and e-newsletters (see Figure 3.1). This tells nonprofit marketers they must use a multichannel approach when communicating with this generation. Relying on one or two channels alone will put them at a disadvantage.

WHERE SMALL NONPROFITS HAVE A BIG ADVANTAGE

At this point you may be thinking, how in the world can my nonprofit achieve this level of outreach? You're in good company: With more than 1.8 million nonprofit organizations operating in the United States today, the vast majority of them are small operations with budgets of less than $500,000 and staffs made up of just one or two people.

Even with these constraints, however, we have seen some of the most remarkable and passionate social media campaigns come from smaller organizations. The advantages these groups have over the large institutional structures are their ability to be nimble, take risks, and not be bogged down by a senior management that is risk-averse or unwilling to open themselves up.

Here are a few findings from the Case Foundation's *Report on America's Giving Challenge* that show the power smaller organizations can have in successfully implementing their social media strategies:[17]

- **Proximity to Personality.** Social media is showing us that people connect to people much more easily than they connect to organizations. Smaller organizations often have the benefit of having a more personalized "people to people" approach.
- **Risk Tolerance.** Small, upstart organizations may be a bit more comfortable with experimentation than larger organizations. Large organizations may feel that a misstep could tarnish their brand somehow. Small organizations know mistakes are just part of the learning process, and it's great to make them (at least for the first time!) early and often.
- **Rapid Adaptation.** Small organizations don't have layers of bureaucracy and approvals. If they have a strategy that's not working, they move to another one quickly. They don't have to send it up the chain of command for approval.
- **Authenticity.** Large organizations have a tendency to overpolish their social media efforts and lose their humanity. In social media, authenticity always wins—and at times authenticity requires imperfection.

Connected consumers are only becoming more pervasive in society and ultimately in your nonprofit organizations. With this in mind, organizations like yours must not only recognize how the landscape is shifting but also keep up and remain competitive in the new social market. Your constituents' expectations are far more complex than they have ever been, and their ability to provide instantaneous reactions and feedback has never been greater.

Eight Practical Tips for Building Your Online Social Media Strategy

This Land Is Your Land. Even if you don't plan on using it right away (or ever), be sure to reserve your online space by creating your organization's Facebook page, Twitter account, YouTube channel, LinkedIn profile, and so on so you have them ready as your organization gets more involved in building its social media presence. The most important thing here is to claim your land before others have an opportunity to do so.

(Continued)

Time to Decorate. People want to get to know you, what you stand for, what you care about, what's in it for them, and who's doing the talking and posting. Take advantage of all that your profile has to offer by sharing photos, information about your programs, links to your website and blog, and anything else that helps prove you're a real nonprofit, doing real things. It also helps to have a real person behind the organization, so take some time to introduce the person(s) who are managing the account on your behalf.

Listen Up Before You Speak Up. Look before you leap, and listen before you speak. It's important to take some time to get to know the territory. See what others who are in your "space" are doing to engage with their constituents. Learn from their best practices as well as their mistakes. Start poking around to see whether there are other nonprofits focused in similar areas and then engage in conversation with them, much as you would if you met someone in person at a conference. This allows you to connect with people who are already interested in the things you do and may be partners or supporters in the future.

Chat It Up (But Hold Off on Your Ask). Once you've spent time finding and listening to those with whom you want to connect, start building relationships. Don't lead with an ask or by promoting your own programs, but first get to know others on a more personal level. Social media is about relationships. Offer to help, share links, retweet others, and engage in conversation.

Identify and Interact with Influencers. Perhaps your cause already has a spokesperson, but whether or not this is the case, there are individuals who have tremendous social media pull. If you can figure out the appropriate ways to engage them, it can amplify your message in ways you couldn't imagine. Influencers can help you reach more people because of the trusted relationships they have already built.

Call Your Army to Action. At the end of the day, doing the steps outlined above has a purpose: to build a community of people who support your organization and are willing to take action in support of your cause. Your online network will respond when you ask *if* you've built real relationships, engaged with people, proved to be a useful resource, connected others, and had an overall positive impact on your online community.

Say "Thx." We all know the Golden Rule: "Do unto others . . ." The same holds true in social media. A thank-you in the virtual world is as easy as a follow-back, a retweet, liking a Facebook page, leaving a comment on a blog, showing up at an event, or any other action that you've asked them to take. Social media is cyclical, and the people who continue to come back and support you are the ones you support in return.

GENERATION CONNECTED: THE MILLENNIAL ENGAGEMENT PLATFORM

Although our world is flatter, faster, and more hyperconnected than ever before, it's still people that make technology matter. In fact, we'd argue that technology is more about a mind-set and the strength of relationships than it is about the latest app or new gadget. The real value of social media comes down to people, relationships, and the way the two intersect.

So how do we move organizations from being users of social media to actually being "social organizations"? And what does today's social organization look like, knowing that technology is the backbone of so much of how Millennials function? Let's take a look (see Figures 3.2 and 3.3).

Figure 3.2
Generation Connected: Millennial Engagement Platform

Leadership Inviting

New media is a necessary utility for functioning in the 21st century, but how it is best leveraged is an evolving process for most nonprofits and businesses alike. Organizations have to make it easy for Millennials (and everyone for that matter) to find them, and once they arrive, nonprofits need to be open to give them what they want, how they want it, and on their terms. This means that executives not only have to be willing to relinquish some control, but they should also develop platforms for listening. Listening is a good way for organizations to orient themselves online, and social media makes listening to large numbers of people easy and inexpensive.

Tangible Transparency

People want and expect to connect in real time to real people, not to logos or avatars. They want the opportunity to engage in real conversations that include an honest and transparent back-and-forth, not one-way communications. The channels that Millennials use to find information and share their lives are highly personal, and the way they interact with technology is incredibly purposeful. The key, therefore, is actually quite simple: Organizations must get smarter about humanizing their interaction with constituents and act more like people, not formal institutions.

Social Connectivity

Social connectivity is a given—but organizations need to think about the value they are providing through their connections. For some it is facilitating authentic conversations—some of which are actionable, others to build relationships. Other times social connectivity is about sharing resources, links, and information without any expectation of a direct return from that person.

Solution-Inspired

Too often organizations look to new media and technology as the solution rather than a tool for deepening engagement. While mobile use is on the rise among this demographic in particular, don't assume you can only connect with them via their phones. Ignoring traditional channels for engagement can result in missed opportunities. That's why we encourage organizations to take an integrated multichannel approach to engaging with prospective donors or volunteers.

BUILD a Better Environment by Engaging Millennials

Be Unified

With Millennials, you either go authentic or go home. It's all about trust and backing up what you say, but this also means that everyone from the top down needs to have an agreed upon and consistent message.

Understand Their Environment

The best organizations on social media understand not only the medium they are using to communicate, but also the individuals to whom they are interacting with. The ultimate goal should be to share information that creates a community of "insiders."

Identify Key Change Makers

There are many individuals and organizations doing online engagement work well. Find them, connect with them, and find out their secret sauce. Social media is about reciprocity and people are more willing to share than you might think.

Lead by Engagement

The key to social media is being "social"—and that means engaging with constituents in ways that resonate with them. But don't be too quick to engage without understanding what drives your audience to take action.

Determine Success

Success in social media is not the number of followers or friends you have. Success is determined instead by focusing on the business outcomes of the account. Define what your goal and method will be, but also be willing to adapt along the way.

Figure 3.3
Generation Connected: Five Key Takeaways

1 Within social media networks, discuss the issues you are dealing with as an organization. Ask your community questions, ideas, and ways to improve on a weekly basis. This can easily be done through polls on social media platforms like Facebook.

2 Millennials are interested in the people behind the social media handles and profiles. Show more of yourself by posting video blogs, stories, and views from what you see with the people you serve. Provide direct contact information (phone, email, social media) for the key people of your organization.

3 Use images and video generously on social platforms to share the stories of your work as well as the people behind them.

4 Create at least one shareable action on each page of your website. For example: "If you like this article, please share with your firends on Facebook."

5 Search social media content (posts/tweets) and comment/provide feedback on conversations relevant to the issue of the cause.

A SPECIAL NOTE TO THE EXECUTIVE LEADER

The business models and hierarchical structures that are all too common in traditional nonprofit institutions will not allow for the same kind of engagement in the connected age. Certainly, Millennials are not the only demographic using social media. But they did come of age when social media was the cool new thing. It is integrated into their daily lives; it's how they connect with friends and understand the world.

This generation engages with brands, channels, and organizations in new ways, limited only by the rate of technological advancement and innovation. You must think about your constituents as consumers and interact with them based on their heightened expectations, and on the platforms and formats they use to communicate and make informed decisions.

A Call to Action

In 2010, while watching the devastation of the Haiti earthquake unfold on TV and across the Internet, twenty-seven-year-old Jake Wood knew he had a special set of skills as a former Marine combat veteran—and he'd be ashamed if he didn't use them to go and help the people of Haiti in the immediate aftermath. But even after four years of service with tours in Iraq as a platoon leader and in Afghanistan as a scout-sniper, Jake knew he would be up against a different kind of enemy.

The day after the earthquake, Jake posted a message on his Facebook page: "I'm going to Haiti. Who's in?" Within hours the first unit was formed, with volunteer first responders, doctors, nurses, and combat vets. Calling themselves Team Rubicon, within days they had $250,000 in medical supplies and donations, thanks to their savvy use of social networking and an eager pool of friends who saw this as a way to lend their support. Within two weeks Wood and his team had saved more than 2,500 lives and livelihoods before the larger humanitarian groups arrived.

But their work didn't stop in Haiti. Since the initial team landed in Port-au-Prince in January 2010, Team Rubicon has been deployed to Chile, the Thai-Burma border, Pakistan, South Sudan, and most recently to Alabama, Missouri, and Texas following devastating tornados in 2012—using their military experience and operational expertise to provide speedy help to victims every step of the way.

Under Wood's leadership, Team Rubicon's military model has created a dynamic new paradigm for disaster relief, deploying rapidly when every hour counts, uniting combat veterans with medical professionals, thriving in the midst of chaos with real-time communications, partnering with members of the local community, and bridging the gap between disaster and response. Moreover, Team Rubicon has ensured that returning veterans are not left alone on the sidelines and that their skills and talents are not wasted, but instead strengthened and leveraged for good.

Team Rubicon: A View from the Ground in Haiti

Personal reflections from Jake Wood, founder and CEO, Team Rubicon

After the earthquake in Haiti, the media showed us images of mass looting, chaos, just absolute pandemonium. We felt compelled to help. We called up the large aid organizations and were turned away. "Thanks but no thanks," they said. "Send us donations instead."

But we didn't have money to offer. We had skills and experience.

Just twenty-four hours after the quake, we had established contact with a group of Jesuits in Port-au-Prince. "Get down here immediately," they said. "You can use our compound as a base."

Team Rubicon was on the ground three and half days after the quake. We knew that once we crossed the Artibonite River from the Dominican Republic into Haiti, there was no going back.

While hundreds of relief workers and supplies sat on the tarmac of the main airport, we trudged into the hardest-hit areas of Port-au-Prince with only what we could carry on our backs. We partnered with trusted local nationals to mitigate risk and better serve those in need.

Team Rubicon treated around three thousand patients during our first mission. While the situation for many relief workers may not have been ideal in the immediate aftermath of earthquake, we thrived in it. We know how to do chaos. We're Marines.

It was then that it dawned on us. Using the skills we had learned in the military—teamwork, decisive leadership, risk management, emergency medicine—we can save lives in that "golden hour" immediately following a natural disaster. Moreover, our skills allow us to occupy a unique niche in disaster response; small, fleet-footed teams can respond and treat victims faster than larger bureaucratic organizations.

The Millennial Generation's flexibility and creativity are remarkable to observe. Like Wood, many Millennials are looking at their next chapters as a time for self-exploration. With the weight of economic and global uncertainty factoring into their every decisions, they're trying to find meaning in their jobs, and many are delaying their entry into the traditional workforce.

For example, Millennials are enrolling in programs such as AmeriCorps in record numbers. More than 582,000 people applied to the national service program in 2011, but due to federal funding limitations, they competed for just 82,000 spots. In the past two years alone, nearly one million AmeriCorps applicants have been turned away from serving our communities. And, despite passage of the bipartisan Kennedy Serve America Act, which set a path to increase AmeriCorps to 250,000 members annually by 2017, the law authorized only the expansion and did not guarantee funding. As a result, Congress has slowly decreased its support over recent years.

Although it's frustrating to see so many turned away, the outpouring of passion to serve is also motivating. Just ask Millennial Zach Maurin, who together with Aaron Marquez founded ServeNext following their full-time year of service with AmeriCorps at City Year in Boston. Maurin, who deferred college to join City Year at the age of eighteen, explained, "People who do service are often the ones who don't want to get into politics. We're trying to change that perception and the way that people think about how they affect change locally and at a national level."

In politics, Maurin explains, "There are highs and lows, victory and defeat, and trying to take on Capitol Hill doesn't always make you feel as good as going to spend two hours mentoring a child where you get immediate gratification and know you're having a direct impact. We're trying to change that."

Marquez, who serves as a first lieutenant in the United States Army Reserve, reflected on the role of service during the height of the Congressional Appropriations process in 2011 and wrote in an editorial in the *Huffington Post*:

> Less than one percent of the U.S. population serves in the Armed Forces, and even fewer have the opportunity to serve in a civilian national service program. While our country is engaged in two wars abroad we have asked very little of citizens at home. The one percent of Americans that serve in the military and their families are bearing an inequitable burden to keep our country free during this time of war. Shouldn't we ask citizens to protect our communities here at home by improving our schools, responding to natural disasters, and bringing clean energy to our neighborhoods? Through national service we can strengthen our democracy, meet pressing challenges, build a more active and engaged citizenry, and live up to America's promise to "form a more perfect union."[1]

Like many Millennials, Maurin and Marquez see a deliberate blurring of the lines between social change and business, but not as much between social change and politics. At ServeNext, the philosophy is first you serve and then you become an advocate. Considering that more than seven hundred thousand

Americans have served in AmeriCorps since 1994, there is a vast pool of talent and energy that can be channeled to help advocate in Washington, DC, and in communities across the country.

For the nonprofit sector, AmeriCorps alumni represent a paradigm shift, an opportunity to harness on-the-ground experience into a massive new leadership generation. Individuals trained in AmeriCorps programs such as Teach For America and Citizen Schools will continue to buoy leadership and education reform in this country. And if they can't find opportunities to serve at home, Millennials are just as eager to head overseas. They might turn their focus to global health inequity through programs such as Global Health Corps, or apply to take a gap year between high school and college through programs like Global Citizen Year (see Figure 4.1).

A NEW BREED OF ACTIVISTS AND DOERS

As Wood, Maurin, and Marquez demonstrate, Millennials have established themselves as a new breed of activists and doers. But for the average nonprofit, understanding how to engage them in volunteer work can be a mystery. Although Millennials are seen as ambitious and hopeful, whether the world will live up to their great expectations is a question yet to be answered.

This chapter focuses on demystifying the Millennial volunteer, because the problems facing our local and global communities call for exactly the values that Millennials believe in: collaboration, teamwork, openness, and transparency. It's up to organizations now to take the first step in understanding what gets Millennial volunteers engaged and, perhaps more important, what keeps them engaged.

According to the 2012 Millennial Impact Report, Millennials who want to support nonprofits overwhelmingly will do so by giving of their time, with 63 percent of them reporting they volunteered for nonprofits in 2011. Even better, 90 percent of respondents say they expect to volunteer as much in 2012 as they did in 2011, if not more. And by a margin of more than two to one, Millennials who volunteer for nonprofits are also more likely to turn to their wallets and give.

According to the 2011 Volunteering in America Report released by the Corporation for National and Community Service, 11.6 million Millennials dedicated 1.2 billion hours of their time to volunteer service across the country during 2010.[2] This accounts for 21.2 percent of all Millennials in the United States.

Figure 4.1
The Future of Social Activism

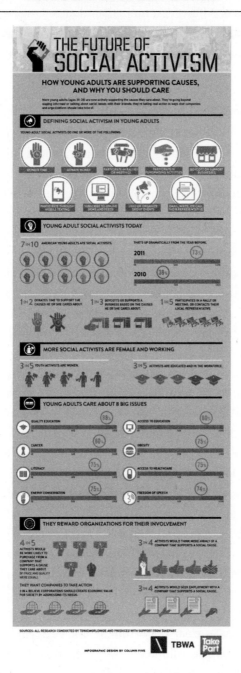

In comparison to other generations, this is lower than the national average, but volunteer rates in this demographic have risen steadily over the years. From 1989–2005, volunteer rates of Millennials more than doubled, from 13.4 percent to 28.4 percent.[3] These numbers underscore the importance of getting them in and getting them set up with meaningful opportunities to contribute their time and talent.

HOW DO MILLENNIALS FIND OPPORTUNITIES TO SERVE?

What's the best way to find Millennial volunteers? According to the 2012 Millennial Impact Report, 81 percent prefer to learn about volunteer opportunities from friends or family members, 72 percent appreciate getting information from email, and 68 percent look to the organization's website for volunteer information.

Given that so much volunteering with Millennials is peer-related, organizations need to create volunteer recruitment campaigns through social media networks such as Facebook. This includes promotion through peer influencers and other online agents of the organization to help spread the visibility and reach of volunteer opportunities. (We'll cover more on peer influence in the next chapter.)

Although today's unprecedented technology allows us to reach new audiences, the call to action must be clear, it must be actionable, and it must show impact. Platforms such as All for Good—the über-aggregator of many of the online volunteer matching sites like Idealist, VolunteerMatch, and Network for Good—are powerful tools, yet they're only as powerful as the opportunities that nonprofits upload. When we enter our zip codes into a search engine and let it work its magic, we don't want to find an opportunity that's outdated or already over capacity. We've taken the first step, and we expect to be matched with an opportunity that makes sense and is available.

This could go beyond providing good volunteer opportunities to creating more of a relational experience between volunteer and organization. Organizations should solicit feedback, provide follow-up, and ask what it could do better. Sites such as Great Nonprofits allow folks to rate their experiences and share knowledge so others can make more informed decisions about where to give or volunteer.

But although platforms can have all the bells and whistles in the world, the big question remains: How do we get nonprofits to use these tools in a smart way that provides up-to-date, clear opportunities for engagement and makes more people want to use them to volunteer? And then how do nonprofits turn those volunteers into champions and supporters?

Organization Spotlight: Giving Sum

In this interview with the founders of Giving Sum, a giving circle of young professionals, Marty Posch and Ryan Brady discuss the challenges and successes of engaging Millennials in a program in which both financial and volunteering commitments are required. Notice the breakthrough they had when it came to working with Millennials and their loved ones. For the complete interview, please visit: www.causeforchangebook.com.

Q: Why did you start Giving Sum?

A: We were looking for ways to capture and expose young professionals in Indianapolis to new ways of involvement with organizations. We wanted to open their eyes to the incredible work of some of the best nonprofit organizations in the city. We also felt that there had to be a better model of giving to nonprofits for this generation than just financial transactions. The Giving Sum model takes a passion, interest, financial, time, and support approach to mobilize a group of Millennials to make an impact locally.

Q: Can you describe the Giving Sum Model?

A: We have three tenets to our work: philanthropy has to be fun, philanthropy has to become part of your lifestyle, and philanthropy must be an independent decision but empowered by others around you. Through Giving Sum, you give $500 to become a member. We wanted a commitment of people new to philanthropy. This would mean they would be invested beyond just signing a piece of paper. We always joke that the experience is better than watching cable, so divert your cable bill to us.

The model provides education, service, and leadership development for members with organizations and thought leaders in the community. From monthly programming to networking throughout the year, we have created an approach where learning about philanthropy and active civic engagement begins to become ingrained in every day life. We realize now that not everyone will be at a super-engaged level. We see the one-third model of engagement happening for us. In other words, one-third of the Giving Sum members will spend at least a couple hours volunteering and coming to meetings, one-third will come to every meeting and some volunteer activities, and one-third are super engaged, serve in leadership capacities, and provide overarching direction for the organization.

Q: How do you get Millennials engaged in nonprofit organizations either as donors, volunteers, or evangelists?

A: It is a together concept. You as an individual need to tell us (the organization) and decide with us how your money and time should be used in the community to help the people that need it most. This is a partnership approach and not an us-versus-them mentality. We are partial to an environment where conversation, education, and the collective group

(Continued)

can produce powerful results. Do not underestimate the power of peers. In particular, focus on couples. We have discovered that Millennials who are just starting to date or are creating new paths of life together with their spouses or partners want experiences together. Philanthropic involvement is an incredible opportunity to provide something for them to do outside home and work. The challenge is that not every organization has volunteer programming or involvement for couples together. For example, if you want to have an experience together, yet the volunteer project has one person in one room filing and the other in a room answering phones, the likelihood of this being a good experience for them as a couple is pretty much zero.

Q: What does the future hold for Giving Sum?

A: We have started to realize that there is a life cycle for our members and Giving Sum. Some will not renew, not because of programming but because we have helped them identify that philanthropic passion and they are running with it. For example, a member the other day just became the chair of the board of a nonprofit. Through us they were exposed to the group and also learned the skills necessary for good governance and leadership. So I would say that we prepare our members to leave.

Giving Sum and its brand have started to migrate beyond meetings and education. We are now implementing citywide days of giving, service, and other options for members outside the formal opportunities we offer. Other organizations and institutions now come to us to help them think through the involvement of this next generation of philanthropists. So we see our role in helping to educate the broader community, in addition to our members, about how to make giving, volunteering, and education a model for others to institutionalize.

PROVIDE EXPERIENCES BASED ON SKILLS

Millennials don't want to just help nonprofits; they actually want to play a role in leading them and making them better by putting their brains, expertise, and skills to work. It's not enough to ask them to sort cans at a food bank or paint murals on the wall of an elementary school. Although these are important activities, Millennials have transferable skills in technology, business development, communications, and other key areas that nonprofits desperately need help with—but rarely do nonprofits take the time to make these deliberate connections.

In the 2012 Millennial Impact Report, Millennials were asked what kind of volunteer activities they preferred, and 48 percent of respondents said they wanted to use their education, background, or professional expertise to help nonprofits build their capacity. The volunteer activities can take many forms: a business analyst for McKinsey might have the skills to help an organization undergoing a strategic planning process, or a young Deloitte accountant might be able to help review materials before an organization's audit. As Figure 4.2 shows in greater detail, there are a number of ways that Millennials are choosing to spend their volunteer hours; using their professional skills leads all other forms of volunteer service.

Recognizing that more and more young people are expecting and in some cases demanding opportunities to give back as part of their professional careers, we are seeing organizations such as the Taproot Foundation taking bold steps to redefine pro bono service. They're expanding the model beyond the legal profession to help ensure that organizations have access to the marketing, design, technology, and strategic planning resources they need to succeed.

The brainchild of Aaron Hurst, the Taproot Foundation was founded with the premise that the eight million business professionals in the United States have the skills and talent nonprofits sorely need. Corporate America spends more than $60 billion on advertising in a year, and nonprofits need succinct clear messages to stand out in that clutter. With four hundred thousand communications professionals throughout the country, Taproot knew they could find individuals who could help them; thus was born an organization that today reaches beyond just communications professionals and provides volunteer opportunities for individuals in industries from finance to technology.

Since 2001, Taproot has engaged business professionals in more than 780,000 hours of pro bono service on more than 1,300 projects in five key cities. What's more, they are behind a national effort, A Billion + Change, that has energized businesses to dedicate nearly $2 billion in pro bono services to nonprofits.

The Millennial generation is hungry for these kinds of volunteer opportunities. Hurst says the average age of volunteers in Taproot programs is about thirty-five, with a significant cohort of professionals ages twenty-six to thirty-five. Not only can younger employees use and improve on their own skills, but they can also gain greater leadership experience managing and overseeing volunteer project teams to address a nonprofit client's needs.

Similar to Taproot, online micro-volunteering platforms such as Sparked and Catchafire (which, incidentally, were both founded by Millennials) are leveraging online communities of skilled volunteers to make it easier for business professionals to share skills without having to quit their day jobs. What's more, these platforms are making it easier for nonprofits to leverage the goodwill of these savvy professionals in return.

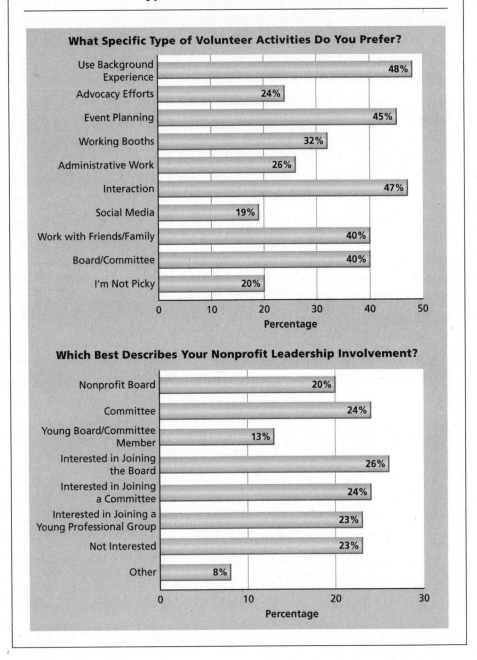

Figure 4.2
Types of Volunteer Activities

What Specific Type of Volunteer Activities Do You Prefer?

Activity	Percentage
Use Background Experience	48%
Advocacy Efforts	24%
Event Planning	45%
Working Booths	32%
Administrative Work	26%
Interaction	47%
Social Media	19%
Work with Friends/Family	40%
Board/Committee	40%
I'm Not Picky	20%

Percentage

Which Best Describes Your Nonprofit Leadership Involvement?

Involvement	Percentage
Nonprofit Board	20%
Committee	24%
Young Board/Committee Member	13%
Interested in Joining the Board	26%
Interested in Joining a Committee	24%
Interested in Joining a Young Professional Group	23%
Not Interested	23%
Other	8%

Percentage

In the case of Sparked, all the projects are entirely web-based, making volunteering mobile and accessible to a generation that is constantly on the move. Projects, or "challenges" as Sparked refers to them, are designed as activities that can be completed collaboratively and entirely online. When a user logs into Sparked, the challenge-matching engine recommends a series of challenges based on the person's skills and interests profile. It's up to the individual to take on a challenge and work toward finishing a project, often in conjunction with others who are completing similar tasks in a crowd-sourced way.

Getting to know your organization's volunteers and the skills they bring to the table is an important first step in bringing them closer to meaningful engagement. Nonprofits that don't offer Millennials the opportunities to both "work in the trenches" and apply their professional skills and expertise run the risk of losing them to other organizations or other life priorities.

We know that time is a precious commodity for Millennials, but as Millennial Impact Report results indicate, it's not about time; it's about being asked. This suggests that nonprofits need to be more direct about engaging Millennials in real decision making and leadership. Give younger leaders the chance to do meaningful work that leverages their best assets, and it's more likely you'll engage them for the long term.

To capitalize on the opportunity presented by volunteer talent, nonprofit leaders need to expand their vision of volunteering, integrate volunteers into their strategic planning, and reinvent the way that their organizations support and manage volunteer talent. And if they want the highly skilled volunteers to stay, they need to create an experience that is meaningful for the volunteer, develops skills, demonstrates impact, and taps into volunteers' abilities and interests. The more people are stimulated and engaged, the more they will make time to volunteer.

Organizational Spotlight: Global Health Corps

Global Health Corps, founded and led by former First Daughter Barbara P. Bush, is a Millennial-driven movement working on the front lines to bring attention to global health inequity at home and abroad. Global Health Corps was built on the notion that the rising generation of Millennials has the passion, energy, and skills to confront today's global health challenges and the opportunity to engage effectively right now. What's more, they have

(Continued)

figured out how to make a very deliberate connection that leverages the professional skills of their Fellows.

Some might be surprised to learn that very few Global Health Corps Fellows have any formal training in the health care profession prior to their year of service. They are writers, teachers, economists, actors, social entrepreneurs, and more. This gap is intentional. As Bush has shared, it's assumed that you can't work in global health if you're not a medical professional. Thus opportunities are scarce for individuals with backgrounds in program management, supply-chain systems, computer programming, or engineering to embark on a career serving public health.

Without these opportunities, too many skilled young professionals are left out and unable to offer innovative approaches to some of the most pressing challenges of our time. This is precisely the bridge that the Global Health Corps is hoping to build through its program, by recognizing that the complexity and scope of today's challenges require people with diverse skills to deliver innovative sustainable solutions.

Take, for example, twenty-six-year-old Ameet Salvi. He studied engineering at UC Berkeley and landed a job shortly after graduation working on supply chain management at Restoration Hardware and then at Gap. Like many other Millennials, Salvi decided he wanted to put his skills to use for social good. He applied and was accepted to Global Health Corps.

As Bush tells Salvi's story, she explains, "His job is to do for the one million people of Zanzibar exactly what he did for the Gap. But instead of getting jeans to the Gap and off to the consumers, he is working to get life-saving medicines into the hands of patients and hospitals that need them most."

Salvi is but one example of how the rising generation is stepping up to address global health inequity. The complexity and scope of global health challenges are vast, but new approaches to solving problems are necessary, and the rising generation of Millennials is delivering results.

THE THREE R'S: RECRUITMENT, RETENTION, RECOGNITION

We know that positive volunteer experiences depend on three key elements, no matter what your age or skill level: creative methods of *recruitment*, concerted efforts around *retention*, and *recognition* for a job well done. The catch is that when it comes to each of these three elements, different age cohorts expect to be treated slightly differently. Here's how we see it break down:

Recruitment

- **Boomers** want organizations to offer opportunities and volunteer position descriptions that show how they will leverage their skills. They want to be ensured positions of leadership. Some of the best ways to reach them are through publicity in newspapers and through religious institutions.

- **Generation X-ers** expect organizations to meet them where they are—and therefore are more inclined to be attracted to family or corporate volunteer opportunities with flexible scheduling. They also want opportunities for independent volunteer service, and they are not as focused on the "group" thing.

- **Millennials** want team positions and opportunities to volunteer in groups; they want to leverage online tools, especially mobile and social media, to reach the audience in authentic ways; and they want to be able to easily invite their friends.

Retention

- **Boomers:** Organizations should reimagine their roles to keep them stimulated and so they take on volunteer management opportunities. Also note that the more hours Boomers volunteer, the more likely they are to come back.

- **Generation X-ers:** Organizations should give this cohort family volunteer opportunities, change processes to adapt to their needs, and respect their skills and opinions.

- **Millennials:** Their needs are similar to those of Gen X, with an emphasis on regular communication, typically through the use of varied channels (both on- and offline).

Recognition

- **Boomers:** Organizations should focus on recognizing their expertise, leadership, and ongoing commitment.

- **Generation X-ers:** Organizations should recognize their creativity and independent contributions.

- **Millennials:** Organizations should recognize their collaborative efforts and recognize the individuals for being team players.

Volunteering and service have been ingrained in this generation for quite some time, with junior and high schools often mandating that students log a certain number of volunteer hours in order to obtain a diploma. But although schools' good intentions are commendable, author Ron Alsop notes that they aren't always entirely selfless.

In his book about the Millennial generation, *The Trophy Kids Grow Up*, Alsop says that some have volunteered for public service projects partly so they could beef up their resumes to impress college admissions officers and corporate recruiters. They're not the only generation that has aspired to change the world, either. Alsop writes:

> Although the Millennials may be quite passionate about changing the world, they are hardly the first generation with such ambitions. Indeed, many Millennials are the children of activist baby-boomers who staged sit-ins and boycotts to protest the Vietnam War or the plight of migrant farm workers, discrimination against women and minorities, and environmental pollution. This may be the generation for Al Gore's *An Inconvenient Truth* documentary about the perils of global warming, but it was the boomers who helped celebrate the first Earth Day in 1970.[4]

Although this is true, and Millennials have their Boomer parents to thank for instilling these behaviors into their routines from an early stage in life, we also know that Millennials are using the tools at their disposal to go about volunteering and engagement in a different way.

BUILDING A NEW CONTINUUM OF ENGAGEMENT

Millennials, for the most part, are politically aware and believe their actions can make a difference. Although most are less inclined than preceding generations to take more active steps, such as participating in a demonstration or writing a letter-to-the-editor, their interest in doing *something*—coupled with their belief that doing so has an impact—serves as an entry point to engagement. Organizations need to develop pathways that lead young adults from interest in an issue, toward easy actions, and then on to increasing levels of commitment.

For example, initial and low-threshold actions such as donating money and goods might be followed by invitations to attend meetings or engage in short-term volunteering. In much the same manner, entry-level or brief volunteer experiences should be followed by opportunities to engage in more in-depth volunteer work and skill development.

We have recognized that there is a changing continuum of engagement, and all nonprofits must begin to create opportunities within that continuum in order to both attract and retain the Millennial volunteer (see Figure 4.3).

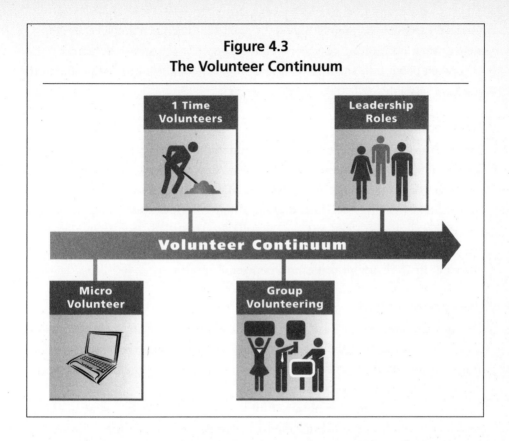

Figure 4.3
The Volunteer Continuum

The Millennial volunteer continuum is a new way of thinking about organizations' volunteer engagement efforts. Its goal is to provide an approach that deepens volunteer involvement over time, and it is structured to offer Millennials opportunities focused on both frequency and skill. Though we call it a continuum, it's less about moving people from one end of the spectrum to the other than it is about giving them the opportunity to see themselves as part of a larger, continuous effort.

The first level provides Millennials with micro-volunteering activities. As defined by Sparked.com, micro-volunteering is "volunteering that you can do in small bits of time—from five minutes to two hours. It's high-impact, high-efficiency do-gooding." Micro-volunteering has the following attributes: It is convenient, crowdsourced, and network-managed.

Convenience

Micro-volunteering is volunteerism that fits into your schedule *when you have time*—typically (but not necessarily) via an internet-connected device such as a personal computer or mobile phone. In practice, to achieve this level of convenience, often no training or vetting by the nonprofit is needed. Volunteer tasks are broken down into small tasks so that you can complete one within the time you have available.

Crowdsourced

For many nonprofits, the idea of crowdsourcing their needs has opened up the door to new perspectives and new volunteers. Organizations will present a need and then ask a larger group for assistance. Micro-volunteers who have the time, interest, and (ideally) the skills and who *may* be previously unknown to the nonprofit will jump in and answer the calls for assistance. This often allows an organization to open itself up to a much broader base of potential volunteers and introduce its work and priorities to a new set of supporters.

Network-Managed

The time demands of the manager (typically a nonprofit staffer) are reduced by distributing as much of the project management and quality review as possible to the network of micro-volunteers. This work management method differs from a top-down model of project management.

To better understand the power of micro-volunteering, let's look at an example from an after-school organization in Georgia that posted the following on Sparked.com as a volunteer opportunity:

Share Your Talent: Help a Kid

We give tuition-free tutoring for children in kindergarten through second grade. I'm a retired educator and I've seen how discouraged a youngster can get when they just can't "get" it and both parents have to work.

So, I have iPads and Android tablets, but I need help locating specific apps that are priced $10 and under to strengthen specific academic skills. The two basic areas are language arts and math. Here are two areas of apps needed:

1-creative writing

2-word problems incorporating $+$, $-$, and simple $\times$

I've downloaded some creative writing apps and deleted them because they were confusing to follow. They have to be simple to follow the directions (especially for us tutors to learn!!). Thank you SO much.

As you can see in this posting, the organization created a *"project brief"* with the specific outcome and result needed for those looking for a small project. Seven volunteers responded with their ideas and advice to help the organization use the appropriate apps for the people they serve. As these seven provided ideas, the online community critiqued their thoughts. This crowdsourced model provided a unique opportunity to find the best solution for the organization. This approach also allowed volunteers to get the project done with a minimal amount of planning and coordination.

The next level of the Millennial volunteer continuum is one-time, specific volunteer opportunities, or what many refer to as a "Day of Service." These may be nationally sponsored days like Make a Difference Day or the Martin Luther King, Jr. Day of Service, or they may be coordinated through corporations or even nonprofits themselves.

Whatever the case, these activities require no more than one day's commitment from Millennials. Although the opportunities are small in comparison to ongoing commitments, they still call for the skills of volunteers and must be meaningful for both the organization and the individual. Your organization should see these days of service as the first exposure a volunteer has with an organization—and you don't want to make a bad first impression. Even though these are short-term projects, the experience that Millennials have with these has a tremendous influence on whether or not you will see them (and their friends) again.

When you are establishing these limited initial opportunities, advanced preparation can help match the skills of the individual with the organization's need. The organization can create online surveys and use social media to understand Millennial volunteers' interests and then match them with volunteer activities that would be most fitting.

For instance, create a simple poll or question about the event on your Facebook page to help the community understand the specific skills, needed hours, and expectations of volunteering. Develop a skills bank in your organization that maps the competencies of your volunteers. This makes it easier to call on the appropriate individuals when the time comes and take advantage of the skills they have to offer.

At the next level on the continuum, organizations offer short-term, project-based opportunities for Millennials. These may represent volunteer activities that have a commitment of more than one day, but still are relatively short-lived, such as a weekend, a couple weeks, or a month. Examples at this level include planning committees for events, serving beneficiaries meals for a week, helping to organize a day of service, or answering the phone three days each month.

One organization putting this level of volunteer engagement to work is KaBOOM! KaBOOM!, a leader in self-organized volunteer engagement that provides a variety of opportunities for the individuals who want to help them. Their volunteer site, Our Dream Playground, provides opportunities for those looking to help for one day and those that want to help plan and get involved in a series of leadership and advisory committees leading up to the playground build day (see Figure 4.4).

The next level on the Millennial volunteer continuum is long-term skills-based volunteer engagement. At this level, Millennials are given consistent opportunities to help lead and serve the organizations of their choice. Some

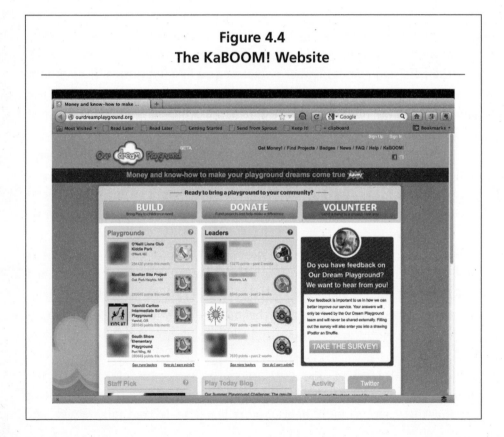

Figure 4.4
The KaBOOM! Website

examples include bringing in Millennials to help with marketing, accounting, technology, and or other services that advance the organization through a regular commitment of time and resources.

As described in the earlier story about the Taproot Foundation, this level of engagement is an opportunity to match that skill to a project necessary for the organization's long-term advancement. Using skills at a deeper level of engagement impacts not only the mission but also the bottom line, since the volunteers are providing higher-level skills that the organization would normally have to pay for or outsource to a vendor.

The last level of volunteer engagement is a year-long commitment of service to an organization through programs such as AmeriCorps or Public Allies. Millennials sign up to help such an organization build its capacity to serve more in the community, address critical issues such as education or poverty, and/or provide the necessary staffing to engage constituents. This level of service has risen in popularity with many Millennials, as exhibited by the volume of applicants each year.

As we examine the continuum, you may be wondering how this can all come together for your cause. The American Cancer Society demonstrates how an organization can provide opportunities at all levels. As exhibited on their website, they offer micro-volunteering and online advocacy, opportunities to take part in fundraising walks and or plan events, and more administrative functions for the organization.

In addition, each American Cancer Society chapter has specific skill-based experiences available that go beyond what is put forth on their website. This continuum of volunteer engagement not only is easy for Millennials to engage in, but also is based on frequency and skills that work for both the organization and the individual.

GOING DEEP: BOARD ENGAGEMENT

As noted in the Millennial Impact Report, 45 percent of Millennials want to help plan events and develop strategy on committees or small groups, and 40 percent said they wanted a chance to serve on a board or advisory committee. However, nonprofits should not respond to these statistics by putting Millennials on their boards and committees unless they're willing to give them real responsibilities and leadership opportunities. Focus group participants made it clear that they do not want to be the token "youth representatives" on a board. They want to engage in authentic leadership, with real tangible impact on the organization.

Almost a quarter of respondents said they do serve on a nonprofit committee, and 20 percent said they serve on a nonprofit board. Why don't more serve? Nearly 62 percent of respondents said they are prevented from board service by a lack of time, but 40 percent said they simply have never been asked.

Even with their bent toward leadership, Millennials are very interested in frontline work as well. Forty-seven percent of survey respondents said they want to work directly with program participants, and 40 percent would agree to do anything so long as they could volunteer as part of a group of friends or family.

As in their school-age days, Millennials' motivation to volunteer is not always entirely altruistic. This ambitious, career-minded workforce seeks challenges and demands leadership opportunities. In particular, the next generation of business leaders views workplace volunteer programs as a two-way street and wants a return on their volunteer investment. In the seventh annual Deloitte Volunteer IMPACT study, half of Millennials (51 percent) surveyed say they want volunteerism to benefit them professionally.[5]

RETAINING MILLENNIAL VOLUNTEERS

Providing opportunities throughout the Millennial volunteer continuum is important, but in order to maintain ongoing engagement with this valuable volunteer base, retention is crucial. Communicating additional opportunities to serve is not enough to retain Millennials as volunteers. For better results, incorporate the following key strategies to incorporate into your Millennial volunteer retention program:

- *Provide flexible opportunities to engage.* Millennials are accustomed to being connected to one another and to their work 24x7. Millennials are also working variable schedules and are accustomed to juggling multiple tasks and responsibilities. They expect a certain level of flexibility in their personal life and careers, and, not surprisingly, they expect and in some cases demand the same in their volunteer life. The more that organizations offer short-term, project-specific opportunities that can be achieved on a flexible schedule, the more likely they will be to attract Millennials.
- *Leverage their extensive personal and social networks.* Millennials want to volunteer, but even more so, they want to feel part of something bigger than

themselves. This often means involving their family and friends in volunteer experiences. Nonprofits must find new ways to tap the extensive networks that Millennials have, while understanding that this demographic is much more likely to show up with their peers to volunteer. But don't stop at on-the-ground engagement. Encourage Millennial volunteers to share your messages of volunteer opportunities, upcoming events, and the case for financial donations with their networks.

- *Provide career-building opportunities.* According to the Pew Research report, "37 percent of 18- to 29-year-olds are unemployed or out of the workforce. This represents the highest share among this age group in more than three decades." By positioning your volunteer opportunities as attractive additions to a resume and skills set, you can attract Millennial volunteers to your positions as a way to enhance their job marketability.

- *Engage Millennials for their skills.* Millennials believe they have much to offer nonprofits and expect to be treated with respect when it comes to sharing their ideas and skills. Engage them for the skills they have to offer, and partner with them as colleagues. In return you will see greater benefit for your organization. When they are engaged as partners at a high level, Millennials will often happily pitch in on less glamorous work.

The best way to lose Millennial volunteers? According to focus group feedback, a bad experience or a situation in which volunteers' time was poorly used will turn Millennials off from future volunteering. That first volunteer experience is critical to establishing a good impression among Millennials and their peers in order to keep them coming back for more.

THE IMPORTANCE OF WORKPLACE VOLUNTEERING

Net Impact's *Talent Report: What Workers Want* in 2012 reveals that employees who say they have the opportunity to make a direct social and environmental impact through their job report higher satisfaction levels than those who don't.[6] In fact, employees who say they can make an impact while on the job report greater satisfaction by a two-to-one ratio over those who can't. This data is backed up by the two-thirds of graduating university students who say that making a difference through their next job is a priority, and by the 45 percent of students who say they would even take a pay cut to be able to do so.

What studies like this and Deloitte's Volunteer IMPACT study also show is a distinct link between volunteerism and employee engagement. Millennial employees who give more outside of work in a volunteer capacity are more likely to give more at work. And although some research suggests that Millennials are predisposed to civic responsibility, it's also clear that they view volunteerism as an investment not only in the communities they work and live in but also in themselves.

Put another way, Millennials will go the extra mile if it builds their personal legacy—the sum of their contributions, large and small. For today's professionals, the most valuable currency tends to be recognition—the kind that raises their profile among their peers and allows them to stand out and be recognized by their managers.

What's more, greater engagement outside of work in volunteer activities has been shown to result in greater day-to-day satisfaction and retention. As you refine your Millennial employee engagement strategies, consider ways you can give all employees an opportunity to go the extra mile and earn visibility in the process.

WHAT DOES IT ALL MEAN?

Millennials want opportunities to serve, and many of them are willing to combine service with giving. To increase volunteerism, nonprofits would do well to provide a range of opportunities, let volunteers know the impact they'll have, and encourage current volunteers to invite friends and family to join them in giving their time.

However, resources spent to engage Millennials in volunteer opportunities will be wasted if you don't ensure that they have a good experience and that their time is used wisely. Here are some guidelines:

- *Provide experiences based on skills:* Millennials are looking for ways to put their professional skills to use when they volunteer. They have transferable skills in areas such as technology, business development, and communications that nonprofits need. Nonprofits must take the time to assess their volunteers' strengths and to make more deliberate connections.
- *Show the impact of your and their work:* It's no secret that Millennials—having grown up in a 24x7 news cycle with instant messaging and the immediacy of platforms like Twitter and Facebook—expect to see immediate results from their work and personal pursuits. The same holds true for their volunteer work. Even if the progress is

only incremental, make sure that you are sharing it with your volunteers. If they can see the value they are adding, they'll keep coming back for more.

- *Always have a clear call to action:* Today's volunteers may be savvier when it comes to finding volunteer opportunities on their computer or iPhone, but they expect an experience that matches the ease with which they found it. Although today's unprecedented technology allows organizations to reach out to new audiences, the call to action must be clear, it must be actionable, and it must show impact.

- *Ensure openness and transparency:* Go beyond providing good volunteer opportunities to creating more of a relational experience between volunteer and organization. Solicit feedback, provide follow-up, and ask what you could do better. Ask Millennials to rate their experiences and share knowledge so that you can improve the experiences for others. For example, the Monterey County Rape Crisis Center solicits feedback both in an online survey and through Facebook (see Figure 4.5) to learn how to better engage their volunteers in the future.

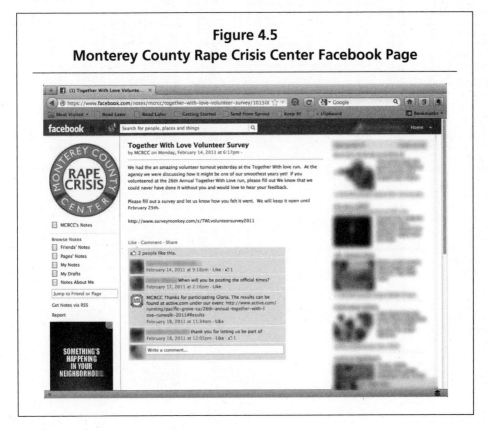

Figure 4.5
Monterey County Rape Crisis Center Facebook Page

Figure 4.6
Call to Action: Millennial Engagement Platform

Leadership Inviting

Develop pathways that lead young adults from interest in an issue, toward easy actions, and then on to more graduated levels of commitment. It's up to organizations to take the first step in understanding what gets Millennial volunteers engaged and, perhaps more important, what keeps them engaged.

Tangible Transparency

Go beyond providing good volunteer opportunities to creating more of a relational experience between volunteer and organization. Solicit feedback, provide follow-up, and ask what you could do better. Ask Millennials to rate their experiences and share knowledge so that you can improve the experience for others to come.

Social Connectivity

Recognizing the role that the peer group has in promoting volunteer activity is central for informing strategies that help increase service among Millennials. Special emphasis should be placed on tapping existing social circles as a method of recruitment as well as highlighting the social or team aspect of volunteer work to make service opportunities more attractive to potential participants. It's what some refer to as a "posse" model of volunteering, which brings together groups of young adults and enables them to volunteer together over time.

Solution-Inspired

Most Millennials do believe their actions can make a difference. Although most are less inclined to take more active steps, such as participating in a demonstration or writing a letter to the editor, their interest to do something, coupled with their belief that it has an impact, serves as an entry point to engagement. Low-threshold actions, such as donating money and goods, might be followed by invitations to attend meetings or engage in short-term volunteering. In much the same manner, entry level or brief volunteer experiences should be followed by opportunities to engage in more in-depth volunteer work and skill development.

BUILD a Better Environment by Engaging Millennials

Be Unified

While today's unprecedented technology allows organizations to reach out to new audiences, the call to action must be clear, it must be actionable, and it must show impact.

Understand Their Environment

Time is a valued and scarce resource for young adults, and all strategies must include tactical provisions that make volunteering time-friendly. Emphasis should be placed on expanding volunteer opportunities that offer a flexible schedule, have options for short-term commitments, and are conveniently located.

Identify Key Change Makers

Understand that this demographic is much more likely to show up to volunteer if they know their friends/colleagues will join them. Take time to identify those network leaders who can mobilize others to join them.

Lead by Engagement

Millennials expect to be able to take on leadership roles even as volunteers. Organizations must think about creating opportunities that expose Millennials to leadership roles on boards and committees.

Determine Success

Millennials are mission driven and always need to know what their efforts will lead to when it comes to community change. Ensure that you have defined measures of success before a project begins so that Millennial volunteers can chart their progress toward the organization's goals.

Although Millennials are one of the most challenging demographics to reach, they are the volunteer force that will help change how your organization affects the community and the people you serve. Remember that volunteer service opportunities must be convenient, rooted in social networks, and facilitate connections to deeper social change. Take the time to invest in a new continuum that will help this generation see connecting with your organization as advantageous for them, rather than focusing on simple activities that don't require or capture their spirit, skill, and eagerness. (See Figures 4.6 and 4.7.)

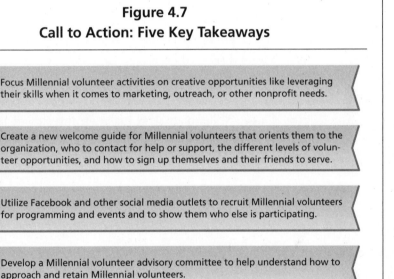

**Figure 4.7
Call to Action: Five Key Takeaways**

1. Focus Millennial volunteer activities on creative opportunities like leveraging their skills when it comes to marketing, outreach, or other nonprofit needs.

2. Create a new welcome guide for Millennial volunteers that orients them to the organization, who to contact for help or support, the different levels of volunteer opportunities, and how to sign up themselves and their friends to serve.

3. Utilize Facebook and other social media outlets to recruit Millennial volunteers for programming and events and to show them who else is participating.

4. Develop a Millennial volunteer advisory committee to help understand how to approach and retain Millennial volunteers.

5. Create new opportunities that allow Millennials to volunteer virtually.

A SPECIAL NOTE TO THE EXECUTIVE LEADER

Most Millennials are politically and civically involved, but they tend to participate when the investment of time and energy is low or when the behavior is well integrated into the course of their regular routine. Although Millennials are most motivated to serve when they think they can make a difference in the lives of others and when they are working on issues about which they care very deeply, their most common forms of civic engagement are what could be called "low-threshold activism," such as signing petitions, donating money, and making purchasing decisions.

Millennials tend to be most generous with their time when working with nonprofits that inspire them. There is no single way that Millennials prefer to engage; instead, most are looking for a continuum of options, from one-time engagements to long-term opportunities. And although they want the chance to work on the front lines delivering services, they especially want to leverage their knowledge, expertise, and backgrounds to help *lead* nonprofits. In particular, Millennials want to see more opportunities to lead on boards and committees.

It is important for nonprofits to create a continuum of volunteer engagement, from one-time volunteer projects to opportunities to volunteer with friends or family to leadership roles that use their professional skills. Moreover, Millennials want to make it clear that they shouldn't be taken for granted, that they can play an important leadership role in your organization even if they can't commit a lot financially right now. Millennials who make an investment of time today and have a positive experience will be more likely to donate when they have the means to do so later in life.

Peer Influence

Brian Elliot was a Harvard Business School grad who found himself on a comfortable path, finishing up a prestigious fellowship with a venture philanthropy firm. Approaching the age of thirty, Brian spent many weekends suiting up and hopping from wedding to wedding, watching his friends settle down, get married, and have kids.

It was around this time that Brian began culling through data on public opinion related to lesbian gay bisexual transgender (LGBT) equality to understand how it compared to the status of laws. What he found was an inexplicable gap. He started to wonder how there could be 50 percent support against housing discrimination, yet his landlord (and landlords in more than twenty states) could kick him out of his apartment for no reason other than sexual orientation. Or why in twenty-nine states he could be fired without question simply because of his sexual orientation.

Brian looked around at young people. He looked in the eyes of his friends' children. He began to wonder what this meant for the next generation, and what it might take to close this gap and accelerate the change for equality.

When he had come out to his friends at age sixteen, Brian said, he'd "never expected to become a professional gay." But he believed the gay rights movement was the civil rights issue of our generation. He also was adamant that gay rights today were missing a crucial component: straight people. So he did what any Millennial who wanted to build a network of supporters would do: he turned to six hundred of his straight friends on Facebook.

Brian started a Facebook page called "Give Brian Equality." Of the six hundred friends he invited to join, half did within the first twenty-four hours. If you think about it, that in itself is an incredible conversion rate; most mass emails receive an open rate somewhere around 15–18 percent and an action rate of 2–4 percent. Brian also created a simple one-minute video explaining that although he might seem just like his friends, he didn't have the same rights or sense of security that his straight friends had.

Within one month more than nineteen thousand people had "liked" the page. Brian knew he was on to something. If there was this much energy around one person's very personal appeal to his friends, what might happen if a bunch of people in the LGBT community could ask their friends to support them?

Thus began his personal quest to build the online social platform that would become Friendfactor. Brian took the equal rights movement of the Millennial generation and built a platform that redefined online action. It also repositioned the gay rights movement, stripping away most of the issues and instead focusing on people, just as he had seen other successful online networks do.

He said, "Gay friends are so much more important than gay rights." After all, his straight friends weren't necessarily interested in the intricacies of gay rights; they were interested in helping their friend Brian. And they did, by sending emails to their members of Congress and raising attention for issues that ultimately affected public policy decisions.

Brian exercised a strategy that is becoming more and more common in our everyday lives, affecting everything from trivial choices, such as deciding which restaurant has the best dim-sum, to serious decisions, such as determining where to channel your personal philanthropic dollars. Our society has become increasingly dependent on friends telling their friends to act—what is commonly called "peer influence."

Peer influence in the nonprofit world shifts the dynamics of organizations in a few key ways that we will explore in this chapter. The evaluation and recognition of peer influence by organizations not only helps empower and sustain a network of supporters but can also increase staff capacity.

Here's what we're beginning to see:

- Donors and organizational supporters are increasingly relying on referrals and guidance from friends, family, and coworkers to make decisions—with Millennials relying even more heavily on their networks and sometimes even on the opinions of strangers.

- Individuals are organizing not just on behalf of organizations and their issues but without organizations at all, as the rise of the "free agent" takes hold.

- Direct communications by nonprofit organizations to constituents and individual prospects are having far less of an impact on decision making than in years past.

- Nonprofits are finding new ways to work with individuals outside of their core networks to tap their most vocal and loyal supporters to be active promoters of causes and organizations.

OLD SCHOOL VERSUS NEW SCHOOL PEER INFLUENCE

It's no surprise that the visibility of peer influence in the last five years stems primarily from advances and developments in social media. But if we go back to the days prior to the emergence of social media, we see that peer influence has always existed; it was just rooted in marketing efforts that emphasized face-to-face communications and personal relationships in a different way.

Although it pains us to mention Tupperware parties in a book about Millennials (most of whom would likely not even understand the reference), think about how friends and family members would come together to make purchasing decisions in the 1980s and early 1990s. An individual would host a party for a small network of friends and family members. The group would engage in real conversations in a laidback style, while the brand was gently presented during the event.

The hostess, by way of direct invitation, was recommending that this group purchase plastic ware to make their lives easier in the kitchen. She would establish rapport in the beginning of the event by telling everyone why they were there, the importance of how Tupperware had changed her life, and then introducing a representative who would show them the latest plastic goods. The event was built on the premise of a strong individual willing to reach out and tell her personal network how important a product or service was to her.

In the nonprofit community, peer influence has been more prevalent in fundraising than in any other discipline in the sector. Capital campaigns, which raise substantial financial resources for physical structures and endowments, have always been driven by committed peers influencing their personal networks to give. Some of the first early capital campaigns at Harvard University for residence halls and libraries included a committed core group of faculty coming together and raising support from their peers for the institution.

The capital campaign models are fueled by the ability of largely high-net-worth individuals, as volunteers and committed constituents, to convince their peers to support a cause they believe in. Language such as "Join me and my spouse in supporting the school," or "Be one of the thousand supporters at this level," or "Become one of the elite few to help the cause advance"—all are rooted in the power of peer influence.

If we fast-forward to the early 1990s, we see peer influence in the nonprofit sector take a new approach to getting constituents involved. Organizations such as the Muscular Dystrophy Association and other major medical organizations began to use peer influence to raise support for special events. From runs and walks to bike-a-thons and bowl-a-thons, peer fundraising began to dominate in nonprofits seeking to raise not capital dollars but rather operating support through events.

Before social media, marketing and public relations efforts also began to incorporate peer influence models to constituent engagement. Although popularized by celebrity and pop culture, movements in the mid-1980s such as Hands Across America were developed with the marketing approach of peer engagement to complete the human chain across the continental United States. By hitting both media and grassroots organizations nationwide, the organizers fueled peer participation by creating materials and messaging that said, "Bring your family and friends to help us for fifteen minutes to stand in support of ending hunger and homelessness." It took major media, marketing promotions, word of mouth, and grassroots organizing at its best to make it possible.

As the 2012 Millennial Impact Report indicates, special-event fundraising structures based on peer fundraising are the most widely engaging mechanism for Millennials to support causes. In fact, 60 percent of Millennials give through these types of events, with almost 40 percent of them raising funds for nonprofit organizations through their peers for or at the event itself. Why does this happen so much more than any other fundraising tool? Millennials grew up with a model wherein the special-event fundraising approach was the norm. Raising support through family and friends was not something new or even popularized when they grew up; it simply was always present.

Today, the popularity of peer influence has been catapulted by the use of technology and social platforms. The concept of sharing important information via Facebook or Twitter enables any organization of any size to be heard. It simply takes a short compelling message, an easy way to act, and a few committed individuals willing to spread that message to their network and infuse it with personal interest and a personal story.

Let's All Buy Together

Group-based consumption has been popularized in the United States because of companies like Groupon and Living Social. Both entities are based on a daily deal model whereby receiving the deal is dependent on the number of individual buyers who purchase a deeply discounted product or service. It plays into the Millennial makeup with a combination of peer/group modeling, technology, instant buying capabilities, and social media.

But will it last?

That is the million-dollar question. Millennials like these sites for the ability to get deals, but "couponing"—as the Millennial-focused blog YPulse points out—appeals to them even more, because it tends to make shopping more like a game. Millennials want to be the first to share their newfound deals with their friends on Facebook just as much as they want to be the first to share a YouTube video before it goes viral. And beyond being the first to share the deals, they also can introduce brand-new local and small businesses to their peers—many of whom use the couponing sites to reach new markets and break into new communities.

Although strong initially with Millennials, these sites are struggling to maintain the audiences they once had. The daily deal sites contain many of the attributes that resonate with this generation, but to maintain relevancy they must sell products and offer deals that appeal to that audience. There is a big lesson in this for many organizations that use technology and other online forms of engagement to attract Millennials: even if you build a product or service based on Millennial attributes, maintaining an audience can be a bigger challenge once the sizzle of the new idea is gone.

WHO ARE THESE INFLUENCERS, AND WHY SHOULD I LISTEN?

The term "influencer" is nothing new to those in marketing and advertising. Influencers are historically known as the individuals who persuade others in their social circles and beyond to purchase, participate, or engage in a product, service, or activity. Marketers have worked with influencers since what seems like the beginning of time to help them broadcast their messages to the widest network possible. With the growing influence and importance of social media in selling ideas and products, a new breed of influencers and brand ambassadors has emerged. And we're finding that online influence isn't about popularity; it's about expertise.

There are social media influencers like Gary Vaynerchuk, who, as a self-trained wine and social media expert, combined his two passions and revolutionized the wine industry. Or Pete Cashmore, who before becoming one of the most followed tweeters in the world—with more than two million followers—founded the website Mashable in 2006 and grew it to become one of the most influential sources in the social media and technology space.

Incidentally, both Vaynerchuk and Cashmore are Millennials, and both have built and leveraged their personal brands in their respective areas of expertise. Nonprofits should take note: in today's world an organization's brand may not be as important as those who are associated with the brand. In the case of Vaynerchuk and Cashmore, the combination of their wide online audiences, their expert voices in their respective fields, and the personal brands they developed along the way led to a powerful shift that enabled them to drive more traffic, readers, sales, and influence for their corporate brands.

So how do you engage these so-called influencers successfully? You must be willing to target them and talk to them in terms that relate to *their* story, not your organization's story. Although organizations may have selfish reasons for engaging influencers for organizational advancement, the influencers must see, in any organization request, the potential for their own personal gain—in this case, by fulfilling their passion and internal motivation to help others because of the organization's work.

What makes influencers relevant is that they can help you connect to an audience in an authentic way, which organizations often find difficult. So engage them early in the process, and after you've gotten them on board, build a relationship that will outlast the initial campaign. Find ways to build an ongoing relationship that is mutually beneficial, so that your organization and their personal brand become aligned as one.

Most important—and we'll reinforce this theme throughout the chapter—give up control of the message and trust your influencers to tell the organization's story through their own words. This is the authentic engagement that their followers appreciate and expect, and it's what will help guide their fans and followers to your organization. We know that influencers are the ones who create and share content about products, brands, and services via social networking websites. They often have an extremely powerful voice and may already have a strong and loyal following online. Nonprofits need to consider who they are marketing to as an important factor. If they can get their message across to a key influencer, then they can spread the brand message using their online influence.

MEET TODAY'S NONPROFIT INFLUENCER

In the corporate world, celebrities lend their personal brand and likeness to help companies sell everything from a new pair of sneakers to a new set of wheels. But in the nonprofit world, there's a new kind of influencer that every organizational professional should get to know.

One of the key findings from the Millennial Donors Study 2011 by Achieve and Johnson Grossnickle and Associates (JGA) was the importance that trust and peer influence held in decision making for Millennials. When asked to describe what motivates them to give, 85 percent of Millennials pointed to a compelling mission or cause, and 56 percent cited a personal connection or trust in the leadership of the organization. Following only slightly behind that were friend or peer endorsements, which compelled 52 percent to give.

That high-profile celebrity or influential leader endorsement? Apparently it's not worth the effort from a strictly fundraising standpoint: only 2 percent of Millennials said that such endorsements motivated them to give. Still, it should be noted that although celebrity influence may not result in actual gifts, it does help raise awareness of causes and their work. We have seen this occur with celebrities such as Oprah and Ashton Kutcher, who use their media platforms to endorse and activate awareness campaigns for causes.

Today's nonprofit influencer looks very different from a celebrity. Yet these influencers are a growing and important element of the social change movement, and when engaged in the right ways they can be a boon to nonprofits by helping them attract new donors, spread compelling stories, or give new faces and fresh ideas to causes and organizations that are in need of a twenty-first-century makeover.

In *The Networked Nonprofit*, Beth Kanter and Allison Fine introduce us to these nonprofit influencers, known as "free agents."[1] Free agents are individuals working outside of organizations who have a common interest in pursuing its mission. Although they don't hold any formal position on the staff or board, free agents do everything from organizing events (both on- and offline) to raising awareness, reaching new audiences, and energizing prospects.

What's more, today's Millennial nonprofit influencer isn't interested in simply spreading messages that are manufactured in an office, with stodgy language that has to be approved by seven layers of management. They want to tell their friends and family about the importance of organizations in their own words. And they are desperate for short messaging and clear calls to action to mobilize their friends, family, and broader social networks.

Influencers don't do this for attention or reward. For the most part, they are enthusiastic champions who believe in the mission. They are moved to help spread the word and tell others because of their experience (or that of a close family member or friend) or their own ideologies calling them to act for the greater good.

Many influencers work directly on behalf of nonprofit organizations, whether or not the organizations know it or "approve" of such activity. More often than not, nonprofit influencers have the ability to look at challenges a nonprofit faces from the outside, and they bring new approaches to develop solutions that might never have happened in the existing structure and confines of nonprofits. Either way, these free agents are shifting the dynamics within and outside of institutions, and because of their unique characteristics and entrepreneurial spirit, the change is being led in large part by Millennials.

To be clear, not all free agents are Millennials, just as not all Millennials are free agents. But there's a powerful dynamic almost built into the DNA of younger generations to serve as ambassadors for the issues and causes of which they are a part. We have seen time and again that Millennials place a premium on peer relationships rather than on institutional loyalty. This has profound implications for activist organizations that are accustomed to building and maintaining support from their donors over long periods of time. In other words, although young people are unlikely to be lifelong donors to their local United Way, they will engage enthusiastically when it comes to targeted campaigns, especially if they feel a passion for the cause or a personal connection.

Still, for many organizations this concept is too foreign to understand or embrace. They dismiss these free agents as novices with neither experience nor depth of knowledge when it comes to the intricacies of the nonprofit sector. But the truth is, in today's hyperconnected world, free agents like Brian Elliot are the ones who are able to organize quickly and generate a real impact, and it is incumbent on nonprofits to find and create ways to work with or alongside these new agents of change.

SEND IN THE FREE AGENTS

Consider as well how social networks are beginning to rebuild our social capital and decrease isolation by increasing trust between the people we work with online. Rather than being critical of the current challenges of mobilizing people for a cause online, we should spend more time considering the solutions and opportunities.

Our online social capital is built on two fundamental elements: trust and reciprocity. First, trust. Let's say you're a Facebook user and see on your newsfeed that three of your friends just donated to an organization. You've never heard of this organization, you've certainly never donated to it, and you have no previous affiliation or connection to it. But you see that these three people—with whom you have a personal relationship and for whom you have mutual respect—have given to the organization.

Suddenly it doesn't matter how much that organization poured into its outreach and solicitation efforts; the chances that the info would ever trickle down to you are pretty slim anyway. But because of the social capital you have with three individuals in your social network whom you trust, you are intrigued and want to learn more about the organization—and maybe even consider a financial gift.

This scenario is not uncommon, as more people are using their online social capital to help one another—also known as "reciprocity in action." Twitter is a great place to watch reciprocity unfold. If you watch an influencer's Twitter feed, you won't see a lot of broadcast messages, but rather an exchange of ideas, links, and knowledge. Twitter users ask and answer questions: What's the best platform for online donations? Who's got a consultant who can help us develop our theory of change? And so on, until the network is fully involved and supported.

As we shared in Chapter Three, Take Back the Pink illustrates the perfect storm of free agent engagement. Six women took control, both independently and in coordination with one another, and figured out how to navigate boundaries, develop new strategies, and construct a division of labor without the politics, policies, or pace of any one institution holding them back and delaying progress.

With all the talk about influence, it should be noted that influence cannot be achieved until you are able to demonstrate relevance. Indeed, the two go hand in hand. Relevance is built when an organization or a person focuses on being indispensable to their audience. They eat, sleep, and dream about helping their audience, and because of this passion they are able to attract followers, create fans, and soon translate their relevance into influence. Being accessible and answering people's tweets or responding to blog posts is good. Being relevant is even better.

Organization Spotlight: Chicago Humanities Festival

The Chicago Humanities Festival's mission is to create opportunities for people of all ages to support, enjoy, and explore the humanities. They fulfill this mission through annual festivals, the fall Chicago Humanities Festival, and the spring Stages, Sights & Sounds, and by presenting programs throughout the year that encourage the study and enjoyment of the humanities.

Organization Overview

- Ten percent of staff time devoted to engaging Millennials
- Six to nine Millennials on staff
- Budget: $1–$5 million
- Twenty staff, three hundred volunteers
- Somewhat of a priority to engage Millennials—As a small organization, they do all that they can to reach a spectrum of different demographic groups.
- Twenty-six to fifty Millennial volunteers
- Over five hundred Millennial donors

Young Professional Focus Group Helps Increase Engagement of Millennials

The Chicago Humanities Festival has created a diverse panel of young professionals to regularly meet as a focus group. The staff is using the young professional focus group to work on audience development and raise awareness and access to Festival events.

"Rather than try to raise revenue from this group prematurely, we are working with our focus group to increase inclusivity and word-of-mouth recommendations, one of our most powerful marketing channels," said Audrey Peiper, director of individual giving for the Chicago Humanities Festival.

"Younger audience members tend to be more last-minute or impromptu in their approach to attending events, which means they miss out on our best events that sell out early. We are surveying this younger population to see what strategies we can employ to address these obstacles," said Peiper. The staff of the Chicago Humanities Festival has considered the perspectives from their young professionals focus group and buyer-behavior and marketing surveys to craft a customized ticket bundle aimed at young professionals.

"With over one hundred programs from which to select, Chicago Humanities Festival audience members are often paralyzed by the sheer number of choices. Combined with their busy schedules and more impromptu decision-making habits, young professionals often find themselves exasperated by information overload or wanting to attend sold-out events. By creating a highly edited menu of events bundled as a unit for convenience, we hope to attract more Millennials with opportunities that will interest them," said Peiper.

Source: Achieve and Johnson Grossnickle and Associates, Millennial Impact Report 2012. www.themillennialimpact.com

WHEN PEER INFLUENCE DOESN'T WORK

One of the biggest complaints we hear in the nonprofit community concerns situations in which organizations try to tap peer influence to get other Millennials engaged in a cause, but the rate of participation is dismal. Organizations may then throw out peer influence as a strategy because the work of the free agents didn't produce. But can we blame the free agents?

Peer influence still requires organizations to create compelling and easy ways to get involved in the cause. Regardless of how good the peer is at telling the story or spreading the message, the organization is still responsible for the peer's network experience with the cause.

Let's say, for instance, that I tell my friends and family about a cause through my social network and provide a link to volunteer with me next Saturday. Members of my personal online network click the link and are taken to the organization's website to read more, be sold on the experience, and sign up. Now imagine you were one of the individuals in my network who clicked on the link. What if it brought you to a website with more than five hundred words describing how to volunteer? What if the sign-up link was in a small font at the bottom of the page? What if there was no information about the upcoming event? How likely would *you* be to sign up or participate?

Both peer messaging and organizational messaging, regardless of who is telling the story, require good design, smooth user experiences, and other fundamental forms of conversion in order to ignite action (see Figure 5.1). You can ensure success by creating a peer influence modeling program that will help you visualize and conceptualize the peer influence from conversation to conversion.

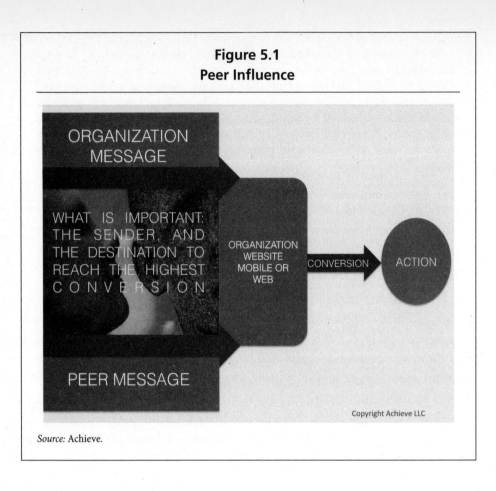

Figure 5.1
Peer Influence

ORGANIZATION
MESSAGE

WHAT IS IMPORTANT:
THE SENDER, AND
THE DESTINATION TO
REACH THE HIGHEST
CONVERSION

ORGANIZATION
WEBSITE
MOBILE OR
WEB

CONVERSION

ACTION

PEER MESSAGE

Copyright Achieve LLC

Source: Achieve.

Organizations must continue to invest in making all engagement pathways and points—from websites and social media to donation forms and action alerts—easy to understand, easy to use, and easy to get excited about.

Remember, that initial contact gained through a social network is your first opportunity as an organization to make an impression. Do you really want to take an enthusiastic new constituent from a glowing peer review to a place on your site that doesn't hold the same passion?

GIVE PERMISSION TO PEER INFLUENCE

Although some organizations stay an arm's length or further from these self-mobilizing and seemingly unpredictable free agents, it doesn't have to be that way. The conversations and connections taking place elsewhere, whether on- or offline, don't have to remain a mystery to you. Give permission for your community to report back, and provide the mechanisms to do so. Find a way to embrace these free agents, bring them into your work deliberately, and create a bridge between old- and new-school approaches to social change.

Some organizations are wary about using free agents because of the control they need to give up. However, you can actually create a multiple win for your organization and your community by giving permission to broadcast and influence on your behalf. It sounds simple, but it's something that nonprofit social media expert Amy Sample Ward has identified as a crucial element of broadening a message while also focusing the community. Because every organizational effort has infrastructure requirements, Amy offered the following steps as ways to give permission and leverage the peer influencers in your community.

- Create a dashboard, a toolbox—a website function with any other catchy name you like—that allows influencers to grab images, videos, files, or messages that are ready to be broadcast.

- Create opportunities for influencers to do something unique or valuable with their participation.

- Monitor how your influence tools are used ("share with a friend," retweet, and so on) to see what content is best or most successfully shared and whether any new influencers are emerging.

- Provide recognition or a spotlight for those who are taking your message into their networks and creating impact.

- Help your staff, team, or organization understand the value in distributing the communications and influence of your work, and help them leverage the network in similar ways across all departments and campaigns.

In short, give peer influencers the information and training, resources, and recognition they deserve in order to help you achieve your constituent goals. This will require thoughtful engagement from the staff and also ownership across several departments, including marketing, fundraising, and communication.

PEER INFLUENCE IN ACTION: TWO CASE STUDIES

Today's Millennial nonprofit influencer is armed with social media tools that enable thoughts and ideas to spread much more quickly and efficiently than ever before. One of the most far-reaching examples appeared in February 2012 with the launch of the online movement against the passage by Congress of the Stop Online Piracy Act (SOPA) and the Protect Internet Piracy Act (PIPA).

According to Google, more than 4.5 million people signed their online petition, more than 2 million people tweeted against the legislation, and 162 million people visited Wikipedia's blacked-out landing page. Even more important, eight million people in the United States looked up their congressional representatives to voice their protest directly to their offices. Millions of citizens engaged in their communities and protested the bills in the House and Senate; both bills were ultimately defeated.

The collective action, especially on the part of Millennials, ranged from people censoring their pictures on Facebook and Twitter to posting status updates, links, and pictures protesting the bills and mobilizing their peers to do the same. What was interesting to watch, though, was that although major influencers in the tech space—like Wikipedia, Google, and Reddit—participated in the blackouts, the communities associated with each of those platforms helped drive the campaign forward. In fact, according to individuals close to the protest, as the Wikipedia and Reddit communities debated whether to stage a blackout—an idea that started with Wikipedia cofounder Jimmy Wales—a group of activists discussed other tactics and messaging on an email list that grew to more than one hundred participants before the protest.

The participants debated how websites should state their objections to SOPA and PIPA and how to most accurately portray the bills. They also worked together on tools to help protesters contact Congress and provided talking points for those discussions with lawmakers. The interaction on the leaderless list led to widespread collaboration, proving the power of the grassroots movement. The biggest lesson learned from anti-SOPA and -PIPA protests was that people act quickly when they realize they have something at stake.

Turning to another example, let's look at the immediate and unprecedented mobilization in the wake of the earthquake in Haiti. For the first time, we had data demonstrating the role that peer influence played during the mobile giving campaign in the aftermath of the Haitian earthquake. The study, conducted by the Pew Center for the Internet and American Life, the Berkman Center at Harvard, and mGive, showed that donors who used their mobile phones to donate after the earthquake actually did more than give.[2] They also talked about their giving, which, in effect, actively encouraged others to follow their lead.

Part of the response's success may be the novelty associated with donating by text message. Regardless of the reason, suddenly there are individuals, many of whom have never donated to disaster relief efforts in the past and most of whom have never "texted-to-give," engaging in a simple act, talking about it, and watching its ripple effect.

All told, text-to-give efforts in support of the Haiti relief efforts raised more than $43 million. Perhaps even more important was the fact that these were not one-time donors. More than half went on to make additional disaster-related mobile gifts over time. These are what managing partner of Arabella Advisors and self-proclaimed "philanthropy wonk" Lucy Bernholz has referred to as "roaming reflexive donors."[3] Their kind of giving isn't committed to a place, cause, or organization; rather, it's "do something and talk about it."

SO WHO'S DOING THE TALKING—AND WHY DOES IT MATTER?

According to anthropologist Robin Dunbar, there is a theoretical cognitive limit to the number of people with whom one can maintain stable social relationships. Individuals have, on average, a social network of about 150 people, known as "Dunbar's Number." Dunbar explains, "the part of our brain that copes with language, thought and personal interaction will max out when our social circles stretch beyond 150."

Professor Dunbar developed this theory in the 1990s, well before social networks took hold. Yet the 150 figure has endured, regardless of whether the relationships are in person, online, in the office, or long distance. Beyond this number, the stability of the relationships does begin to break down, and connections are not as meaningful.

Think about this in the context of your personal online social network. You have your close friends and family, those with whom you desire to share everything from the mundane (your frustration with your commute) to the fantastic (your daughter's first steps). This is largely because of pre-existing relationships, trust, and connections that you've developed with individuals in the offline world.

Then there are those with whom you have looser connections—people you meet at conferences, or folks with whom you enjoy a happy hour beverage. You have a mutual interest in networking and sharing information, most likely because of overlapping interests or professional connections. But there is a limit to how much you might personally share with them.

The third grouping—individuals with whom you'd like to be friends—makes up the outer ring. This can encompass celebrities, news reporters, social media personalities, or any other individual you look to for entertainment and information.

Now think about how you make decisions about purchasing major items from electronics to vacations, even applying for credit cards. If you're a Millennial, you're actually more likely to turn to the opinions of complete strangers over those of your friends and family. According to a study by the social marketing firm Bazaarvoice, about 51 percent of Millennials are more likely to be influenced by user-generated content (UGC) produced and posted by strangers than by recommendations from friends, family, and colleagues. Compare this to only 34 percent of Boomers who are equally enthusiastic about trusting the opinions of strangers.

Millennials' reliance on reviews and ratings is disrupting all areas of business. Why does this matter to nonprofits? Increasingly, brands and organizations are recognizing that although those 150 people who fall within your social network as "friends" are important, what's even more powerful and important are those well-connected communities of people who are organized around a single topic.

These communities make up what is known in the digital world as "interest graphs." In the simplest of terms, if a social graph is the relationships among the people we know, then an interest graph is the relationship map of the things we like. There may be some overlap between the two, but not necessarily. It could be a map of wine aficionados, new moms, cat lovers, or social entrepreneurs. All are organized around an object, cause, or issue and can be targeted through a specific lens according to that interest.

For nonprofits, the idea that the interest graph could be more powerful than the social graph is an exciting prospect. After all, organizations have spent a good portion of the past five or six years laser-focused on combing the Internet searching for supporters and cause champions, which has led to the development of complex interest graphs.

The LIVESTRONG Foundation has in essence created an interest graph of those who are committed to finding a cure for cancer. The Humane Society is an interest graph made up of people who are committed to finding safe homes for animals. The Red Cross has built an interest graph of first responders and blood donors. And with any of these scenarios, the interest graph is a game changer for nonprofits who are looking to engage their supporters in deeper and more meaningful ways.

Here's the catch: Although these examples are related to specific nonprofits, the interest graph model overall allows people to organize themselves outside of individual nonprofits. This concept goes back to the beginning days of self-organizing and human behavior related to the nonprofit sector—which means it's time for nonprofits to begin thinking about interest graph optimization. How can you best take stock of your online fans and followers and use the information about their common interests to increase your visibility in that space?

HOW TO LEVERAGE THE INTEREST GRAPH

Millennials will be the first to tell you: you're going to need to relinquish some control if you want to fully leverage the interest graph. For all the time you've spent building up donor prospect lists, wooing volunteers, and capturing email addresses over the course of the past few years, the interest graph operates differently. In fact, you don't own the relationship at all. Your donors, volunteers, and prospects do because they're the ones driving the change.

So get to know them. How are you being useful to them? Are you sharing information, offering resources, listening, and experimenting with messaging and approaches? The way in which organizations choose to share information will ultimately lead to how they are seen and viewed—as relevant or not—on people's timelines and in their social streams.

When Facebook made significant changes to its platform in late 2011 with Open Graph applications, they reinvented the way that users can interact with brands and nonprofits—essentially making any action expressed on Facebook a branding opportunity (depending on the user's privacy settings). Suddenly individuals moved from simply "liking" their Starbucks coffee or the World Wildlife Fund to being able to emphasize activities and how much they care about them; for example, Lisa is *drinking* a Starbucks nonfat soy latte or Kenneth is *volunteering* with the World Wildlife Fund.

The more a user interacts with your app, the more integrated it becomes with the user's interest graph. This becomes much more beneficial to nonprofits, because users can actually choose the updates they'd like to share more often.

In the old Facebook, if a person regularly listened to his playlist using the music-sharing site Spotify and was also a regular volunteer for Children's

Hospital, both activities would appear with the same weight in their social stream, based entirely on the frequency of interactions. However, if that same person can now place more emphasis on that social activity than on the last song he listened to, the interactions with the organization's page become more prominent on his profile. And this, in turn, allows more family and friends to take note and engage with the content.

It's now clear that supporters want to control their own engagement experiences. They want to be able to define and customize how they are communicated to—from setting email frequency to going paperless altogether—and they want to be able to develop their own content, which has led to the rise of UGC on sites across the board.

EXPAND USER-GENERATED CONTENT ON YOUR SITE

Here are a few techniques for organizations to consider as they experiment and expand opportunities for UGC on their own websites:

1. Add UGC to your homepage and anywhere else your services are featured. This could be as simple as inviting donors to leave a public comment after they make a donation, or sending a link to volunteers after a service project so they can share their experiences with their friends and with the world. You can also use sites like GreatNonprofits, which offers a badge to place on your homepage, letting visitors see and submit reviews of your nonprofit directly through the organization's website.

2. Ask people to respond. Don't just make the opportunity available to individuals; go to the extra effort of inviting them to contribute. The response rate of Millennials in particular goes up dramatically when you ask them to respond, but you have to make it easy for them. If Millennials can't find an easy way to take action, you're going to lose them, and they probably won't come back.

3. It's not enough to invite response—you need to respond yourself. The Millennial generation expects quick recognition and an understanding that their voice has been heard. Respond even if you don't have an answer; it shows that you value them, and it helps build the trust that is so vital to Millennial engagement.

As you read in Chapter Four, the true value of social media comes down to people, relationships, and the meaningful actions between them. As such, value is measured through the exchange of social currencies that contribute to one's capital in each network. Through conversations, what we share, and the content we create, consume, and curate, we individually invest in the commerce of information and the relationships that naturally unfold—and we can see the returns in the power of peer influence.

Figure 5.2
Peer Influence: Millennial Engagement Platform

Leadership Inviting

Nonprofit executives must understand that the best way to reach Millennials is to welcome their perspectives and give them and your community both permission to report back and the mechanisms to do so. Find a way to embrace free agents, bring them into your work deliberately, and create a bridge between old- and new-school approaches to social change. Although some organizations are wary about using free agents because of the control they need to give up, you can actually create a multiple win for your organization and your community by giving permission to broadcast and influence on your behalf.

Tangible Transparency

Our online social capital is built on two fundamental elements: trust and reciprocity. These two factors are dependent upon organizational transparency, which is vitally important to Millennials. More often than not, nonprofit influencers have the ability to look at the challenges a nonprofit faces from the outside and to bring with them new approaches to develop solutions that might never have arisen within the existing structure and confines of nonprofits.

Social Connectivity

Today's Millennial nonprofit influencer is armed with social media tools that enable thoughts and ideas to spread much more quickly and efficiently than ever before, in addition to the tools and applications that drive conversations, organizations must also understand the underlying connective issue that exists in the social graph and open graph. Consider as well how social networks are beginning to rebuild our social capital and decrease isolation by increasing trust between the people we work with online. Rather than being critical of the current challenges of mobilizing people for a cause online, we should spend more time considering the solutions and opportunities.

Solution-Inspired

Millennials are solution-oriented and might not feel meaningful connections with an organization until they are part of working toward whatever problem the organization is setting out to solve. With this in mind, organizations must continue to invest in making all engagement pathways and points—from websites and social media to donation forms and action alerts—easy to understand, easy to use, and easy to get excited about. Better solutions come with clear access to this information.

BUILD a Better Environment by Engaging Millennials

Be Unified

Give peer influencers the information, training, resources, and recognition they deserve in order to help you achieve your constituent goals.

Understand Their Environment

You must be willing to target and then talk to peer influencers in terms that relate to their story—not your organization's story.

Identify Key Change Makers

What makes influencers relevant is that they can help you connect to an audience in an authentic way—one in which organizations often find difficult. Engage them early in the process; after you've gotten them on board, build a relationship that will outlast the initial campaign.

Lead by Engagement

In today's hyperconnected world, free agents are the ones who are able to organize quickly and for real impact. It's incumbent upon nonprofits to find and create ways to work with or alongside these new agents of change.

Determine Success

Create a workplace dashboard system that details the goals and vision of the organization, and show how Millennials' and other employees' contributions will help the organization achieve the desired outcomes.

Figure 5.3
Peer Influence: Five Key Takeaways

1 Invite peer influencers to informal discussions with the leadership of the organization every quarter in order to share important information and upcoming opportunities to attend events.

2 Develop a group of online advocates to spread messages, write content, and develop online conversations for you. Let them become your personal journalists.

3 Reward influencers for the number of online mentions of your organization, and recognize them on your site.

4 Give sneak peeks of new initiatives, provide information to your loyal evangelist, and create a unique community site for these loyalists to receive updates and other forms of impact from donor support.

5 Track peer influence by discovering the Millennials who share, retweet, and like your content.

A SPECIAL NOTE TO THE EXECUTIVE LEADER

One of the biggest complaints we hear from nonprofits about the concept of peer influence is that organizations try to tap Millennials to get their friends engaged in a cause, but it ultimately results in dismal participation. Organizations may then throw out peer influence altogether as a strategy because the work of the so-called free agents didn't produce.

But perhaps the free agent or peer influencer isn't completely to blame for the dismal results. Taking advantage of peer influence still requires organizations to create compelling and easy ways to get involved in the cause. Regardless of how good the peer is at telling the story or spreading the message, the organization still has ownership of the experience that the peer's network has with a cause. This requires organizations to create compelling and easy ways to get involved, take action, and ensure that the cycle of engagement continues.

The Millennial Donor

The majority of today's nonprofit leaders see the sheer size and makeup of the Millennial generation and almost immediately—and perhaps naively—sees dollar signs flash before their eyes. They start crafting strategies they believe will engage the rising generation. And although we now know that Millennials collectively share about $300 billion in purchasing power, with $69 billion of it being discretionary, the challenge for nonprofits is much greater than simply competing with a Millennial's daily habit of a grande nonfat soy latte. It's about changing behaviors and finding compelling ways to connect on their terms and in ways that resonate with their everyday routines.

We know that Millennials do give, and when they do, they can be very supportive of the causes they choose. But there is a disconnect between the way they give and the way they are being cultivated as donors. Organizations see a nearly endless pool of potential Millennial donors, yet they lack the understanding of how to connect with them; they choose to instead target high-net-worth donors and those with whom they share a long or deep history. Because of this misplaced focus, organizations are seeing disappointing returns when it comes to engaging the next generation as philanthropists, which only perpetuates their lack of interest in engaging them in the future.

Much of the data throughout this chapter comes directly from research led by Achieve and its partner Johnson Grossnickle and Associates (JGA), who together over the past three years (2010–2012) have set out to understand the giving habits of Millennials. Each year the study has offered new insight into the generation, giving rise to new tactics and theories. And each year the research has helped the nonprofit field understand more about the inner workings and mind-set of the Millennial philanthropist.

With three years of research on Millennial giving and engagement now completed and in the public domain at www.themillennialimpact.com,[1] three clear themes have arisen: the impulsive nature of Millennials' giving habits, their innovative uses of mobile technology, and their strong preference for event- and peer-based giving. Every leader must grasp these targeted areas before seeking financial support from the rising generation of Millennials.

IMPULSIVE GIVING HABITS

As we have discussed, Millennials are often sought after in the consumer marketplace simply because of the magnitude of their spending power. From the time they wake up to the time they go to sleep, they receive endless messages embedded into their daily routines that invite them to purchase goods and services. Because of this cacophony, nonprofits are competing not only with each other but with everyone for Millennials' attention.

Therefore, organizations must be quick, compelling, and inspirational— sometimes in less than the 140-character limit of a tweet. This can be challenging for some organizations, whose traditional case statements and support materials take pages upon pages to convey the impact of their work.

But the research today indicates that Millennials desire immediate access, actions, and participation if they are to be persuaded in that moment. This means the organization must constantly be ready, have the technology established, and be capable of handling inspirational giving in the moment when it arises.

MOBILE IS NO LONGER OPTIONAL—IT'S ESSENTIAL

After the successful text-to-give campaign by the American Red Cross in the wake of the 2010 earthquake in Haiti and then the 2011 earthquake and tsunami that devastated much of Japan, every fundraiser dreamed of replicating that model and ensuring a mobile giving strategy for their organization. But though the campaigns were an important breakthrough in giving for the nonprofit sector and raised an enormous amount of money through individual small donations, it steered nonprofit leaders incorrectly down a path through the use of mobile.

Organizations immediately looked at mobile and said, "We need to have a text-to-give strategy." What they failed to think about was the way in which individuals and Millennials in particular are using their mobile devices. As we discussed in Chapter Three, Millennials use mobile as an opportunity to engage with organizations when they encounter an impulsive message of support, action, and participation. They connect with nonprofits and learn about the stories they read in the moment. They sign up and purchase event tickets, read about the latest happenings, and hear how they can sign up to help the nonprofit in some way. Although financial support is sometimes a part of the Millennials' mobile activity, it does not necessarily mean that they will give through text in that moment.

Given this behavior, why aren't organizations looking at a constituent's mobile phone as a tool for ticket sales, volunteer sign-up, or strategic communications, rather than going straight to text giving? Indeed, organizations must consider how they message support and inform Millennials in order to help them better understand the need for support and how to help—all through a mobile device.

CAN WE BLAME THEM FOR LIKING EVENTS?

Millennials have grown up surrounded by special event models. As discussed in Chapter Five, Hands Across America mobilized more than five million Americans, from New York City to Long Beach, to form a human chain, raise money, and bring awareness to homelessness and hunger in the 1980s. In the 1990s, events like Hurricane Andrew off of the coast of Florida helped draw attention to the need for relief efforts during natural disasters. And of course there were the tried-and-true bike-a-thons, walk-a-thons, bowl-a-thons, and other forms of event-based peer fundraising models that surrounded Millennials and trained them to use these models to raise awareness and support for causes.

Other early forms of engagement for this generation occurred in school-based programs that benefited organizations like the Muscular Dystrophy Association, American Heart Association, and American Cancer Society. They created forms of classroom- and event-based models to engage schoolchildren in raising support for these causes. As a result, these behaviors became embedded into young people's routines.

Moreover, this taught a generation how to leverage event-based models to raise support. It's no wonder, then, that we see research indicating a strong preference for event-based models and a high level of activity around peer endorsement and support for their participation in special events.

Organization Spotlight: The Penn Fund at the University of Pennsylvania

In this interview with Dvorit Mausner of the Penn Fund, she discusses the reasons why and how the Penn Fund is working with Millennials at events in a group capacity to increase participation in their campaigns. Pay particular attention to how she describes the approach they use when Millennials are invited to alumni and fundraising events. For the complete interview, please visit www.causeforchangebook.com.

Q: Why did the Penn Fund decide to engage Millennials?

A: When we started the current capital campaign, there was no specific intention to focus on this age range of alumni. I proposed to engage students about what the outcomes of the campaign will do for them. Young alumni are the future. They will be the major donors of the next campaign. Therefore we need to get them ready for this by getting them more involved in more young alumni programming; otherwise we'll miss a huge opportunity.

Q: Describe the YPenn program.

A: We started the program to provide opportunities for younger alumni to get involved in Penn's campaigns. We create programs and events in conjunction with activities currently going on with our campaigns. YPenn offers the opportunity for young alumni to participate in programming such as a reception with their fellow peers, making it purposeful for them to come out. Most of these people are not drawn to university events unless there is a social event where they can see people similar to them. They are also more likely to go if there are younger alumni around handing out business cards. The original thought was to get more events connected to campus so people would stick around for a drink and connect with other young people. YPenn essentially became a VIP experience for the next generation, and people were very responsive to this option. The primary purpose from a fundraising perspective is that this young alumni base will hopefully contribute back to the university community through their participation and involvement. But the key to making that happen is to ensure that we improve the communication of how they can be involved after every event and what they can do next—that critical call to action of stewardship. This involves finding clearer connections in events and then to annual giving. This has really been growing since the start. It feels grassroots and then becomes very professionalized.

Q: How do you steward Millennials to show them you seek more than just a pure transactional relationship?

A: We use a combination of different stewardship messages—*here are other ways you can stay connected, here is how you do things, I need your feedback*. You want to find out from them how you can excel as an entity with their gifts. You must keep continuing to listen to Millennials, because they think once you have their money you should hear them more. An event is the door opener, and they are able to give based on their initial participation. Stewardship is in recognition of the program and can help them make a connection from a donor to the next step. As a fundraiser, they are my VIP's; they are on my radar, and I have to facilitate the relationships. The impact on the individual level is that they are adding to the university community—building the relationship beyond the thank-you.

PEER FUNDRAISING OCCURS ALL THE TIME

We discussed the importance of peer influence in Chapter Five, and the same principle holds true for giving. Research shows that peer fundraising is the preferred method most endorsed by Millennials, and it's a reliable trigger for participatory giving. Millennials trust their peers' recommendations more than others', not only when deciding to get involved with an organization but also when deciding which organizations to support financially.

If you truly want to get Millennials to give, harness the power and energy of the peer leader to help you raise money for your cause. More than 70 percent of Millennials responding to surveys say they have raised money on behalf of nonprofits. Combined with their interest in using the event model, this means that Millennials are most likely to help raise money by spreading the word, promoting a fundraising event, or participating in a walk, run, or cycling event, usually relying on friends and family to support their cause.

Millennials are also using new online giving platforms—such as Razoo, Fundly, and Crowdrise—that focus on the power of peer fundraising. These platforms make it easy for individuals to create their own fundraising campaigns to raise support for the cause of their choice. For example, Razoo (razoo.com) is a social fundraising application that enables individuals to create minifundraising campaigns for nonprofit organizations. Whether users come as individuals or as part of a team, Razoo provides the technology and mobile tools to help them use social media, email, and a dedicated website to raise funds. This type of platform is ideal when Millennials seek support from their friends for events, walk/runs, and other types of social-based activities for organizations.

In addition to Millennials themselves using peer models to raise funds, some organizations have developed business models that rely on peer-based fundraising

Figure 6.1
Millennials Raising Money for You

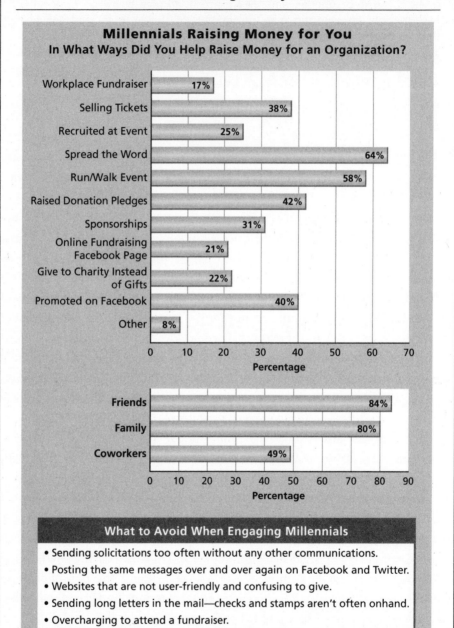

Millennials Raising Money for You
In What Ways Did You Help Raise Money for an Organization?

Category	Percentage
Workplace Fundraiser	17%
Selling Tickets	38%
Recruited at Event	25%
Spread the Word	64%
Run/Walk Event	58%
Raised Donation Pledges	42%
Sponsorships	31%
Online Fundraising Facebook Page	21%
Give to Charity Instead of Gifts	22%
Promoted on Facebook	40%
Other	8%

Category	Percentage
Friends	84%
Family	80%
Coworkers	49%

What to Avoid When Engaging Millennials

• Sending solicitations too often without any other communications.
• Posting the same messages over and over again on Facebook and Twitter.
• Websites that are not user-friendly and confusing to give.
• Sending long letters in the mail—checks and stamps aren't often onhand.
• Overcharging to attend a fundraiser.

to raise substantial support for the cause. charity: water developed a birthday program that encourages donors to redirect what they would have spent on birthday gifts to raise support for clean water in developing countries. Through a custom technology platform that enables the individual fundraiser to promote and engage friends in the fundraising project, charity: water provides a dedicated page that details the location of the water project and the benefit to the local community.

In addition to charity: water, numerous organizations have branded peer fundraising campaigns that speak to the characteristics of Millennials and their giving habits. Here are some brief overviews:

- The Michael J. Fox Foundation created a branded website called Team Fox to encourage individuals to raise support for Parkinson's research. The site allows individuals to create dedicated web pages to get their friends and family to support the foundation. In addition, the foundation provides resources and mentors, recognizes top fundraisers for their efforts, and provides creative tools through social media to spread messaging about the campaign.

- The American Cancer Society created a branded peer campaign called More Birthdays. The concept of More Birthdays is to raise support and awareness to help the American Cancer Society find a cure. Through personalized e-cards, awareness building social media images and messages, and personalized web pages, individual fundraisers can raise money for the organization.

- Feeding America introduced their Virtual Food Drive program as a way to engage friends and family to support hunger relief throughout the United States. Individuals can create a web page that displays the virtual food drive of items to help their family and friends donate online to Feeding America. With social media and other online tools, it is easy to spread the message of how important it is for everyone to support efforts for hunger relief.

Crowd funding has also gained in popularity with the Millennial generation. Crowd funding means a large group of individuals pool resources together to support a particular project or organization. This is different from typical peer fundraising because the project or goal is usually larger than one individual's network can support. Therefore it takes a large "crowd," or several groups of networks or nonpeers, to come together and support a project.

Usually this type of fundraising occurs through an online application developed by an organization to encourage individuals and their networks to support particular projects. Here are a few of the most well-known crowd funding platforms attracting Millennial supporters:

- DonorsChoose (Donorschoose.org) is an online platform for teachers to upload classroom projects that need financial support to enhance student understanding of a particular area of study.

- Kiva (Kiva.org) is a microfinance organization that enables individuals to lend money to a borrower, typically in a third-world country, to start a business that will lead to self-sufficiency.

- KaBOOM! (kaboom.org) created Our Dream Playground as a tool to help local communities and stakeholders raise support for new playground equipment and parks.

Organizational Spotlight: One Percent Foundation—Giving Circles the Millennial Way

In 2007, two passionate young men looked at their annual giving and realized they weren't giving to the causes they felt most passionate about. They felt they couldn't *afford* to give, didn't *know* where to donate, and didn't believe their small individual contribution would make an *impact*. During an epic road trip, they had a total *aha!* moment in which they realized that giving doesn't have to be massive or flashy; it can start with just 1 percent. And so, together with thirty friends, they launched the One Percent Giving Circle.

The One Percent Foundation (www.onepercentfoundation.org) is a nonprofit organization that makes philanthropy accessible to Millennials and empowers them to change the world together. The Foundation's goal is to inspire all young adults to give at least 1 percent of their income to philanthropic causes.

OPF's core program, the One Percent Giving Circle, has grown to become the largest online giving circle in the country, with hundreds of active members nationally who have collectively awarded over $200,000 to nonprofits. Composed of anyone eighteen to thirty-nine years old who makes the commitment to give 1 percent of his or her income to philanthropy, the One Percent Giving Circle engages members in identifying, assessing, and selecting grant recipients. The OPGC also features educational programs and a participatory grantmaking process that empowers members to engage in thoughtful, lifelong philanthropy.

The One Percent Foundation has found that three key barriers limit Millennial philanthropic engagement:

- Affordability: Millennials think they can't afford to give.
- Knowledge: Millennials don't know where to give or how to evaluate the effectiveness of organizations.
- Impact: Millennials believe their limited funds can't make a difference.

The OPGC model successfully breaks down these barriers and makes giving accessible, engaging, and meaningful. By engaging Millennials in sustained and strategic philanthropy when they begin to earn an income, OPF empowers them to be more generous over their lifetimes, to meaningfully affect the organizations that reflect their passions, and to lead their communities on the critical issues of the day.

HOW DO MILLENNIALS GIVE?

Understanding how and why Millennials give is important for fundraisers and executives as they launch new engagement platforms. What follow are findings from the Millennial Donors Study 2011 and the Millennial Impact Report 2012, reflecting the reports' most salient takeaways. Fundraisers should look at the data to better understand the nature of giving and the trends but also keep in mind that this is a long-term strategy to giving and involvement. The results of the surveys and research presented here should not be used for short-term gain. It is your challenge to harness this power and energy for long-term success and look for a participatory engagement strategy that helps Millennials involve themselves in the support areas of the cause.

The Givers' Gap: All-In or All-Out

The most striking aspect of the Millennials' giving and volunteering history may be its polarization: Millennials tended to either give generously of their time and money or give hardly at all.

Although the largest single segment of Millennials said they had donated $300 or more in the past year, the next largest segment had given less than $50. A question about their giving plans for the coming year yielded a similar gap, but responses did suggest that Millennials plan to be more generous, with slightly more saying they would move to the higher end of the giving spectrum and a smaller segment expecting to fall into the bottom group. Other responses were spread fairly evenly in the gap between those extremes.

As one might expect, this age group does not tend to make large single contributions. Asked about their largest donation to a single organization in the past year, the biggest chunk of the Millennials reported it as less than $100. Still, nearly 15 percent of the Millennials gave at least one gift of $1,000 or more.

Questions about volunteering yielded similar gaps: less than 30 percent of the respondents reported volunteering more than thirty hours for nonprofit organizations in the past year, but even more said they volunteered five hours or less. Asked about their plans to volunteer in the coming year, a third said they likely would volunteer thirty hours or more, and a quarter said they expect to volunteer five hours or less.

Only a small amount of this donated time is spent in board meetings, according to the report's findings. Only 16.6 percent of the respondents currently serve on nonprofit boards, and only 33.1 percent have ever served as board members.

More than anything else, the giving and volunteering polarization in this age group (as well as their board involvement) would seem to be simply a product of the respondents' personal and professional progress. Typically, those who have successfully entered the workplace and settled into careers would be more generous, whereas those who are still finding their footing would have considerably less to give in terms of time and money.

As such, we don't expect this polarization to continue as this generation matures. On the contrary, we expect that, as the bulk of the generation acquires greater wealth, more of these donors will emulate their more generous peers—underscoring the importance of forging relationships with them now, regardless of their means.

Takeaway: Focus on the participation of this generation as donors (first-time and renewable gifts) rather than the amount of their gifts. This strategy will ensure that your organization is effectively creating an engagement program that honors engagement and involvement rather than short-term revenue.

Connected with a Purpose: Give Me Substance

No one would be surprised to learn that Millennial donors are technologically savvy and highly connected; what might be underestimated is what they want to know about an organization, and how they want to receive information.

Nonprofit organizations often assume that the best way to connect with younger donors is through activities and events, and the study results do reflect a high level of interest among these donors in knowing about such opportunities to gather and connect. However, the respondents showed an even higher interest in information about the organization and its fiscal health. By a large margin, they reported being most interested in hearing about a nonprofit's programs and services (86.3 percent), and more than half (53.9 percent) said they want to receive updates on the organization's financial condition.

However, a desire for thorough and meaningful communication does not necessarily suggest a desire for frequent contact. Most of the respondents would prefer to hear from organizations on a quarterly basis; slightly more than a third would welcome a monthly communication. Very few would be satisfied with only an annual report; by the same token, almost none (only 2.4 percent) expect a weekly update.

Having established what information Millennials want to receive and how often they want it, we turn to their preferred methods of communication. As expected, when asked what technologies they use to stay in touch with friends and colleagues, they cited Facebook and texting in strong numbers (83.4 percent and 66.2 percent, respectively). But many more, at 99.2 percent of respondents, rely on a relatively well-established communications tool: email. Other options—such as blogging, Twitter, and instant messaging—are used much less frequently.

This email inclination rose to the top again when the Millennials were asked about their preferred methods of receiving information from organizations they support. More than nine out of ten respondents said they prefer to receive information from organizations via email, with Facebook coming in a distant third, behind even print communications.

And although many of these donors rely on email to learn about organizations, Google serves as their primary resource when looking for information, with Facebook again surfacing as a popular choice.

Takeaway: Based on these findings, it's apparent that organizations would be mistaken to rely on stereotypes when communicating with Millennials. Yes, these donors do embrace social media, and they are interested in hearing about activities and events. But email still carries a lot of weight, and this generation is as interested as any other in receiving substantive information on a regular basis. Lastly, organizations need to be acutely aware of how they're showing up in Google searches and how they use Facebook; those platforms are integral to reaching this group.

Two-Faced: Find Me on Facebook, Meet Me Face-to-Face

As important as technology is to Millennials' lives, many of the respondents' survey answers demonstrate that personal connections and close relationships are even more important, and that, although technology can be a useful tool for reaching donors, it is not the best way to establish lasting connections.

Despite some of the media attention paid to massive, one-hit social media campaigns, the study results suggest that the vast majority of respondents are unlikely to volunteer or donate to an organization the first they hear about it. In fact, fewer than 1 percent of respondents are likely or very likely to give time or money based on first impressions, and more than six out of ten will want more information before donating or volunteering.

The results also suggest that a personal connection to an organization can play a significant role in decisions to give: Although only 28 percent of respondents said they prefer to volunteer with an organization before donating, a big portion of them—83 percent—donate to organizations from which they have received services or with which they have participated in programs. This result seems to contradict the long-held notion that organizations cannot solicit support from those they serve.

Certainly, technology can play a big role in reaching these donors—and, again, email and Facebook are the most favored technologies. Email is by far the most effective technology for inviting these donors to volunteer, with Facebook ranking a distant second. More than three-quarters of the respondents also said they have used email to donate, and more have used texting than Facebook to give (18.2 percent versus 14.3 percent). However, it should be noted that this survey was done shortly after the Haiti earthquake, when a number of highly visible text-based fundraising campaigns were under way.

Even email falls considerably from favor when juxtaposed with personal contact. When asked how likely they would be to donate based on methods of asking, 66 percent of respondents said they would be likely or highly likely to respond to a face-to-face request, whereas only 37 percent said they would be likely or highly likely to give if asked via email. Results were similar when the donors were asked how likely they would be to volunteer based on methods of asking. Only 9 percent of the respondents said they were not likely to give or volunteer if asked in person.

The person doing the asking also has an impact on how likely these Millennials are to give or volunteer. By far, friends and family members carry the most weight with their influence over a Millennial's gift of both time and money. Coworkers fell to a distant third in both categories.

Another key factor in urging these donors to give is the nature of the request. The more specific the request, it seems, the more likely they are to give. Very few of these donors are likely to respond to a general, nonspecific request, and more than half said they will not respond to an annual donation call. On the other hand, more than half are likely to respond to a specific request for a particular project, an emergency situation, or an appeal that explains exactly what the money will be used for. Responses were similar when survey recipients were asked how likely they would be to volunteer based on the nature of the request.

The donors also prefer specific information to special events or recognition gifts. Although more than half said they would not be likely to donate based on their attendance at a private reception or a recognition gift, nine out of ten said they would be at least somewhat likely to donate if the request is for a specific and unique need.

About one-fifth of respondents said they would be likely or very likely to donate after attending a private session with friends and coworkers, although quite a few more said they would be somewhat likely. Again, specific information is important: nearly eight out of ten respondents said knowing how money would be used would influence their decision to give, whereas only 28.2 percent said the person who invited them to the event would be a factor in the decision. The results also suggest that organizations hosting an event might do well to consider who delivers the evening's speech. Eight out of ten respondents said they would be at least somewhat likely to give after an event with an influential speaker.

Takeaway: Successfully soliciting funds from any generation can be a complex process that relies on many factors, but organizations seeking to reach Millennials may be able to simplify their strategies considerably: employ a multichannel, high-tech process to reach these donors, but rely on face-to-face contact when making the ask.

Big Givers of Small Gifts (in Various Ways)

The easiest way to sum up the Millennials' giving habits might be with the phrase, "A little to many by various means."

Overall, the survey respondents are generous: 93 percent of them donated to nonprofit organizations in 2010, with 21 percent of them giving $1,000 or more over the course of the year, and another 16 percent giving between $500 and

$1,000. However, that giving was distributed mostly in small increments to many organizations. Although 62 percent of respondents donated more than $150 to nonprofits in 2010, more than half of all respondents—58 percent—said their single largest gift was less than $150. Overall, only 10 percent gave single gifts of $1,000 or more, and 61 percent of all donors gave to three organizations or more.

Although that generosity is good news to nonprofits, the results hint that the future holds even better news. If trends suggested by this study hold true, Millennials will become even more generous over time. Forty percent of respondents said they expect to give more in 2011 than in 2010, and 54 percent said they would give the same in 2011 as in the past year. Of the remaining respondents, 5 percent said they would give less than in 2010, and only 1 percent said they do not plan to give to charitable organizations at all in 2011.

Providing further support to this budding trend is the fact that increases in giving correlate to age, as the survey results show higher levels of giving and numbers of organizations supported as donors age: Millennials falling into the thirty-to-thirty-five age range gave significantly more in 2010 than donors aged twenty to twenty-four or those twenty-five to twenty-nine.

Let's examine for a moment how Millennials *do* give. Seventy percent of respondents said they gave online, 39 percent gave in response to a personal ask, and 34 percent gave after receiving a letter in the mail.

This data supports the idea that multichannel fundraising efforts with Millennials will continue to be important rather than relying on a single tactic. According to the 2011 donorCentrics Internet and Multichannel Giving Benchmarking Report by Blackbaud:[2]

- It has become increasingly common for new donors to give their first gift online.

- In aggregate, online-acquired donors have much higher cumulative value over the long term than traditional mail-acquired donors.

- Every year, large proportions of online-acquired donors switch from online giving to offline sources, primarily to direct mail.

- Without the ability to become multichannel givers by renewing support via direct mail, online donors would be worth far less.

Although this preference for personal contact is consistent with the Millennial Impact Report 2012, new information suggests that, although this reflects how Millennials give, it doesn't reflect how they would *prefer* to give. When Millennials were asked how they prefer to give (see Figure 6.2), 58 percent of them pointed to online giving as their preferred method. Still, 48 percent do prefer to give as a result of a personal request.

A similar action/preference split appeared when it came to giving via mail and email: although 30 percent of respondents gave after receiving a letter in the mail, only 21 percent said they prefer to give in response to a mailed solicitation. In verbatim comments, many respondents suggested they would like to

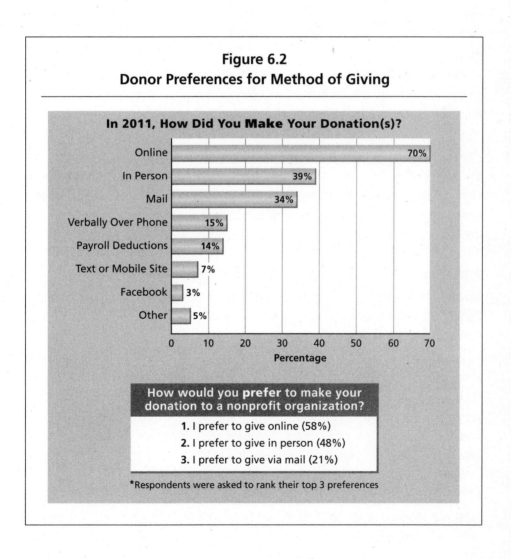

Figure 6.2
Donor Preferences for Method of Giving

In 2011, How Did You Make Your Donation(s)?

Method	Percentage
Online	70%
In Person	39%
Mail	34%
Verbally Over Phone	15%
Payroll Deductions	14%
Text or Mobile Site	7%
Facebook	3%
Other	5%

How would you prefer to make your donation to a nonprofit organization?

1. I prefer to give online (58%)
2. I prefer to give in person (48%)
3. I prefer to give via mail (21%)

*Respondents were asked to rank their top 3 preferences

give regularly through payroll deductions, and several would prefer to maximize their giving through company matches.

Those organizations investing heavily in social media approaches might want to rethink that approach. Only a small number of Millennials donated via text (7 percent), Facebook (3 percent), phone (10 percent), or mobile apps (1 percent), and none of those vehicles was heavily preferred.

As for the emerging trend of giving circles, Millennials are fairly lukewarm to the concept. Only 28 percent said they would participate in a giving circle. On the other hand, only 22 percent rejected the notion outright, with half of all respondents saying they simply are unsure about the idea—suggesting that, although the idea has not caught on yet, it might be worth exploring in the future.

Takeaway: Continue to pursue a multichannel approach to attracting Millennial donors, but be patient as entry-level givers focus on small gifts to multiple organizations; more mature donors give larger gifts.

Furthermore, the disconnect between the ways Millennials give and the ways they would prefer to give suggests that organizations are not offering Millennials the giving tools they prefer. Although it seems that Millennials are dedicated enough to giving that they'll use whatever methods are available, organizations would be wise to embrace giving methods their targeted donors prefer. Failing to do so might mean losing donors to organizations that do.

A Matter of Trust: Givers Who Follow Their Hearts

When it comes to motivating a Millennial to give, successful nonprofits should focus on clearly communicating their mission and trustworthiness—and skip the celebrity endorsements.

A compelling mission or cause will move the vast majority of Millennials to give—especially if that mission or cause centers on education, human services, faith-based causes, or art and culture. Two-thirds of respondents said they supported education organizations in 2010, with 59 percent giving to human services organizations, 40 percent contributing to faith-based causes, and 39 percent supporting art and culture organizations.

When asked to describe what motivates them to give, 85 percent of Millennials pointed to a compelling mission or cause, and 56 percent cited a personal connection or trust in the leadership of the organization. A friend or peer endorsement compelled 52 percent to give; a nudge from a family member prompted 42 percent to give. Slightly more than a third (34 percent) gave as a result of a workplace fundraising drive. A compelling video won over 12 percent of donors, whereas fundraising contests inspired only 5 percent to give. What about the high-profile celebrity or influential leader endorsement? Apparently it's not worth the effort from a strictly fundraising standpoint: only 2 percent of Millennials said they were motivated to give by such endorsements.

When making decisions to give, Millennials value trust above all other factors. In fact, they put such value on trust that 84 percent said they would be somewhat or very interested in donating to organizations that they can fully trust, and 90 percent said they would stop giving to an organization that they could not trust.

To gain givers' trust, organizations should network strategically. More than three-quarters of Millennials (77 percent) said they would trust organizations endorsed by friends or family members, and 64 percent said they would trust an organization if they have met its leadership. Transparency also is a key factor in trust, as 70 percent of respondents said they trust organizations that report how financial support makes a difference.

Other factors that play a key role in giving decisions are specific information and matching gifts. Eighty-two percent of Millennials said they would be very or somewhat interested in donating to organizations that describe the specific purpose for which the money will be used, and 82 percent would give if the organization specifies where the money will be going. Finally, 71 percent of Millennials said they would be interested in giving if they could increase their impact by seeing their gifts matched by another donor.

Takeaway: Make your messages as compelling as possible. At the same time, though, acknowledge that no cause will win Millennials' hearts or dollars if it fails to win their trust. Therefore, as you work to hone message and fundraising efforts, also work to win and protect donors' trust.

Party with a Purpose: Donors Seeking Fun Connections

Just about everybody loves a party, and generous Millennials are no exception. The trick for nonprofit organizations seeking Millennial donors is throwing the right kind of party. Fortunately, our survey questions revealed no big surprises when it comes to fundraising events. Sports- and game-related activities and opportunities to mingle with peers rate high with Millennials; events that require further donation beyond an entry cost rate low.

Dinner parties with entertainment appealed to 63 percent of donors, social cocktail parties with peers drew positive answers from 62 percent of respondents, and 55 percent said they were somewhat or very likely to attend a small private event or gathering. Half of all respondents said they would be somewhat or very likely to attend an event with an information speaker or presentation.

Asked whether a fundraising activity including a sports event or game tournament would appeal to them, 58 percent of respondents said they would be somewhat or very likely to attend; 56 percent responded positively to questions about a fundraising walk or run.

Asking for money at an event is generally frowned on by Millennials. Less than a third of respondents said they would be likely to attend or participate in events including a silent auction, with similar numbers saying they would be attracted to raffles or scavenger hunts.

Takeaway: Choose events carefully, focusing on the opportunities they create for donors to connect, and eschewing those that would attempt to get more money from donors after they've walked through the door.

Make It Easy: Enable Impulse-Inspired Giving

Most Millennials put their money where their passions are. In 2011, the majority of survey respondents supported numerous organizations, and most expect to support as many or more in the coming year—assuming nonprofits make giving easy.

Three-quarters of the Millennials responding to the survey made a financial gift to a nonprofit organization in 2011. Although the majority of those gifts (58 percent) were $100 or less per organization, the typical Millennial supported five organizations in 2011, and 87 percent said they expect to support at least as many organizations in 2012.

And those gifts have the potential to grow: 27 percent of respondents said they give larger amount to a few organizations they care about. Slightly more than 15 percent gave gifts of $500 or more, and about half of those gave $1,000 or more.

When they do give, surveyed Millennials prefer to work through the web, with 70 percent of respondents saying they made 2011 gifts online through a nonprofit's webpage. However, 39 percent said gifts were made to a person or at an event, and another 34 percent said they sent a gift in the mail, although it's unclear whether direct mail or some other form of appeal prompted the gift.

Although Facebook is popular with Millennials, its popularity doesn't often translate into Facebook giving. Fewer than 10 percent of responding Millennials had used Facebook to make donations to nonprofits. Of those who have not given via Facebook, nearly half would consider doing so, but 48 percent of those who would not give through Facebook said security concerns—mostly having to do with Facebook policies—make them hesitant.

Regardless of how they gave, though, many of the surveyed Millennials can be expected to act quickly when they are moved. In focus group discussions, Millennials said they like to give "in the moment," but that does not mean the gifts are haphazard or random. Millennials described a willingness to give based on emotion and in moments of inspiration, but they still want to know that their gifts will have an impact, and they're more likely to give larger gifts to organizations with which they have strong relationships. When asked to choose the phrase that best describes their giving preferences, 42 percent of respondents chose "I give to whatever inspires me at the moment."

Takeaway: Organizations must not ignore "small" Millennial donors but instead should build on those relationships and inspire a greater sense of connection to their causes. They also should be sure to make online giving convenient, and, again, make it accessible to mobile phones so it's easy for Millennials to give when inspiration strikes them. Remember that mobile giving does not mean text giving only; it often means Millennials are accessing your organization's website via smartphone.

Give Them a Reason—Show Them the Impact

Of course, understanding Millennials' giving patterns does you no good unless you also understand their giving motivations. According to the Millennial Impact Report 2012, most Millennial donors want to know their gifts will make a difference. Asked what messages would most likely motivate them to give, 54 percent of respondents said they would respond to the message, "Your support will make an impact; here's how . . . ," and 31 percent would be attracted by the message "Your gift of $25 will help us [do XXX]."

Focus group participants responded well to programs that provide tangible examples of what the nonprofit can purchase or provide for constituents at certain levels of giving. How compelling are such examples? Half of the respondents said the way the request is phrased wouldn't matter as long as the organization explains how the money specifically will be used.

In that same vein, when asked to select their biggest pet peeve about non-profit fundraising, most respondents chose the answer "When I don't know how my gift will make a difference." Other top turn-offs are getting long letters in the mail, being told how much to give, and getting a gift in return for a donation.

Takeaway: Fail to communicate your impact, and you'll fail to attract Millennials' support—and run the risk of never engaging them at all. An organization's appeals and general information must be clear about impact and how donated dollars are used, and they must provide tangible illustrations about how gifts will be used. In addition, be sensitive to the audience's financial sensitivities, invest in cost-effective and efficient appeals such as online approaches, and don't ask Millennials to spend money to simply engage with your organization.

Friendly Persuasion: Put Peer Pressure to Work

Even if they can't give as much as some other demographic groups, Millennials nonetheless are willing to help raise funds, usually by calling on friends and family. More than 70 percent of Millennials surveyed said they have raised money on behalf of nonprofits. Of those who have not, almost half said it's because they simply haven't had the opportunity.

Nearly 64 percent of the survey respondents said they have helped raise money by spreading the word or promoting a fundraising event; 59 percent have participated in a walk, run, or cycling event; and 42 percent said they have raised donation pledges for an event. Even in their fundraising, Millennials showed their technology preferences: slightly more than 40 percent of respondents said they have promoted a nonprofit on Facebook and posted a link for friends to give, and 21 percent have set up an online fundraising page for their favorite cause.

When Millennials do raise money, they like to keep it close to home and make it personal. Eighty-four percent said they typically call on friends when they're fundraising, 80 percent reach out to their extended families, and 49 percent will make the rounds at work.

Millennials might not give as much as other groups, but they can bring a lot of energy and enthusiasm to your fundraising efforts. Leverage their social (and social media) skills to attract new supporters, and offer them plenty of exciting and active opportunities to help you raise money, always remembering that, if you engage them, you're likely to gain access to their friends, families, and coworkers as well.

FINAL THOUGHTS

Millennials do give, and they are incredibly generous to the organizations they support. Although their gifts may not match the capacity of major donors, their support can bring with it friends, new constituents, more awareness, and public acknowledgment within spheres of online networks. This can be far more valuable than a single gift of money alone.

Technology is a tremendous tool for nonprofit organizations, but it is the means to a relationship with organizations and should not be the sole driver of any relationship building that an organization wants to do with its Millennial donors. Beyond technology, you'll need to establish trust and authentic relationships in order to help Millennials come closer to the causes they support.

This means fundraisers still have a duty to connect with their Millennial donors and focus on helping such donors understand the true impact of their gifts, show the tangible transparency this generation wants, and demonstrate how they can have an impact beyond their financial support with the organization. We recognize this will be challenging, as fundraisers have limitations on the time and effort they can contribute. Therefore development departments will need to seek the assistance of Millennials to reach out to their peers and amplify the organizational messaging.

Lastly, the fundamentals of giving haven't changed. Millennials, like any other generation, respond to in-person requests for support. The old saying is true: "I never gave, because I was not asked." With data still supporting this solicitation method, fundraising departments will need to combine traditional and new approaches together in a coordinated manner that yield the response they want from Millennials.

What does this mean for nonprofits? View online giving as an entry point for impulsive action, and start building honest, ongoing relationships based on authentic conversations in social media that you can then elevate through conversation in person.

The Millennial donor is influenced by peer and family in a very connected world. With so many Millennials using smartphones to connect and educate themselves on nonprofits and their current happenings, impulse messaging will be important to Millennials so they can quickly respond to calls for support.

In addition, Millennials have grown up with the concepts of event-based fundraising that incorporates peer strategies. From the "walk-a-thon" model to the after-hours party for an organization, Millennials are drawn to an organization if such offerings are readily available and at a price they can afford.

But keep in mind that pursuing only one approach to fundraising with Millennials will hinder your success in obtaining their support and interest. Safeguard against assumptions that Millennials will react only to online solicitations. Research indicates differently, and you may be surprised by the results of offline methods and personal asking approaches. Use the peer to influence the Millennial donor through various channels such as direct mail, in-person asking, social media, and email.

Figure 6.3
Millennial Giving: Millennial Engagement Platform

Leadership Inviting

It starts with the leadership when it comes to asking Millennials for support. The executive leadership of the organization should create opportunities to bring Millennial supporters together to create a new relationship based on trust. Just as with older donors, connectivity to leadership is imperative in strengthening the connection between individual and organization. Once a month, invite Millennial donors to the organization and/or a local coffee shop to talk candidly and informally about what is happening with the organization.

Tangible Transparency

Organizations must take a transparent approach to Millennial solicitations. Whether it is online or in person, organizations should discuss the specifics of gifts and how their particular support will be used. This is an opportunity to open up your doors and not hide how the money contributed by donors is used. Consider using infographics or other forms of design and data in order to make tangible transparency a part of everyday donor communication.

Social Connectivity

Peer endorsement is crucial in moving Millennials from constituent to supporter. The social connections established through peer networks will be very useful as a fundraiser tries to raise support from Millennials. One of the first tasks of any fundraiser to any fundraiser is to identify social networks and the influencers leading engagement of their peers. In addition, use social connectivity to open a dialogue online in social media about how each follower's or fan's support is important and where donations go specifically. Use images and text that is shareable—easy to copy and post/tweet. Long explanations of how money is used will be ignored and not shared among Millennial donors and their peers.

Solution-Inspired

Consider Millennial donors as some of your best advisors. Use stewardship communication as an opportunity to ask financial supporters what ideas and approaches should be used to strengthen the program. This could even be done through social media conversations and dialogue created between the Millennial donor and their peer. Here is your chance to bring the Millennial donor closer through conversation about how the organization, its programs, and even fundraising efforts can be better. Do not shy away from this important aspect of the Millennial engagement platform, even if you receive negative feedback about your existing work.

BUILD a Better Environment by Engaging Millennials

Be Unified

Everyone in your organization needs to understand what the message to the Millennial donor is. Debrief internally before campaigns to review the message specifically targeted toward the younger demographic.

Understand Their Environment

Review recent research on Millennial giving at TheMillennialImpact.com. Take this opportunity to help others internally understand the power of the peer, impulse, and event approaches on this generation when they give.

Identify Key Change Makers

Millennials react positively to other Millennials. If you have staff who are part of this generation, let them be the change makers. This is also a chance for the organization to publicly showcase the generations that are involved in helping shape and engage a new group of supporters.

Lead by Engagement

Do not make solicitation your first step in engagement. Try to use a peer and their network of Millennials to come together in small sessions and at events to discuss ways to improve the organization. This is a time to show Millennials you value more than just money.

Determine Success

Establish both participation benchmarks and reasonable financial goals when attracting Millennials. In the early years of seeking support from Millennials, focus on participation metrics. Establish a simple and easy participation goal such as the total number of Millennial donors from each campaign. This should be the only metric your organization cares about in year one.

Figure 6.4
Millennial Giving: Five Key Takeaways

1 Recoginize donor involvement by thanking Millennials for their time and skill beyond just giving.

2 Focus on participation in the fundraising process by creating micro giving campaigns that start at the $5 or $10 level.

3 Use email and mobile-optimized donation pages to ensure that Millennials can transact in the moment and on the go.

4 Communicate how their money has been used at least quarterly to ensure the Millennials are involved in the stewardship process.

5 Devote resources and time to convene Millennial donors in informal discussions (coffee shops, social venues, etc.) with leadership and discuss how their gifts can help enact their ideas.

A SPECIAL NOTE TO THE EXECUTIVE LEADER

If you lead an organization, there is a small chance you picked up this book to try and figure out how to raise money from this generation. Most executives like you are struggling with both connection and expectations when it comes to Millennials—partly due to the hype of unique situations such as text-to-give for disaster relief or online campaigns such as Obama for America.

Try to establish manageable expectations for Millennial giving with your fundraising staff. Millennial donors, like all first-time donors, are experimenting with giving and how they want to be philanthropic with your organization. You can do so much more with Millennial donors if you challenge your staff internally to create experiences that involve conversation, dialogue, and interaction between the staff, executive leader, and beneficiary and the individual supporter. Financial support will come when they trust you, and when that trust transcends their peers and connects with them personally.

chapter SEVEN

Millennials in the Workplace

*T*he following story traces Derrick's journey to obtain full-time employment in the nonprofit sector:

We all have stories of our first job. In grad school, I had been working closely with an organization that helped K–12 schools around the country incorporate service and philanthropic education into mainstream curriculum. Although I was beginning to look for employment beyond this graduate-level post, I had inquired about the possibility of staying on in a role that did not exist. I think this was the beginning of my Millennial approach to employment.

The organization had not embarked on a coordinated national effort to reach more schools and teachers nationwide. There was a clear opportunity for the organization to develop a new approach to partnerships and collaborations that could yield this coordinated growth. The role I envisioned would be focused on developing new relationships with K–12 stakeholders in an effort to garner support for the mission, spread the work we did into new schools, and elevate the brand of the cause. It would be my job to convince the seasoned executive director to take a chance on me.

My supervisor, a representative of the Boomer generation, admired the energy and excitement of individuals like me. Despite her being my boss, she never treated me as what I was: a graduate assistant making barely minimum wage. She was always responsive, inviting, and transparent about the work of the organization and how it ran. I felt comfortable pitching the new role to her.

At that time, she and I worked in different states, so I drove more than six hours for a meeting about a job I thought was so important but that had a slim chance for approval. After I arrived, we spent some time talking about how work had been going and the challenges of the organization, from brand awareness to mass engagement from the schools. We talked and laughed about the countless hours everyone spends to bring this important work to the next level. I knew it was my time.

I paused for a moment and reflected on the current conversation. It would be insane not to find the resources to make this position possible. Instead of talking about the endless possibilities of why I thought the job was important, I talked about the "collective together"—about how we had not yet gathered the people in the community who would advocate and promote our cause on our behalf. I said, quite bluntly, that my skills in relationship building—coupled with my desire to bring people together on our work—were not just nice, but necessary.

I could tell she was a little surprised (though not overwhelmed) with my idea about the new position. She sat back, looked at me, and said, "Derrick, one of my mentors told me that in leading a company or organization you will always be persuaded to do things because of new ideas and innovations. But you should always think beyond those ideas and recognize the people that talk and ignite the passion in us to take action. That is where you should always make investments. I believe in you, and I also believe in your abilities—good people who are good at what they do bring good success to any organization. I agree and will pitch the board on our idea and the new position."

I was so excited I could not believe it. Still, a bigger group of people now needed to be convinced. The organization's board consisted of some of the most seasoned nonprofit executives in the country. It included funders, association leaders, and corporate executives, all with at least twenty years of service in the field. They were experienced, thoughtful, forward thinking, and, most important, generation-neutral.

When my boss pitched the idea of the new hire, they understood the opportunity to bring in someone with the skills that I had. They understood the desire to create relationships and build those into successful endeavors for the organization. And they understood the need to build a new infrastructure that would help expand the brand of the organization and seize opportunities on a nationwide scale. I was later told that at the board meeting they spent little time discussing the concept and more about what the goals of the new position should be.

They approved the hire—and me to be their key person. They could have chosen anyone to fill the position, but they saw value in my work, my abilities to connect and build relationships, and my age. They recognized the potential in having someone of my generation go out and overcome some of the barriers to success.

When the board walked out of the room, the board chair passed me on her way out to her car. As she was leaving, she took my hand and said, "We are proud and excited to have you on the team. It is going to be hard work, but I know you will be successful. I am here if you need me as a support, but I will champion everything you do. Call on me when times get tough, but also call on me when you need help figuring out how to navigate a system that is not friendly to people like you. You have my best."

At first I didn't quite understand what she meant about navigating a system unfriendly to "people like me." But later, I realized exactly what she meant. She recognized early on that I would have trouble with some who viewed me as too young, too inexperienced, and lacking the institutional knowledge necessary to engage in high-level discussions. There were times I did call on her for help—mainly for someone to listen and hear me out on the challenges I faced. She became a remarkable mentor.

I could not have asked for a better situation in landing my first job. I had an understanding, transparent, and authentic leader who told me, more than once, to conquer the world regardless of what people say. I had coworkers (some more than double my age) who never treated me any differently than they would a peer, even when I was charged with leading them in certain initiatives.

Lastly, I was never told it couldn't be done. We were a small team and lived in an environment in which a committed group of people made everything possible. And it showed. At our peak, in 2005, we had more than a hundred thousand teachers downloading materials from our website every month—all made possible by a team of six.

To this day, I still connect with this team of people and admire everything we did together and the impact we had. It was a wonderful time. I will be forever grateful to them for giving me a chance.

But I am a lucky one. Not too many Millennials have an experience like I did when finding a job. Today some of my Millennial friends are still searching for their dream job and an open organization like the one I found. They struggle to fit in and be as creative as they can, given the formal structures of the organization they work for. This chapter is to help you, the nonprofit executive, take advantage of this generation's skills and desires in order to enhance your organization's work product and community impact.

MILLENNIALS AND THE NONPROFIT WORKPLACE

The current economy has affected traditional coming-of-age decisions, from careers and marriage to parenthood and schooling. In addition, it has possibly contributed to a broader change in social norms about when "adulthood" actually begins. This is especially true as Millennials tend to linger in the comfort of their parents' homes and on their parents' health care plans—much longer, in fact, than generations before them, who were eager to break free, get married, begin their families, and climb the corporate ladder.

In spite of this shift, the pressure to constantly improve and build on existing structures is relentless in today's organizations. We are living in a world with new problems that need new answers. As a result, we're building a lot of new stuff—a new economy, new media, new politics, and even new cities. The idea of centralized organizations and one-way communications is being replaced by networked approaches with multichannel dialogue. Now we are discovering that the key to organizational success lies in openness and transparency between and among employees, volunteer boards, stakeholders, constituents, and the wider audience that organizations touch through their work.

A NEW LADDER OF SUCCESS

Although the rungs of the corporate ladder are arguably quite different for Millennials from what they were for prior generations, some would say they are coming of age without a ladder at all. The traditional ladder is still seen in professional fields such as law, where you know the process for being indoctrinated into the legal profession. You begin with undergraduate school, study for the LSATs, get into law school, find a summer internship at the best possible firm, and then take the bar exam. The route is formal, prescribed, and bureaucratic in nature.

The nonlinear career path of someone setting out to find meaning and change the world is much less defined. The new path has a combination of chance encounters, being at the right place at the right time, following one's passions, finding meaningful work (however you define it), and developing relationships with mentors in a given field that you hope will lead to exciting projects and a career of service and community entrepreneurship.

Although older generations might scoff at such a loosely defined approach, Millennials have a different set of career priorities that go beyond the corner office, six-figure salary, or cushy retirement plan. It's incumbent upon organizations to understand these new priorities and adapt to them. If they don't, they run the risk of losing the exceptional talent of Millennials who choose organizations with a culture and mission more closely aligned with their interests.

For nonprofits, this often means losing out to more nimble, leaner start-ups with a social mission or to double- or triple-bottom-line companies with quicker paces of change, flat(ter) structures, and cultures that allow for work–personal life blending. The growth of new business models that both turn a profit and do good gives those entering the professional world a new option. College graduates no longer have to choose; they can do both.

So how do we alter the ladder of success to resonate with today's younger generation? Millennials want to have a career that is meaningful; they want an opportunity to be challenged and to challenge others; and they want to feel that their bosses, peers, and community value their work.

The State of Young America, a poll issued by the Young Invincibles, found that 48 percent of young adults feel that their generation will be worse off than their parents. This statistic is highlighted through record unemployment rates, the soaring cost of higher education, and the issues of inequality facing our increasingly diverse generation. On the other hand, the same report found that approximately 77 percent of young people personally believe they can achieve the American dream, as defined by hard work, education, and a strong community. In this duality lies the problem and the opportunity that the Millennial Generation and nonprofits must seize and solve together.

Millennial Views on Meaningful Work

Find Meaning:

"My job is an extension of who I am as a person, and I want to make sure that it aligns with my personal beliefs. A company in today's day and age can't just be about the bottom line. I need to know the impact of my work is also benefiting society."

"I want my work to be a continuation of my passions. Any place where I invest such a significant portion of my time needs to show it is having an impact in the broader community."

(Continued)

Be Challenged and Challenge Others:

"There's a misconception that my generation is lazy and looking for the easy way out, when in fact, we are actually looking to be intellectually challenged. We want to be surrounded by people who are motivated, driven, and passionate, and we tend to seek out opportunities that will provide for that in an office culture."

Feel Valued:

"I want to know that my thoughts and opinions are not only heard but valued. It's one thing for organizational leadership to ask what I think, but it's another thing to actually have them adapt a process or project based on my feedback."

WHY TODAY'S WORK ENVIRONMENT IS SO DIFFERENT

The nonprofit work environment has changed dramatically over the last ten years. Ten years ago, work environments centered on providing their employees the structure, the resources, and the means to complete their work. Treating employees well was important, but the focus was on how the company or organization could help them accomplish the work fast and effectively through incentives, benefits, and salary-based models.

Boomers and other older generations were also put into hierarchical structures that screamed, *Work hard and do well and you will advance up the corporate ladder*. Employees had to spend a certain amount of time working their way up to larger executive positions. This "put in your time" approach to corporate advancement made its way into the nonprofit sector as well.

In contrast, the essential design of today's workplace can be seen as a strategic tool that reflects and expands on an organization and its goals. With this in mind, nonprofits must consider the impact of Millennials in the workplace and realize their potential in helping create a dynamic and highly effective work environment. Such an environment goes beyond traditional systems, processes, and hierarchies, and instead focuses on the work product itself.

Wondering what your organization should be thinking about as it creates a twenty-first-century work environment? Perhaps the most important thing to keep in mind is that business as usual is a thing of the past. This is not to say that the new entrepreneurial way is the only way, or even necessarily the better way. But if you're stuck in a "this is how we've always done it" mentality, you may want to reevaluate how you view your organization's culture and approach.

Millennials on the upper end of the age cohort have now spent about a decade or more in the workforce, and they are developing noticeable trends that are influencing organizational change. Allison Fine presented this shift in a *Harvard Business Review* article about "The New Professional."[1] She sees a new definition of professional behavior developing in this social world: "Social media enables people to be their best selves: honest, open, fallible, funny, and connected, but too many people and organizations are still trying their best to imitate automatons." Your organization, reputation, logo, and staff are living, breathing entities that need to be out in the world to be effective. The transition is unfolding as follows:

Old Professional	New Professional
I am closed to the world.	I am open and accessible to the world, strengthening my relationships with people.
I can't make mistakes in public.	I am human; when I inevitably make mistakes, I apologize quickly and sincerely.
I don't reveal my personal interests to the world.	My interests, hobbies, passions make me interesting and attractive.
I am expected to have the answers to questions.	I am searching for answers with my network of colleagues and supporters.
Power is taken and held.	Power is shared and grown.

Successful strategies during times of great change are possible only if we allow ourselves to change the rules. Our continued reliance on top-down decision making is—given today's rapidly changing environment—a recipe for disaster. At nonprofits with traditional hierarchical structures, there is a gap between the people who make strategy and the people who are tasked with actually making that strategy come to life. In the post-digital world, where Millennials are beginning to outnumber their Baby Boomer colleagues, the gap between those developing the vision at the top and those realizing the vision will continue to grow until we are willing to embrace the somewhat messy culture found in collaborative enterprises.

Indeed, a new collaborative system is needed, one that author and management strategist Nilofer Merchant refers to as *The New How* in her book of the same name.[2] According to Merchant, a collaborate system enables everyone to contribute, lets insights and strategies begin anywhere in the organization, and helps executives and workers learn from and collaborate with one another as they build a powerful shared understanding that integrates strategy and execution to produce new results. The New How is about bringing many people together, regardless of their title or position, to define the strategic direction. That's not to say that all decisions must be made in this light; rather, the approach recognizes that the best strategic thinking can be derived from the collective wisdom of the group as well as from the C-suite.

Merchant also asserts that managing at today's accelerating pace of change requires a high level of cross-silo collaboration. She observes that collaboration is more a function of systems and processes than it is about behaviors and attitudes. With collaborative organizations, success becomes far less dependent on one individual's idea and instead is based on collective decisions made across the organization. This allows more people to share in the celebration when things go well—and the realignment when they do not.

Many organizations will aspire to build an open and collaborative enterprise in an effort to remain competitive and attractive to the rising generation. However, keep in mind a few key attributes of a true collaborative organization:

- More people are empowered to make decisions, more stakeholders have a voice that is respected and heard, and more people are able to identify problems and then take action.

- Organizational values are clearly defined and shared with everyone across the organization.

- Leadership is recognized throughout the organization as the ability for anyone to adequately respond and move forward. There's an appreciation that better solutions may be found by engaging multiple people across departments.

- Those in positions of leadership are there to encourage, not stand in the way of, the people who have the resources and capacity to meet the organization's goals.

- Information is shared in a centralized way so that all have access to what they need, when they need it.

THE WORK PRODUCT VERSUS PROCESS

In traditional methods of work, we see a great deal of focus on the systems, processes, and operationalization of an organization's work, services, and products. With the advent of structured-based approaches to work product in the for-profit world, it was not surprising to see nonprofit organizations incorporate similar programs internally to help them build the necessary infrastructure. For some organizations, this approach has really helped operationalize the impact of their mission in the community.

Today's Millennial, however, is starting to tear down the formal structures of process in an effort to design, craft, and create an environment that will yield even greater impact in the community. With that formal process replaced by the new, more conducive environment, it is astounding to see the drive of Millennials seeking to create solutions; no matter what barriers exist, they continue their quest for impact.

The important aspect of the Millennial mind-set is that they are trying to help people who are helping others, by bringing together their supporters and other individuals to create a lasting approach to social challenges. Although the process of creation is important, it is not the focus. Therefore they seek people around them who share a common interest in building the next solution, no matter what hierarchy exists to help them create it. Rather than "waiting their turn," they start gathering people together to meet the goal.

Occupy Everything

On September 17, 2011, several hundred people marched to an empty park in Lower Manhattan. They erected tents and built makeshift institutions—a field hospital, a library, and even a department of sanitation. Within a few short weeks, Occupy Wall Street had spread beyond Zuccotti Park and served as inspiration for dozens of protests in cities across the country and around the world. Within the space of just a few months, the Occupy movement had not only changed the conversation about income inequality—a point of unity for the movement—but likewise heightened the potential influence of leaderless movements. Occupy was founded on the notion that, "The one thing we all have in common is that we are the 99% that will no longer tolerate the greed and corruption of the 1%"—a reference to the statistic that the top 1 percent

(Continued)

of households in the United States own somewhere between 30 to 40 percent of all privately held wealth.

Occupy's organizational presence in New York and cities like Chicago, Atlanta, and Oakland operated on a consensus model of decision making, whereby anyone could join in and propose ideas, rather than issuing top-down directives. This model of participatory democracy would strive to create opportunities for all members of the group to make meaningful contributions and broaden the range of people who had access to decision making. Specific issues such as food, medical, legal, and security were each handled by individual working groups of citizens.

Even so, it's unclear whether the Occupy movement truly resonates with mainstream Millennials. As Michelle Nunn, CEO of the Points of Light Institute, wrote in a *Washington Post* editorial, the Occupy Wall Street group does not represent mainline Millennials who continue to be more interested in changing business from the inside out than via protest. Referring to the next generation's focus on finding careers that have a social impact, she says, "The Occupy Wall Street movement is largely fueled by a relatively small set of young people who view the protests as a fight for their future. The vast majority, however, are getting up and going to work every day—or wishing they could. These individuals are part of a less dramatic but, perhaps, equally powerful movement of Millennials shaping the future of business."[3]

It's also unclear whether Occupy Wall Street will have staying power, given its loose structure and anti-establishment ethos, but we know that the movement played a pivotal role in challenging nonprofits and foundations to think differently about how they approach and engage others in their work. Looking at the Occupy movement and its dozens of spinoffs across the country, we see that they were able to achieve in just a few months what nonprofits often spend years trying to build. They created a foundation of passionate and dedicated volunteers and activists and a recognizable brand, which allowed them to garner broad media attention; and they managed to do this on a minuscule budget—roughly $650,000 was reportedly raised three months into the campaign. It is unclear whether the impact of Occupy Wall Street will be lasting or brief, but the story of how it unfolded and the ability of the movement to seize control of the national conversation were remarkable.

Even as the Occupy movement brought with it a new and dramatic wave of online activism and engagement, we've only begun to figure out what that activism can or should be able to achieve. As Brian Reich, author of *Shift and Reset*, explains,

What we have seen this year, and last year for that matter, was an understanding of how to focus the energy and attention of a community in opposition to something. The crowd can help to bring down a government, force an organization into reversing a bad decision, scare legislators into changing their position on an issue—but have we figured out how to direct the crowd toward building something constructive? Have the activists lent their collective intelligence to the effort to create a better governing process? Have the protesters stepped up to write better legislation? Aside from raising money, have people who opposed helped to ensure a better, more constructive approach to solving problems gets developed?[4]

Yes, there are lessons to be learned from Occupy, but there is also a desire to find ways to bridge an old way of organizing with the new energy that something like the Occupy Movement brings to our cultural ethos. Sure, you got people's attention, and—in the case of the protests in Tunisia, Egypt, Yemen, and Libya—overthrew a government. But now what? How do we create a structure with clear leaders to move to the next stage of development?

A NEW FORM OF BENEFITS

Benefits give you a unique opportunity to show employees that you care about them. Organizations have long created employee benefits programs that feature salary, retirement, and health care perks. Though still important, these are not as attractive to Millennials as the benefits they see from untraditional nonprofit organizations. This generation of employees seek a different set of benefits—one that supports them in their growth and development as future leaders. These include access to technology, flexibility and balance, a particular organizational culture, and a particular environmental culture. Let's consider each in turn.

Access to Technology

When the *Cisco Connected World Technology Report* asked whether the Internet was a fundamental human necessity, one in three college students and young employees (ages twenty-one to twenty-nine) responding said they believed the Internet to be as important as air, water, food, and shelter.[5] The study, which provides insights into challenges that companies face as they strive to balance current and future employee and business needs, also found that two in five respondents said they would rather accept a lower-paying job with more flexibility in regard to device choice (that is, laptops and mobile phones), social media access, and mobility than a higher-paying job with less flexibility. Millennials clearly want their technology, but they want it on their terms.

Organizations should also consider setting aside resources for Millennials to test new technology to enhance the work environment. For instance, some organizations tell their Millennial employees they can have a certain budget amount to purchase a software program that will enhance the work of the organization in either program or operations. This type of benefit enables Millennials to create new ways to improve the organization while also playing into their interest of experimentation and technology.

Flexibility and Balance

If Gen X introduced the concept of work-life balance, given their strong desire to devote more time to their families and personal well-being, Millennials have taken that concept and morphed it into work-life blending.

What does this mean in practice? Millennials want policies that provide for a more sustainable balance of work and personal life. At work they want the freedom to access social networks, take personal calls, chat with friends via instant message, and use their own tech devices. Then outside the office, they'll happily take work calls from home, check their email on off-hours, and even view coworkers as friends in real life and online. (Some workplaces have even gone to a no-vacation policy whereby employees can come and go as they please, but this type of benefit may be a challenge for some nonprofit leaders who have employees from other generations who are used to specific policies for time away from the office.)

This new view of the workplace is reflected in the findings of a new study from Millennial Branding and Identified.com. They examined the profiles of four million Facebook pages, and found that, on average, Millennials are connected to sixteen coworkers on Facebook. Because of this they will often become an organization's biggest evangelists. Don't be surprised to see a Millennial leader up at night sending emails and texts and chatting it up with friends and social networks in order to tell the organization's story.

Organizational Culture

Culture comprises the unspoken rules that foster creativity and transparency in the workplace. We spoke with one nonprofit made up of an all-Millennial workforce that implemented "virtual Tuesdays," allowing their employees to work from anywhere they wanted one day a week. This could mean they work from home, a coffee shop, their mom's house, or from noon to 8 P.M. it didn't matter, as long as their work was getting done. They found that giving this flexibility and allowing employees to take care of what they need to do allowed for a positive workplace culture that contributed to personal happiness and a better organizational work product.

Environmental Culture

Building on the organizational culture, the environment or physical (and, in many cases, virtual) space given to do one's work is just as important. Although Millennials value their privacy and appreciate an office, they also desire open communication and collaboration. As such, they tend to prefer flexible spaces where they can mix and brainstorm over single-use spaces such as offices or conference rooms.

"NO COLLAR" WORKERS

In its *No Collar Workers* study, MTV looked at how the eighty million members of the Millennial generation were reshaping the workforce.[6] Beyond the fact that they are hyperconnected, tech savvy, entrepreneurial, and collaborative, the study also found they favor fast-paced work environments, want quick promotions, and are not exactly fans of traditional office rules and hierarchy.

As interpreted by their largely Boomer managers, these survey results might indicate that Millennials want too much, too soon. They are seen as "picky" or "self-important," with too little respect for the traditional way things are done. However, this analysis sells the Millennial Generation short. It's more an expression of needing to connect deeply with their work, creating new ways to work, and wanting to be respected and considered hard-working by senior managers. For example, in the MTV survey, "loving what I do" outranked salary and a big bonus, and half of all Millennials would "rather have no job than a job they hate."

If not money, what do Millennials want most? The vast majority (83 percent) are "looking for a job where my creativity is valued," and more than nine in ten Millennials are "motivated to work harder when I know where my work is going" and want supervisors, managers, and executives to listen to their ideas. Millennials walk into CEO offices to tell them how to fix things, and whether or not their boss always takes their advice, they want to know that they are being heard and that their opinions and insights matter. The MTV study found that 76 percent of Millennials think their boss could learn a lot from them, compared to only 50 percent of Boomers.

We looked at MTV's survey together with a survey conducted by the nonprofit consulting group CompassPoint that shed light on how institutions and organizations should be adapting to align with the rising generation's leadership style.[7] CompassPoint identified nine characteristics that show how next-generation leaders are transforming their organizations, which include the following:

- Being impact-driven
- Believing in continuous learning and shared leadership
- Being wired for policy change
- Being multicultural and culturally competent
- Believing in the ambiguity of work-life boundaries
- Viewing constituents as thought partners
- Adding value to board discussions and decisions

Overall, the data and feedback point to a generation primed to give the workplace their all, but who will also call for meaning, mentorship, and meritocracy in a workplace that can channel their contributions. We've drawn several conclusions that help set the foundation for the next generation of nonprofit workplaces and can help organizations reshape the way they work for long-term impact on all generations in the workforce.

- **Clear systems support good workplaces.** Clarity about decision making, job requirements, and evaluation are important factors for creating a positive atmosphere in the workplace. This includes transparency and input into decision making, opportunities for management and leadership skills training, and workplace flexibility. Even with clear systems, however, Millennials find hierarchies difficult to understand because they didn't grow up with them. They believe that an "ideocracy" should reign in the workplace, and that everyone should be heard and the best ideas win out, regardless of who comes up with them.
- **Explicit paths for career advancement are key.** Most people know their job descriptions, but many don't know whether they are doing their jobs well.

Along with older generations, Millennials in the workplace want to know the paths of advancement, what determines success, and how salaries are decided. For the most part, Millennials aren't fans of having to wait six months or a year to get a formal review of their work. Boomers, on the other hand, are more likely to prefer a structured system where feedback is given at certain times of the year. Workplaces can balance these preferences with a combination of management styles and review processes, such as weekly one-on-one meetings with managers as well as formal biannual reviews for employees.

- **Mission-driven organizations are essential.** A crucial aspect for Millennials in deciding where they want to work is a strong belief in the mission of the organization and knowing how their work contributes to its success. It was no surprise to see that Millennials want to see the impact of their contribution. Their commitment is to a cause, not necessarily an organization, and Millennials (as well as Generation X) will gravitate toward organizations and groups that demonstrate a clear ability to create change.

TEN QUALITIES OF SUCCESSFUL MILLENNIAL-FRIENDLY NONPROFIT WORK ENVIRONMENTS

The issue of how institutions will be structured and organized in what's being called the "Connected Age" is an ongoing process. For the first time ever, we have four generations operating under the same roof: the Silent Generation, Baby Boomers, Generation X, and the rapidly maturing Millennial generation. What's more, the sheer size of the Millennial generation means that as Baby Boomers retire or move out of their current positions, the leadership roles they have occupied for so long will need to be filled. And because Gen X is too small to fill the void, Millennials will have to quickly assume the responsibilities of many of these positions.

Meeting community demands while trying to raise enough resources also complicates the work environment of nonprofits. Most organizations are working toward the shining goal of sustainability, and as part of that effort they have had to resort to certain management and cultural changes that affect their ability to help Millennials advance.

For example, we have seen organizations strip professional development from their workplace culture—the very benefit that Millennials rank above salary. This is a generation yearning for professional advancement and ongoing learning, so it is hard for some Millennials to get excited about their prospects when they no longer have access to training in management, technology, marketing, and fundraising.

Moreover, the environment at a nonprofit can be incredibly busy and over-worked; the norm for some Boomer leaders there has been to work long, hard hours to maintain the status quo. Although this struggle for work-life balance is well documented in for-profit work environments, it becomes especially pro-nounced in the nonprofit sector where, to a certain extent, Millennial employees work the same long hours for less pay. Yet it's not the hours worked that chal-lenge this generation; it's the expectation that Millennials need to be physically present and onsite in order to accomplish the organization's mission, thus under-cutting their highly valued flexibility.

But even amid these challenges and shortcomings, Millennials continue to shape the current work environments throughout the nonprofit sector. When we look at how Millennials are affecting the way organizations are managed, mak-ing decisions, and delivering their goods and services, we see some key trends that nonprofit leaders outside the Millennial generation should note in order to maximize workplace productivity.

We hope leaders read the following ten recommendations not as negative challenges, but rather as opportunities to invite and encourage diversity within the workplace culture. Of course, each trend and opportunity may not be right for every organization. But overall, they can help influence how nonprofits today innovate internally to maximize the potential of Millennial employees. Detailed discussions of the recommendations follow this list:

1. Make transparency a given.
2. Level the playing field.
3. Give feedback.
4. Change to drive greater impact.
5. Ensure a networked workforce.
6. Support risk taking.
7. Understand mission-life balance.
8. Recognize that the mission exists outside these walls.
9. Partner to build strength.
10. Build an army.

1. Make Transparency a Given

Millennials join the workforce today expecting honesty and transparency. Transparency, however, goes beyond simple weekly staff meetings or periodic email updates. It's about letting Millennials into the boardroom during meetings. It's about letting them hear directly from their leadership about how the organization is doing, see the financial papers that show the strength and stability of the organization, and witness the strategic direction and advice provided by board members to the staff.

This level of transparency can be hard for some older generations who have been taught to hold information close to the vest. It can also challenge some nonprofit boards that seek to drive the organization's strategic direction directly with the CEO and often have difficulty finding ways to engage lower-level employees. This isn't to say that all board members need to be attuned to the needs of the younger employees; it's more that, given the opportunity, Millennials are interested in pursuing access to and relationships with these leaders. Being able to work side by side with boards and senior leadership can help Millennials increase their vested interest in the organization and fuel their passion to network for the cause's programs.

2. Level the Playing Field

Millennial employees have difficulty with the typical hierarchical structures of nonprofits. Although titles can help provide structure or a chain of command, it is not surprising to see some Millennials ignore titles altogether and instead search for systems that allow access to anyone on staff regardless of department or rank within the organization.

Note that Millennials are not against structure altogether. What they won't accept are organizations that refuse to take steps to improve their systems. This generation wants to build networks internally that help meet a goal, accomplish an objective, and drive change for constituents. The "structure" most often used by Millennials is a team-based approach to drive social change. No matter the expertise of the individual members, the goal is to accomplish a solution-based approach to help meet the strategic direction of the organization.

The goals of every organization hiring Millennial employees should be to bridge existing structures with a team-based approach to productivity. Teams are focused less on department hierarchy and more on leveling the playing field of employees who are interested in tackling an issue.

3. Give Feedback

Millennials want and expect feedback on their work product and performance. Feedback, both positive and negative, is necessary for Millennials to understand their current standing, how their work compares to their counterparts', and how they can improve. And don't be surprised if they offer you their feedback on how *you're* doing as well.

Nonprofit leaders need to create both formal and informal feedback mechanisms when working with Millennials. Formal feedback programs include normal human resource suggestions, such as six-month or annual reviews of performance. In addition, organizations should consider formal processes such as mentor and peer review.

Informally, the organization should provide ongoing feedback based on performance, changes in personal or professional work styles, and areas of improvement. From weekly informal check-ins to coffee shop discussions with the Millennial employee, the nonprofit leader should not be concerned about possibly overcommunicating with Millennials about their performance overall. This ongoing feedback mechanism is a consistent approach to building long-term trust from and engagement with the Millennial employee.

4. Change to Drive Greater Impact

It can be said that Millennials love change, but not just for change's sake. They usually are working within a certain context that provides the background and reasons behind their perceived need to change. In terms of nonprofit work, we see that Millennials seek change in order to elevate the cause and the ultimate mission. Usually this change is driven by their passion to spread the work of the cause in the community and to help others come on board to support and lend their volunteer time and resources to the cause.

For leaders of Millennial employees, it is useful to demonstrate where change can lead directly to greater impact. This includes providing workplace challenges, employee team–based contests, and even incentives and rewards for providing solutions and changes that further the mission. Leaders should also consider inviting Millennials' participation during operational and program review periods to help brainstorm new approaches to solving current local needs addressed by the organization's work.

5. Enable a Networked Workforce

We have observed throughout this book that this generation is networked and well connected. Nonprofit leaders should embrace the generation's need to network with fellow workers. This means that the leader must be willing to enable such communication to occur as long as it helps deliver the results and outcomes desired by the organization. For example, leaders should consider joining in chats and online discussions with employees to help them accomplish tasks. Using Skype or other chat formats such as instant messaging can help create a networked work environment that some Millennials are used to in their personal lives.

Nonprofit leaders should also examine how goals and task outcomes are communicated back to the leadership and how networked technology solutions may aid in the reporting structures of these important benchmarks. For instance, dashboards can help transparently communicate the larger goals and outcomes desired by the nonprofit. Using network techniques such as private Facebook chats through the organization's Facebook page, Google+ Hangouts, or Skype programs for teams can give leaders opportunities to communicate and understand progress, participate in meetings, and provide the information necessary to help employees reach their goals. These techniques can provide the real-time support and leadership needed for some Millennials to increase their productivity in the workplace environment.

6. Support Risk Taking

Millennials are risk takers. Moreover, they are not afraid to take a risk in the context or confines of a system or structure that may already exist. In the search for more effective, simpler, and easier forms of program delivery, Millennials will try different methods in the hope that a new approach can help more people. This type of risk is usually within the confines of program experimentation and operational effectiveness.

It is not uncommon to see Millennials experiment with new program models, which may include technology-based solutions. The opportunity to change and take risks may involve new online tools to communicate with and manage the people receiving services. Don't be surprised if a Millennial on staff asks detailed questions in an effort to find a new approach to delivering the same program but through a different medium. This probing can be a healthy addition to the program-effectiveness efforts currently under way in the organization.

Millennials may bring limited experience into the work environment. Nevertheless, these workers can sometimes fearlessly seek new ways to improve operations or reimagine how an organization manages its internal work processes. It is not uncommon for some Millennials to develop new internal communication approaches that involve a networked approach in an effort to build a more communicative and team-based setting. Look for Millennials to challenge the way things have operated internally in order to bring the group closer together.

This is a key opportunity to let some Millennials and other generations work closely together to change the manner in which work processes, product, and services are managed and executed. This may be important for some older generations to latch onto as they acknowledge how current environments may need to change but can't fully conceptualize how such change should occur.

7. Understand Mission-Life Balance

The term *work-life balance* is commonly used in the for-profit setting, but in the nonprofit field we see a new approach rising: mission-life balance. Millennial nonprofit workers are socially conscious and cause-passionate. This type of mind-set doesn't shut off when the clock hits 5 P.M. The idea of changing the world for the better is alive within them, and the time of day does not matter.

Millennial employees are not averse to working long hours to get the job done. What they prefer is to work the necessary hours in a smart manner and have the flexibility to balance those hours with time off and support for personal pursuits on their own time.

Consider mission-life balance during the hiring process by asking questions that reveal potential Millennial employees' personal drives and how they want to integrate or set aside personal time to accomplish their own goals and agenda. This type of conversation and dialogue provides the nonprofit executive with important details on how Millennials will weave together their personal interests with the mission and vice versa.

Executive leaders should also understand that Millennials continue to work after hours in different ways than those common with other generations. We have seen that Millennials will have late-night coffee shop discussions and network with friends in small group settings to evangelize about the cause, plan the next event, or find ways their family and friends can get involved. This type of informal working should be rewarded and also recognized, even if they are not on the clock. Some executives struggle to conceptualize this because they see other older generations turn the work switch off after they leave the office. Don't be surprised if you arrive at the office one morning and a Millennial says, "I was with a group of my friends and they had some great ideas and ways to get involved. Can I tell you all about it?"

8. Recognize That the Mission Exists Outside These Walls

Millennials want to help people regardless of where they are physically. The confines of a place-based model can be constrictive for those Millennials who gain energy with networking, being with people, and going where the movement is. This can be seen in the work of Millennials seeking to bridge an internal service delivery model with external outreach in their effort to go and meet the need head on rather than wait for the beneficiary to come forward.

When seeking to build new program models, executive leaders should consider the ideas and approaches of their Millennial workers. Their concepts and ideas for using mobile technology and other connected platforms such as social media may help expand the reach and potential of the organization without an increase in costs. Furthermore, allowing Millennials to explore opportunities in the local community is an exciting proposition for some looking to tackle the next challenge. Think of this as an opportunistic approach to helping spread the message; rather than being confined to one location, bring services to others.

9. Partner to Build Strength

The word "partnership" means many different things to many different people. Nonprofits often use this term for an approach to collaboration and inclusiveness. However, it's also loosely associated with "name only" partnerships focused on the marketing aspects of both organizations. To Millennials, this is a lost opportunity.

Millennials look at partnerships and question how they came about and how they are advantageous for the cause. Partnerships in the form of both program and marketing or outreach are usually top of mind for Millennials. Finding those partner organizations that will help deliver aspects of the program and enhance the existing program is a first step in collaboration, often culled from Millennials' own networks, connections, or individuals within their personal spheres of influence.

In addition, Millennials look to partners to hold events, activities, and other efforts to build the marketing and awareness of the organization. This could include partnerships on fundraising activities or special events that will bring in new friends to the cause. Millennials see these as opportunities rather than challenges or threats—such defensive sentiments being common for some older generations seeking to maintain niche interests of the organization.

It's important that executive leaders allow Millennials to explore these opportunities and encourage such dialogues openly among other organizations. This is a time when executive leaders could bring together leaders from partner organizations and their Millennial employees to explore potential collaborations. Such exploration offers a great learning and professional development opportunity for Millennials who may not yet understand the complexities of partnership development.

10. Build an Army

Millennials want to bring awareness and people to the cause. They see the work of the organization as an opportunity to excite their networks, family, and friends. Building an army of new constituents through personal networks and connections is second nature to them. But will executive leaders allow such building to occur? Usually they do, but within certain guidelines.

Millennials want nothing more than to help others see the importance of a cause. This could be done through minimal means, such as social media or greater marketing efforts. No matter the resources, the executive leadership of organizations should maximize this interest and build in new ways to use Millennials to spread the organization's message and let new ideas bubble up through traditional marketing efforts. Allow Millennials to experiment in small groups with connections and network new ways to approach telling the story of the organization and its work. This will encourage ongoing communication and marketing growth while also providing an outlet for the Millennials to build an army of others behind the cause.

We are at a critical juncture when thinking about Millennials and their workplace environments. These new employees in our traditional workplaces can help us advance rather than impede the organization's efforts. Finding that balance of being supportive and nurturing in a professional environment can be tough for some organizations that are rooted in more traditional modes of management. But you can see this new wave of employees as an opportunity to reexamine workplace processes and culture. You may find that a more open and inviting, team-based, results-focused environment appeals to all generations.

MENTORING MILLENNIALS

Although Millennials can be fascinating people, and they are undeniably the future of all change efforts, they're also young and make the mistakes that young people make out of sheer enthusiasm—perhaps they blog something inappropriate, are impatient, or have a short attention span. There is an opportunity for organizations and organizational leaders to act as mentors. Mentoring is a key component to successful work cultures, particularly in those with employees that span across all generations. Traditionally, mentorship is seen as one-way; it's an opportunity for younger or less-experienced employees to learn about the organization's work and overall professional skills from their colleagues. However, we strongly believe we can expand the traditional notion of mentoring to include the following three types of mentorship: cross-generational, professional development, and board to staff mentoring.

Cross-Generational

Simply put, organizations should think of mentoring as two-way and provide mentorships for Millennials with other generations within the organization, not only so they can learn from the more experienced workers, but also so they can share their own experiences. Although a Millennial might need help understanding budgeting or finances, a Boomer might need help understanding how to leverage social media to share a message. The collaboration between multiple generations gives everyone involved an opportunity to build both skills and institutional knowledge. Also consider pairing Gen X and Millennials together; Gen X employees can be great mentors to Millennial employees new to the nonprofit organization.

Professional Development

Professional development mentorships are structured to help Millennials develop their content expertise and skills. Specifically, these can provide Millennials with access to new concepts and ideas when organizations don't have a deep budget to send individuals to conferences and convenings. Organization leaders should consider finding professional development mentors outside the organization. Professionals from other organizations and retired individuals, or members of your local trade association, can expose new Millennial workers to new concepts and ideas beyond what they're learning at the organization.

Board to Staff Mentor

Perhaps one of the best opportunities for mentorship is with an organization's own board members. Millennials are very interested in the leadership of the organization, and the board itself represents a unique opportunity to help new Millennial employees learn from those who are making the decisions about the organization's path and direction. Given that Millennials seek transparency in their relationships, board members must be prepared for the encounter and trained in how to relate with the generation, provide transparency with relation to the organization's direction, and help the Millennial understand the interrelationships of paid and volunteer leadership.

It's helpful if someone on the leadership staff owns and oversees the mentorship program. If a program has been established but its promised relationships do not come to fruition, Millennials will see it as a lost benefit—a perception that will ultimately hurt the Millennial employee's relationship with the organization.

PUTTING IT ALL TOGETHER

Any nonprofit that chooses to ignore the transformation taking place does so at its own peril. The rapid pace of disruption in our institutions and the rise of networked approaches to problem solving guarantee that the only certainty right now is change.

It may take a few years, but one outcome is inevitable: The institution you know today won't look the same three, five, or ten years down the road. Change will occur with or without you, so it's not just about embracing these new approaches but about how quickly you can integrate them into your work environment. Is your organization ready?

MILLENNIALS IN THE WORKPLACE: THE MILLENNIAL ENGAGEMENT PLATFORM

To recap, Millennials are highly social and connected individuals within any institution. They tend to create solutions, be driven by tangible results in a transparent environment, and yearn for learning and mentorship with a goal of advancing in the organization.

Figure 7.1
Millennials in the Workplace: Millennial Engagement Platform

Leadership Inviting

Millennials want to join the leadership in managing and crafting the vision of the organization. They want to learn and be a part of the leadership team that is making the decisions necessary to affect the community and the people served every day. Take the time to spend conversing individually with Millennials about leadership, management, and the things you have learned while leading the organization. This can be done in private one-on-one sessions or as a group.

Tangible Transparency

Millennials want to understand the health and viability of the organization. They want to hear how decisions are made, why decisions are made, and who will make the decisions that will steer the organization in a certain direction. Take the time to help Millennials understand these key tangible transparent elements that make the organization operate. This should be done at the beginning of employment and during crucial times when important decisions are made.

Social Connectivity

Millennials are socially inclined in nature and will look for ways to connect with their peers both online and offline. Inspire that connectivity and level of engagement by encouraging dialogue and conversation about the organization. Using social chat tools such as Skype and other forms of instant messaging about the organization will speak to the social connectivity of the generation.

Solution-Inspired

Millennials want to create solutions for the organization. The need to "change the world" is a notion that transcends helping others in the community to helping your organization create a better workplace that will be more effective. Create a forum where employees can develop solutions to both issues affecting the people you serve and the way that you operate. Consider weekly feedback mechanisms such as forums, chats, or discussions around improvement of the programs and services to the management of the organization.

BUILD a Better Environment by Engaging Millennials

Be Unified

Ensure that the board understands the workplace changes that will take place to create a promising Millennial work environment.

Understand Their Environment

Provide educational sessions for the board and staff on Millennial communication and management styles.

Identify Key Change Makers

Create a feedback and identification system for managers and executive members to identify promising Millennial leaders.

Lead by Engagement

Provide an opportunity for Millennials to craft new benefits, HR policies, and other important workplace culture rules.

Determine Success

Create a workplace dashboard system that details the goals and vision of the organization and how Millennials and other employee contributions will help the organization achieve the desired outcomes.

Figure 7.2
Millennials in the Workplace: Five Key Takeaways

1 Communicate to senior staff the neccessary changes that encourage a Millennial-friendly work environment.

2 Create a leadership and mentor track for Millennials interested in advancing within the organization. This can include educational, skill-based, and professional development opportunities for Millennials who take initiative to broaden their role in the organization.

3 Provide educational sessions for development, marketing, and fundraising based on Millennial engagement through social media, so they better understand social connectivity.

4 Provide opportunities for Millennials to run meetings and lead discussion forums for the entire staff.

5 Allow Millennials to create new workplace goals for the organization. For instance, provide guidelines for an incentive program and allow Millennials to define how the plan will be implemented, the particular incentives to be received if goals are attained, and how the organization will publicly recognize those who achieve success.

A SPECIAL NOTE TO THE EXECUTIVE LEADER

Designing a new Millennial work environment can take time. It is important to design a new workplace environment through several phases and help all generations in the workplace participate. Swift changes to work culture can be challenging for any generation, so take the necessary time to implement a culture that will work for you, the board, and the staff.

The platform we present in Figure 7.1 is the ideal scenario for any work environment involving Millennials. We realize that not every nonprofit can implement every component presented in the figure. At the very least, take the time to discuss with senior staff the five key takeaways from Figure 7.2 that will help the entire organization achieve its overall desirable goals. Then take some of those components and implement them as you see fit. Be sure to help Millennials understand why some ideas were implemented and others not. This form of transparency can help you form a stronger connection with your employees and will create a healthy dialogue internally.

chapter EIGHT

Millennials as Nonprofit Leaders

Today's Millennials are tomorrow's CEOs. They are tomorrow's university presidents and trustees. And in the years to come they will begin to fill more seats on the boards of nonprofits of all shapes and sizes. With the influx of their new styles of leadership, the institutions they lead will in turn look, feel, and operate quite differently from the way they do today, in large part because these new leaders are wired differently from their predecessors.

When Millennials look at the nonprofit sector today, they realize that much of the way in which these organizations are working isn't exactly working. They see well-intentioned systems and processes that haven't kept up with the times. And they are looking for new ways to bring about social change in a more effective way.

So the nonprofit sector, in facing a rolling wave of retirements, also faces both a challenge and an opportunity. Organizations can choose to sit back and watch as these new leaders take hold over the course of the next five, ten, or fifteen years. Or they can spend time today more deliberately planning for this transition.

When it was announced that Paul Brest would be stepping down as president of the $7 billion Flora and William Hewlett Foundation earlier this year, nine progressive nonprofit organizations—including Friends of the Earth, the National Committee for Responsive Philanthropy, and the National Council of La Raza—came together and offered an open letter to the Hewlett Foundation board outlining what they felt should be among the top considerations as the board began its process of searching for a new leader. Among their recommended attributes:

- Someone who maintains the foundation's historic commitment to philanthropic effectiveness

- Someone who understands the role that race continues to play in determining life opportunities in America
- Someone with deep experience and passion for the highest-impact grant-making strategies of grassroots advocacy, community organizing, and civic engagement
- Someone who understands the limits of "strategic philanthropy"

Although these are all important attributes for a philanthropic leader, and particularly the leader of a multibillion-dollar institution, we think they are overlooking some questions. Here are the questions we would pose to a twenty-first-century leader, someone who is willing to approach the sector with an open mind and an understanding of the interconnectedness and interdependency of today's society:

- How do your life and professional experience reflect the interconnected global society of which we are a part? Have you lived, traveled, and explored the world abroad?
- What is your style of leadership? Is it top-down and hierarchical, or do you value shared leadership and collaboration among internal and external networks of people and organizations?
- In the scope of an institution, how do you spark innovation in a time when it is easier to form networks and innovation outside of the formal structures of hierarchy?
- What is your level of comfort with technology, and do you use it in your personal and professional life to learn and share?
- When faced with challenges, how do you work to define solutions, and what value do you place on creating an environment of transparency?

These questions provide a glimpse into what the Millennial leader not only thinks but also embodies. Look at it this way: to a Millennial, traveling and exploring new areas throughout the world has been an experience not only desired but accomplished. More Millennials have spent time living and working abroad for entire semesters or during their summer breaks than the members of any other generation.

In 1995–96, the last year before the first Millennials began entering college, fewer than 90,000 American students opted to leave home and study abroad. Over the next decade, the number of study-abroad students radically increased, by over 8 percent a year, to the point where a decade later the annual rate had more than doubled, to 220,000 students in 2007. They have a more worldly view because they've been out and seen the world before they ever set foot in the office.

Millennials also enjoy creative problem solving. They want to tackle challenges head-on and develop new innovative approaches in an effort to change their environments for the better. As we discussed in the previous chapter, they seek to create a new approach to connectivity in the workplace, and many prefer the ability to both use and access technology there—placing a greater value on that than on other kinds of flexibility or even higher pay.

When looking at this generation's leaders, we can characterize them as connected and network driven. But leaders today want so much more than that. They are looking not only to talk about change, but to be the change agents within organizations. They are not waiting to see what happens and hoping the next board meeting will be a promising time to unveil their new ideas; they are ready to take those ideas and create action immediately.

This is a new call to serve nonprofit organizations. It's a call to be a risk taker in a time when others think risk should be squelched because of economic uncertainty. It's a call to lead a team while others seek to maintain operations as the status quo. It's a call to change their environment, not because their boss or their board has told them to, but because their gut says that change is necessary and it should happen now.

Millennials don't actually consider themselves to be revolutionaries. They don't necessarily want to tear down the system; rather, they want to build it, reimagine it, and yes, even run it. They look deliberately at the structure of institutions, and then decide whether or not that structure is compatible with their own way of creating social change.

The biggest social issues our country and world face today dwarf the capabilities of even the most well-resourced, well-managed nonprofit. Nonprofit leaders need to look beyond simply building their organizations internally; they must begin to build capacity outside of their organizations. The scope of this effort isn't limited to other nonprofits; it entails an appreciation for the power of cross-sector collaborations that bring together the best and brightest people and resources. This requires leaders to focus on their broader mission, beyond their organization—a departure for even the savviest of nonprofit executive leaders.

This is a model that twenty-first-century organizations will need to embrace if they want to capture and take advantage of Millennial leadership. This transition will not happen overnight, and it will take support from all levels within an organization to adopt and adapt to these approaches. More people will have to see themselves as creators and participants in institutions and on a scale and with a level of diversity that no one organization will ever be able to fully achieve. The networked model of engagement is one we believe to be well suited to address our world's complex problems, in large part because of its appeal to those who want to help solve them.

SO, DESCRIBE THE NEXT GEN LEADER

It can be difficult to summarize all the specific qualities that may embody a generation representing more than eighty million people. But we do know that Millennial leaders tend to exhibit qualities that have led to the institutional changes we are beginning to see take place in organizations throughout the country. Throughout our interviews and focus groups, some of the most common characteristics of Millennial leaders that emerged were as follows:

Proactive

Focused

Dynamic

Resilient

Self-Aware

Ambitious

Visionary

Relationship Master

Risk Taker

Transparent

Going Against the Norm

Failing Forward

We thought it important to delve a little deeper into these characteristics and the Millennial leaders who exhibit such qualities and traits. The Millennials we profile in this chapter are solving social problems because they saw an opportunity to make life better and went for it. They want to change the world, and they don't care whether they do that through business, nonprofits, government, or even their own self-organized groups of friends.

These individuals are the true change makers of communities across the country and around the world. They heard it could not be done, and still they persisted. Some spent long nights in coffee shops plugging away; others traveled tirelessly, crashing on friends' couches and leveraging free WiFi wherever they could—all in the effort to tell their story to stakeholders three times their age.

The stories of influential and inspiring Millennials could go on and on; we'll continue to share their profiles on the Cause for Change website. For now, consider these powerful examples.

Proactive

Leaders once were praised for their ability to react to difficult situations; the Millennial leader "thinks forward," analyzing the future and minimizing obstacles that lie ahead. This is done without stopping until the ultimate goal is achieved. This approach requires anticipating challenges, cultivating consensus on desired outcomes, and developing and implementing processes for reaching goals.

Next-generation leaders take time every week to scan the environment of the community they serve and creatively develop solutions and/or mechanisms to ensure that the organization serves the community even during the most challenging times. Millennial leaders aren't waiting to see what happens; they're out *making* it happen for the benefit of the organization and the people who rely on it. In essence, being proactive becomes their driving force.

Zeke Spier is the executive director of the Social Justice Fund, where he has worked since 2007. Over that time, he has engaged hundreds of people as donors and helped to move millions of dollars to grassroots organizing in the northwest United States. Under his thoughtful leadership, Spier has helped many other Millennials take a proactive approach to supporting grassroots and community initiatives. Through education, volunteer experiences, and relationships with organizations on the ground, his model of engagement has helped countless numbers of next-generation philanthropists understand their role as a stakeholder.

Focused

Millennial leaders remain focused on the larger goal of changing the world for the better. They are determined to seek a solution or accomplish an achievement for the betterment of the cause. All other tasks are pushed back in order to maintain focus. The Millennial leader will remain focused on developing strategies, executing plans with staff, and ensuring that the organization is equipped to develop and vet new ideas, programs, or opportunities in a personal and passionate way. It's no surprise that Millennial leaders will create impact measurements on a highly visual dashboard that tracks overarching strategies, programs, and results—all to achieve a greater goal.

Rachael Chong says she won't rest until every professional can volunteer their skills and every nonprofit has access to skilled volunteers. As an investment banker, Chong was shocked by the lack of opportunities for her to volunteer her professional skills while keeping her day job. Frustrated by this barrier to serving the greater good, she left corporate finance to work in microfinance. A year later, Chong helped start up BRAC USA, the U.S. affiliate of BRAC, one of the largest nonprofit organizations in the world. At BRAC USA, Chong created a strategy to effectively mobilize dozens of skills-based volunteers that freed up her time and the president and CEO's time to raise $40 million in less than nine months. She also started Catchafire, a micro-volunteering platform to help connect business professionals with nonprofits that need their skills.

Dynamic

Commanding attention requires a commanding presence. Millennial leaders are dynamic in demeanor, presentation, and action. They understand how to captivate an audience, drive an agenda, and present in a manner that attracts a following in order to share the information. Furthermore, these individuals understand how their team operates effectively and find avenues for success. But dynamic communication is not enough; the Millennial leader also gets people to jump into action.

Erica Williams is a self-proclaimed pop-culture junkie and political commentator, and she's a dynamic leader who has inspired her peers to action. Her life's work is to ensure that everyone has an opportunity to offer their voice and make positive change happen. She's lobbied, organized, protested, trained, and tried to give sharp, clear commentary on all of the ins and outs of the political process in ways that are meaningful to people like her: Gen Y, culturally and technologically savvy, from diverse backgrounds, not rich; who don't consider themselves highly political; who have passions, read gossip blogs, and are too busy trying to survive to deal with Washington politics every day. Williams is currently a senior strategist at Citizen Engagement Lab (CEL), an incubator for people projects that use digital media, technology, and culture to build communities through cutting-edge campaigns.

Resilient

The challenges of a tough economy, poor participation numbers, or financial set-backs don't deter strong Millennial leaders. They attack these challenges head-on, develop solutions, and drive others to act on them. They avoid placing blame on outside forces; instead, they focus on solutions. And when they suffer the inevitable setbacks, they recover quickly, get back on their feet, and push on to the next challenge. Millennial leaders focus on how to overcome the obstacle, not on the obstacle itself. To them, changing the world means looking beyond barriers—to opportunity.

This is something Daniel Epstein fundamentally believes. He sees entrepreneurship as the answer to nearly all of the issues we face today and has dedicated his life accordingly. By the time he received his BA in philosophy, Epstein had already started three ventures; recently, he has shifted his focus to ensuring that aspiring social entrepreneurs around the globe have the resources and skill set to do the same through the Unreasonable Institute.

The vision of the Institute is "to create a world in which no one is limited by their circumstances"—to be a social venture that gathers others like Epstein who want to use profit to drive change. Now in its third year, the Unreasonable Institute gathers twenty-five social entrepreneurs in Boulder, Colorado, where they'll live under the same roof with each other for six weeks and interact with a robust network of world-changing investors and entrepreneurs.

Epstein recognizes that business is not business; business is people. And he places a premium on ensuring that those relationships are handled with great care.

Self-Aware

Millennial leaders understand their limitations and do not take on initiatives and programs outside their own or the organization's strengths. Instead, they pass opportunities on to other individuals or organizations better suited for them. If necessary, they look for partners to work closely with if the idea or concept is a fit but not as strong as others.

Furthermore, Millennial leaders are candid with donors (individuals, foundations, corporations) and develop relationships whereby the donors are very aware of the leaders' interests. These leaders limit asking or accepting gifts for programs outside the scope of the organization. What's most impressive is that they have those conversations while still maintaining—and often strengthening—their relationships with key stakeholders.

Take, for example, Dvorit Mausner and her work as the associate director of Young Alumni Participation at the University of Pennsylvania. She helped encourage her board to look beyond the giving capacity of Millennials and instead focus on helping them understand the need and the reason they should join the Penn Foundation initiatives. By moving beyond traditional methods of fundraising, Mausner has acquired more than 1,200 Millennial donors in just one year and has compelled the trustees and executives at the University to think differently about how they engage with their alumni.

Ambitious

Millennial leaders are ambitious. Although some want work-life balance, a significant number of new Millennial leaders will focus on meeting the larger goal for their chosen cause and work tirelessly to ensure that it is achieved. Their ambition and drive is overwhelming, and their passion for helping others underpins that ambition.

When they walk into the room, you can tell they are driven by their work and will stop at nothing to ensure that you too are passionate for their cause. Do not be surprised if you leave a conversation with a Millennial leader and are somehow moved to give or take action because of their message.

Zach Maurin founded ServeNext as an undergraduate after watching Congress nearly kill funding for AmeriCorps, a program he participated in between high school and college. Maurin—who traveled around the country sleeping on friends' sofas and often deferred a paycheck simply to follow his passion and enable more people to recognize the power of national service—was ambitious and determined. He was willing to go out there and recruit his peers to engage in public policy that would convince Congress to maintain funding for this vital program.

But Maurin was also willing to work across generations, because he recognized that although most of the individuals serving in these service programs were Millennials, members of other generations were running the programs and mobilizing their networks to save AmeriCorps. He quickly figured out how to always have a seat at the table, and ultimately his work paid off. ServeNext merged with Be the Change, Inc., to ensure an even greater presence in the service field.

Relationship Master

Many organizations have a single approach to persuading others to join their efforts: they make their case by talking about past success and how you should be working with them because it is for a good cause. Millennial leaders offer a multifaceted case for support, discussing the issues, challenges, and solutions confronting the organization today and casting a vision for the future. They are masters of relationships with individuals that go beyond just asking for money or trying to get someone to listen. They invite, engage, persuade, and ultimately lead others to their cause.

Their ability to build meaningful relationships developed because since their youth they have been exposed to the power of relationships, within and outside of technology. Millennial leaders will have positive, effective relationships with foundations and other large-scale institutional funders because they find ways to use these relationships beyond financial support. They spend time focusing on their expertise and explaining how the cause they are leading is a driving economic, political, or social force that must be addressed.

Maya Enista Smith is the chief executive officer of Mobilize.org, a growing and innovative Millennial organization whose mission is to improve democracy by investing in Millennial-driven solutions. Twenty-eight years old at the time of this writing, she has been leading efforts to help Millennials around the world take their ideas and make them a reality by providing startup investments.

This isn't Smith's first time helping to organize and build a new generation of change-makers. She began her career as the East Coast coordinator for Rock the Vote at age seventeen, a position in which she registered over thirty thousand young people. Smith believes that in order to create long-term, sustainable, and community-based solutions to the challenges facing her generation, Millennials must authentically engage their peers in identifying problems and proposing solutions. Most important, they must work together to implement these solutions in communities and campuses across the country.

Mobilize is doing just that. They are pioneering an innovative engagement model that leverages the unique characteristics of the Millennial Generation—collaboration, diversity, technological savvy, and an entrepreneurial spirit—to ensure that Millennials actively participate in our democracy and have the skills, resources, relationships, and support needed to move our communities and our country forward. Mobilize.org provides opportunities for members of the Millennial generation to move from passive to active citizenship and to seize leadership opportunities at every age and at every level. Moreover, they are given the tools along the way to build meaningful relationships.

Visionary

When Millennial leaders speak, they often try to offer a visual roadmap for where the organization is going—the story that will drive action, the steps it will take along the way, and the resources needed to get there. Millennial leaders are clear with staff and boards about challenges and strategies, and they provide staff and colleagues with a strong sense of the organization's direction and purpose— all to encourage those around them to jump on board and help out.

Take David Smith, the former executive director of the National Conference on Citizenship (NCoC). Although NCoC is a traditional organization by historical perspectives, Smith offered a new wave of leadership that redefined how today's connected citizenry engage in their community. He took a congressionally chartered organization in existence for more than sixty-five years and brought new life to its work through tracking, measuring, and promoting civic engagement with the goal of building a more informed, engaged, giving, and trusting citizenry.

By hiring a bright new team and pushing his board to think in new ways about active engagement, Smith has helped champion new programs that would keep true to the mission of the NCoC while pushing boundaries and taking risks to help them break new ground. It's not often that an organization would allow someone such as Smith to come in and propose such new and at times seemingly radical changes to an institution; however, the board gave him flexibility to move in a new direction, and it has paid off in the long term.

Risk Taker

Millennial leaders are risk takers. To change the world, sometimes risk is necessary and important. When Millennial leaders come into an organization that has been historically risk-averse, they jump in feet first to change the infrastructure necessary for some risk taking to occur. There are times, however, when institutions are simply not the right place for Millennial risk takers, and they must instead build their own infrastructure to be able to go out and make a bold statement.

That's exactly what Yael Cohen saw was needed when her mother was diagnosed with cancer three years ago. Cohen looked at the cancer field and the organizations that were helping patients like her mom, and realized that something was missing. She founded and is now the president of F*ck Cancer, an organization determined to make a real impact in the cancer space.

Cohen's organization activates Generation Y to engage with their parents about early detection and teaches supporters how to proactively look for cancer instead of just finding it. Over the last two years, she has grown F*ck Cancer into an inspirational and influential player in the nonprofit space, and attracted a host of A-list celebrities to participate in the movement and use their influence to help garner support from the public.

Cohen has brought a unique and younger demographic to the traditionally conservative field of cancer by using her skills in marketing and communication to create an edgy platform that resonates with her generation. It's a movement unique in its emphasis on early detection, its young target audience (not the typical demographic that most cancer organizations are focused on), and its fresh approach to combating the disease.

Transparent

Millennial leaders, for the most part, don't know how to be anything *but* transparent. Given their use of relationships, technology, and interpersonal skills, transparency is second nature. They are transparent to ensure that a goal is met, an outcome is achieved, and the larger vision is made possible. Transparency is exhibited in both workplace culture and external relationships.

Jeff Slobotski is the founder and chief community builder at Silicon Prairie News, an Omaha-based company dedicated to highlighting and supporting entrepreneurs and creatives. When others claimed it could not be done, given that Omaha wasn't located on one of the coasts, Slobotski went ahead and created an emerging model for a grassroots entrepreneurial ecosystem encompassing Omaha, Des Moines, and Kansas City.

His idea of openness and transparency helped connect and highlight the work of the region's creative class. He has organized events such as BarCamp Omaha, Creative Capital Pitch Sessions, and the annual Big Omaha conference to connect people focused on start-up culture, entrepreneurship, and innovation. Under Slobotski's leadership, his events have brought together more than six hundred entrepreneurs and innovators from across the United States to openly discuss how they can collaborate to create new forms of companies and social good organizations.

Going Against the Norm

Millennial leaders are not content with the status quo. They constantly try to improve how they do their work and consistently but appropriately have an ever greater impact. They know the pulse out in the field and understand the needs they are addressing. They know how to differentiate their work from others' and clearly articulate their value to the community.

When they discover a new way to deliver a service, they consult with their program peers, funders, and experts to ensure that the new approach has the potential for long-term impact. They build consensus and then form a new approach to test the method appropriately. They bring others with them as they perform this test and engage with funders early on to ensure that they have support when appropriate.

Josh Nesbit is the CEO of Medic Mobile, a nonprofit using mobile technology to create health systems that save lives. Nesbit also founded Hope Phones, a recycling campaign designed to engage millions of Americans in global health efforts. He and his team have worked in fifteen countries in East and West Africa, Asia, and Latin America, using mobile technologies to support a wide range of programs—from infectious disease surveillance in rural Malawi to emergency response after the 2010 earthquake in Haiti.

Social entrepreneurs like Nesbit think globally, create networks to solve big problems, and tackle almost unimaginable challenges. He didn't hesitate when it came time to coordinate an emergency SMS communications system in Haiti after the earthquake. He and a makeshift team just did it—and eventually managed to handle nearly a hundred thousand emergency text messages after the earthquake hit.

Fail Forward

Like leaders in preceding generations, Millennial leaders are not immune to making mistakes; it's inevitable that they, too, will mess up. There will come a time when they make a bad hire, jump into a project that requires too many resources, or say something that they regret to a donor or a potential partner. Sometimes, when in pursuit of their larger goal to ignite action, they move too quickly and have an unintended or inappropriate outcome. But when this happens, they move on. They learn to create a filter before accepting new programs and projects. They learn to be more articulate, to ensure that the appropriate message is heard. They also learn to not be afraid to take responsibility for their actions and ask for input along the way. And their relationship building with constituents throughout this process never wavers.

Ben Rattray is the founder of Change.org. He created the website to translate people's passion for a cause into effective action through social media. This simple concept helps more than seventeen thousand campaigns a day get started around the world. When Rattray first launched Change.org in 2007, it was seen more as a social networking site for nonprofits. Five years later it has become the fastest-growing site of its kind, adding roughly two million members per month. Now its focus is a bit different. After a few organizational pivots—or failures, as Rattray boldly admits—the site now focuses almost exclusively on petitions.

It's fair to say that Change.org has repositioned the online petition, giving it meaning as an effective tool in an individual's quest to activate a network of like-minded activists. The site is giving more people access to change in their communities and around the world. Some of the most notable Change.org campaigns are the one to end Bank of America's highly unpopular $5 debt fee, which we discussed earlier in the book, and a petition with more than 2.5 million signatures demanding an arrest in the Trayvon Martin case.

All these attributes point to an important understanding of Millennial leaders. They are not afraid of going against the status quo, challenging a board member, or confronting a community that doesn't care or a system that was established way before their time. Some would say this is a negative quality. But the best entrepreneurs, activists, and leaders in history have been unafraid to rise to the challenge and go for it. Millennials acquired this attribute at a young age; we cannot and should not suppress it when they grow up to lead social causes.

WORKING WITH THE BOARD

As a board, when working with a Millennial leader, in your conversations together you will see the traits just highlighted. The Millennial leader has little concern about hierarchy when it comes to the board and CEO relationship. This leader is focused on achieving the broader vision of the organization and interested in how the board can step into a role of evangelizing and promoting the work in order to reach the stakeholders to gain the support necessary for change.

Rather than spend time focused on hierarchal structures, Millennial leaders would rather roll up their sleeves and work with the board to help the organization achieve a broader goal. Under Millennial leadership, the relationship between the board and the CEO will come to resemble new forms of shared leadership that the board may not be used to.

Visionary Partnership

The Millennial leader seeks board members who can share the vision of the organization with outsiders. They see partnerships with these board members and build relationships that can help articulate the broader vision to those in the community who can help enable change. The Millennial leader will also look to the board to help create ideas and generate opportunities to make the vision possible. This brainstorming and idea generation comes with excitement and passion from the Millennial leader. How the board reacts to the vision and process will determine the Millennial leader's interest in working closely with them to improve the organization.

Outreach Versus Operations

Millennial leaders are relational by nature. External constituent-building is a focus in their quest to achieve the vision of the organization. The challenge for both the board and the Millennial leader is ensuring that operations and financial duties are fulfilled appropriately. It's important for both sides to come together and talk candidly about how to run the business of the organization, while also building the operations to effectively engage the external stakeholders and constituents.

This is not to say that Millennial leaders aren't interested in working on the financial or operational needs of the organization; they just tend to be more interested in spreading information and sharing with others the need to join in promotion of the cause. This is where the board can advise and counsel to ensure that the operational components are in place for Millennial leaders to continue their external efforts.

Specific Expectations

The relationship needs to be focused on specific expectations between the board and the Millennial leader. Research suggests that Millennials look to specific needs and ways that they can help create solutions and design methods for problem solving. Therefore the board should be explicit and specific with the Millennial leader about its expectations for the work of the organization, communication, and overall management. The Millennial leader thrives when expectations are clearly defined in an environment in which the board is open and interested in supporting opportunities that may have certain elements of risk.

Encouraging Each Other

Millennial leaders seek encouragement from their board members when executing and developing solutions to challenges. But this encouragement should not be one-way. We see the best relationships between board members and Millennial leaders emerge from an ongoing system of accountability and encouragement. Further, it's vital that the encouragement comes not just from the chair to CEO or vice versa, but rather from all members.

We also see this in the form of mentoring. Maya Enista Smith put it best when she describes a mentor relationship she has experienced with not only board members but also community stakeholders:

> The idea of creating mentoring relationships seems like a really hard or unnatural thing to do because you're almost fabricating organic interactions. The people on whom I've relied the most are people who don't actually view themselves as "mentoring" me. Instead, we've developed peer-to-peer relationships where they feel like they have something to contribute to my development and I have something to contribute to theirs.
>
> I am fortunate to have some pretty remarkable "mentors" in my life. But we've never had that conversation, nor would it feel authentic to have that conversation. I've never had a formal sit-down with the people whom I truly see as my mentors and asked them to serve in that role. On the flip side, I've had some unsuccessful mentorship relationships where I have been sought out by people who say, Maya, how can I help you establish your leadership trajectory—how can I help you? But this one-way value doesn't work for my generation.
>
> Sometimes, I think to myself, "Really, you want my opinion?" I think that the people whose opinions I value and advice I listen to are people that would say the same about me. I think this has changed over generations; it used to be people would say, "Put in your time, I'll tell you how I got here, and you can follow my footsteps." But now I think we're just a whole bunch of people across generations who are thrown into situations and forced to make it up

as we go along. So having a support mechanism of those people is really useful.[1]

WORKING WITH STAKEHOLDERS AND FUNDERS

It's not uncommon to hear from leaders of foundations and other institutions whose sole purpose is to give away money that the relationships they hold with their grantees and partners are strained from the challenges of developing authentic relationships built on trust and honesty. With the Millennial leader's characteristics of transparency and relationship building, we can expect stronger relationships with funders. These leaders move beyond surface-level discussions based solely on funding; they focus more on an advisor-to-advisee role in which they instead talk about the organization's real work, its on-the-ground challenges, and so on.

Michael Maness, vice president of journalism and innovation at the Knight Foundation, explains that working with Millennial leaders within his portfolio of grantees can be a rewarding and exciting adventure:

> Millennial leaders are not hierarchical, which is an interesting establishment given that the foundation and funding community is. Millennials are more attracted to building groups and followings than their counterparts are, and in today's economically challenged environment this is needed to ensure the limited resources are directed to those that can work together.
>
> I also find the Millennial leader to be adventurous when it comes pioneering innovation. They are very post-institutional in their makeup. They don't rely on universities or existing governments to ensure things will happen in the community or needs will be met. They will figure out new things to do, the networks to enable them to go outside institutions in order to influence the institution itself. This is a vital aspect we encourage because it brings that transparent crowdsourcing model to the heart of the organization. This ultimately leads to additional resources, support, and awareness for any cause.[2]

At each stage of the relationship, Millennial leaders are poised to be opportunistic while also treating the stakeholders as investors. True investors, in their eyes, receive ongoing notifications about the latest methods for the program delivery to achieve new impact, or the approaches that didn't work. For most institutional stakeholders, the Millennial leader has been a breath of fresh air in an environment in which usually only constant pitches and success stories are presented in order to get support. The stakeholder–Millennial leader relationship is built on trust, interest in the impact of the cause, and high-level dialogue.

We sometimes see Millennials take certain actions with stakeholders and key constituents because of the life stage of the cause they are leading. For example:

- **Startup stage: Putting a stake in the ground.** During this initial phase of the relationship, the Millennial leader is putting a stake in the ground with the key stakeholders and telling them about how and why the leader is so passionate about the cause. Citing some stats but weaving in more stories, the Millennial leader is persuasive when telling the cause's origin story. The leader is able to paint a vision that draws in the stakeholders to the point that financial support (or any other type of support) is not only possible but also necessary. During this startup phase, the Millennial leader spends time to ensure connection with the stakeholder whenever and wherever possible. This type of communication is usually informal and sets a foundation of trust for longer-term relationships.

- **Mid-stage: Being the expert.** In this stage of the relationship, the Millennial leader positions him- or herself as a storyteller expert and also as a thought leader on the issue. The stakeholder will look to the Millennial leader to respond to challenges, criticisms, and other inquiries about the issues relevant to the cause. When a story is published in a local or national paper, the Millennial is quick to respond and provide evidence in support of or in contradiction to it, using both personal and institutional beliefs and evidence. Overall, the Millennial leader becomes a great source of content and information for the stakeholders while continuing to deepen the informal relationship established in the startup phase.

- **Fully engaged stage: Honesty leading to opportunity.** In this stage, the Millennial leader has developed the relationship to the point where the leader can be completely honest about what works and what doesn't. The leader has been leading the efforts for some time and has been in the position long enough to determine whether something is working or needs to be fixed. Over time they have also been extremely candid with the stakeholder about how the organization has grown and the challenges along the way. These transparent and authentic discussions enable the Millennial leader to help the stakeholder pivot or move in a new direction in order to accomplish the broader vision. The leader is able to tell a new story of cause and effect while also holding true to the organization's larger vision in the community.

Organization Spotlight: People for Urban Progress

In this interview with Michael Brinker of People for Urban Progress (PUP), he describes how he and his colleagues created an organization in spite of setbacks and governmental challenges. He describes a unique model to leading an organization through shared executive talent. For the complete interview, please visit www.causeforchangebook.com.

Q: How did People for Urban Progress get started?

A: PUP started in 2008 when the RCA Dome was set for demolition. The roof had interesting material. We were curious what the material was made out of and what could be done with it. We found out they were going to put the material in the landfill. After finding out the material was useful and could be reused, we reached out to many organizations to help us get our hands on it.

Q: What was the reaction to the concept of this idea to reuse the material of a professional sports stadium?

A: They didn't understand the motivation to do it. I was confused why they weren't already trying to do this. We didn't just go in; we had a plan of how it could be useful. We had pages of research and reached out to the company who made the fabric. It's not like we were approaching with a complaint; we were approaching with a solution but didn't have the means to do so. The city seemed confused by this.

Q: What was it like when you heard the city would not be able to help you? Where did you go after hearing this?

A: We pushed ahead. The demolition company said if we could find a way to transport the material they would find another way to tear it down. This gave us a new, simpler problem, so we went back to the city and targeted the parks department. When we talked with them about reusing the materials, they were glad we came to them, because it could be a resource for parks so they helped transport the material for us. We saved about 90 percent of the roof. Felt like more of a battle then it needed to be, but we got the issue resolved. So the next problem is what do we actually do with this now that we got what we wanted.

Q: So now you have this material, where do you go from there?

A: We thought the best use of the material would be to put it back into the public, in the form of shade structures and pavilions, because it is roof material. But we weren't in the position to fund a project like that. We were in the position where we could buy sewing machines and work with local designers to make smaller things out of it. How we operate now, as a nonprofit is this "small things funding big things" model. Every one of our projects has a financial component so that we generate some of our own income even as a nonprofit. This model means we are not locked in to grant funding—not that we don't want grant funding, but we have more leverage as we shape our organization.

So that's where we started; we bought a sewing machine and started working with designers to make items and sell them. The number of people getting involved started expanding. After our items were shaped, we started working with local retailers to sell them. So these items were touching a lot of hands, and these people were getting paid for it along the way. I think this is very important because for Millennials, those services are becoming increasingly important—but people are expecting them for nothing, especially for nonprofits, but I feel that almost devalues the work.

Q: You created this solution out of a problem; do you see other people in your generation doing this and succeeding?

A: Yeah, I think so. I know a lot of people who are doing start-ups. A lot of people I know are closing the gap between design and fabrication; they are kind of making, doing, and solving things by themselves. People have an idea, they need some financial support, they put it on something like Kickstarter, and then their idea is crowdsourced with support. I think it's a combination of factors. The economic troubles we have have kind of sparked this wave of new entrepreneurship. I also think younger people don't need a large staff to make a difference; all they need is computer and a network or connection to people. That's where the magic is.

(Continued)

Q: If somebody had to characterize Millennials, [as one of them yourself] what would you say?

A: I think Millennials right now are a group who understands that their future is not going to come from a single career. They don't think that way at first, so they enter a more traditional career where the company provides for you. I don't think that is as desirable anymore, and it's not as reliable. So we have to be much more savvy and nimble in terms of making money. But I think that flexibility fits perfectly with the more creative mind-set. You do a project for a couple months, then move on, or you dedicate part time to a project and also work for corporate America. It's becoming more a freelance group than a career path.

BUILDING NEW PARTNERSHIPS

Partnerships are an opportunity to take relationships to the next level. Millennial leaders have discovered that true partnerships will help their cause reach more people, have broader impact, and also be advantageous for their cause. They still feel a certain level of competition, but not to the extent of other generations, whose members tend to be more territorial with their work, funders, and ideas.

This generation sees competitive nonprofits as opportunities and finds ways to collaborate with them or move on. Over time, the Millennial leader may assay programs without partners and quickly realize that joining forces for program delivery or other reasons could work better.

One shining example of a partnership driven entirely by Millennials is that of the Energy Action Coalition, which today is made up of fifty youth-led environmental and social justice groups who work together to build the youth clean energy and climate movement. The Coalition, which upholds many of the Millennial traits we've discussed in this chapter, is committed to building a diverse and inclusive movement to solve the climate crisis and address environmental and economic injustice.

What started as an outgrowth of the Climate Campaign, an effort of six campuses in the Northeast back in 2003, has now brought together hundreds of campus and youth groups, dozens of youth networks, and hundreds of thousands of young people. The Coalition and its partners have united a burgeoning movement to win local victories and coordinate on state, regional, and national levels in the United States and Canada.

Jared Duval, author and former director of the Student Sierra Coalition and participant in the Energy Action Coalition, recounts the success of the movement in his book *Next Generation Democracy*:

> The motivation for our coming together started with a stark realization: The climate challenge we collectively face is of such an enormous scale that none of our organizations could ever hope to catalyze in isolation a movement broad and diverse enough to meet it. . . .
>
> Part of the reason for this growth and success has been a continued faith in our organizing model. The goal was to simultaneously create space for collaboration and relationship building while also respecting the individual creativity and autonomy of each group. Doing so allowed us to build a more powerful and vibrantly diverse new movement: Today, the coalition has expanded to include a wide-ranging array of fifty active and supporting organizations.[3]

When Millennials see an opportunity to engage in partnerships for the betterment of their cause, they approach the relationship in the manner detailed in the following descriptions.

Capitalize on More Human Capital

Millennial leaders understand the need to manage and make use of people in order to create a movement. The more people they can involve, the more relevance in the community they can possess, which ultimately leads to a stronger organization. The Millennial leader approaches other partners to build or expand their "army" of supporters, or to have broader impact and serve more in the community, or both. This may include developing special event programs and cobranded marketing efforts and even sharing online awareness campaigns to amplify the activism power of both organizations' networks.

Their aim is to combine organizations' strength to drive toward stronger positioning in the community and with the people they serve. Their methodology and process for involving the partner are focused on how to build a stronger movement together and accomplish a shared vision, rather than to compete in a vacuum.

Strengthen Their Fundamental Role in the Community

Millennial leaders understand the organization's fundamental role in the community: it provides core services that citizens see as important to the community's fabric and vitality. They have discovered how to create a simple message and translate that into a powerful story about how the cause they lead can change their community. To take it to the next level, the Millennial leader develops a core group of partners who, through shared programs and operational support, help deepen the organization's role in the community. These vibrant partnerships enable the organization to spread deep and wide without compromising program impact.

Seek Opportunities to Drive Change Together

Millennial leaders seek not only change but also the opportunity to drive that change. When the challenge of change is too great to meet alone, they find a relevant partner to help make it possible. This means if they need support from a partner to advocate for an issue, they find a way to join forces to get everyone in the community to care.

The Millennial leader forms partnerships that help the community meet a goal that is bigger than their organization's alone. This usually means bringing together multiple entities, all serving various locales and niche programs, to concentrate efforts on a larger vision. The Millennial leader brings to the table the drive and vision in a collaborative approach that helps the partnership achieve the broader goal.

HIGH EXPECTATIONS

This chapter began with a statement of what we believe the next generation leader embodies. Although a one-size-fits-all definition is tough, from our observations we can conclude that Millennial leaders are born to change, be aspirational, and take the necessary risks with their colleagues in order to reach a broader vision for the community. Further, among the communities and constituents that Millennial leaders serve, we see a vibrancy built through trust and relationships.

We can see why movements like that of the Arab Spring in 2011 garnered so much attention—Millennial leaders led them with a broader sense of relational engagement than we have seen before. Through networks interconnected with networks, they drove change by facilitating a conversation and telling a story about what was possible. More important, they removed the barriers to challenges and created support mechanisms that helped weave the fabric of the community.

If Millennial leaders can do this with new concepts and ideas, imagine what they can do with traditional nonprofit institutions that exist today. Millennial leaders can make it possible for the community to embrace, engage, and trust the institutions that are there to help—a skill that can go a long way in today's culture of division and distrust.

In today's world, leaders need to work across cultural, economic, and geographic boundaries, while also recognizing how technology and transparency are impacting our institutions. Cynthia Gibson and Nicholas Longo noted in their book, *From Command to Community: A New Approach to Leadership Education in Colleges and Universities:*

> Periods of uncertainty can be fertile ground for seeding change, which is why we believe that there could be no more auspicious time than now to experiment with new forms and approaches to leadership. Clearly, we have little time to lose given the unprecedented amount of failed leadership, from the economic collapse and a global environmental crisis to pervasive poverty and widening inequities between the haves and the have-nots, that we faced in recent decades. . . . We need to shift our ideas of what exactly leadership is and, most important, what we expect from leaders—and from ourselves in relation to them.[4]

There is significant work to be done to prepare society for the wave of Millennial leadership that is about to rock traditional institutions as we know them. Currently, we have a culture where expectations of the Millennial Generation do not match the hope that Millennials have for themselves. More urgently, these low expectations don't meet the pressing needs that our country—and our world—have today. The time is now to take the generation's interest, optimism, and opportunistic approach to start a new movement in partnership with organizations.

MILLENNIALS AS NONPROFIT LEADERS: THE MILLENNIAL ENGAGEMENT PLATFORM

When looking at this generation's leaders, we can characterize them as connected and network driven. But leaders today want so much more than that. They seek not only to talk about change but also to be the change agents in their organizations. They hear a new call to serve nonprofit organizations.

Figure 8.1

Millennials as Nonprofit Leaders:
Millennial Engagement Platform

Leadership Inviting

With the fast pace of change in all organizations today, it is essential that leadership is encouraged and discovered at all levels. Explicit paths for career and leadership advancement are key. Most people know their job descriptions, but many don't know whether they're doing their jobs well or what will take them to the next level. When seeking clarity about their jobs, Millennials want to understand clear paths for advancement, know what determines success, and understand how salaries are determined. In addition, help Millennials succeed by providing opportunities for leadership: mentor them to be successful, and invite them into conversations that will help them grow professionally.

Tangible Transparency

Given Millennials' use of relationships, technology, and interpersonal skills, transparency is second nature. Millennial leaders will be transparent in order to ensure that a goal is met, an outcome achieved, and the larger vision made possible. Transparency manifests in both workplace culture and external relationships. Clarity about decision making, job requirements, and evaluation are important factors for creating a positive atmosphere in the workplace. This includes transparency and input into decision making, opportunities for management and leadership skills training, and workplace flexibility.

Social Connectivity

The connected workplace is an environment foreign to some generations but essential for Millennial leaders. They seek to create a new approach to connectivity in the workplace; many prefer to be able to both use and access technology, and they place a greater value on this than on other kinds of flexibility or even higher pay. Millennial leaders must be able to feel networked with their colleagues, both on- and offline; this helps build trust and transparency. And they are able to build meaningful relationships because they have been exposed to the power of relationships both within and outside of technology.

Solution-Inspired

Mission-driven organizations are essential for Millennial leaders. A crucial aspect of determining where Millennials devote their efforts is a strong belief in the organization's mission and knowledge of how their work contributes to its success. Millennial leaders want to see the impact of their contribution. Keep in mind that their commitment may be to a cause—not necessarily to an organization—so Millennials will gravitate towards the groups that demonstrate clear ability to create change.

BUILD a Better Environment by Engaging Millennials

Be Unified

Board members need to rally and support Millennial nonprofit leaders when they embark upon new ideas, risky ventures, and potential failures. This is an opportunity to show unified support for the Millennial's workplace culture and environment they are creating.

Understand Their Environment

Millennial leaders will often have better relationships with foundations and other larger-scale institutional funders because they are finding ways to use these relationships beyond financial support.

Identify Key Change Makers

Nonprofit leaders must help other leaders excel. Within the staff and workplace environment, Millennials should identify and motivate nonprofit leaders and change makers that can make programs successful. Create an environment where staff and Millennial nonprofit leaders can celebrae their role as changemakers.

Lead by Engagement

Millennial leaders are often dynamic in demeanor, presentation, and action. They understand how to captivate an audience, drive an agenda, and present in a manner that attracts a following in order to share the information.

Determine Success

Millennial leaders tend to share more rather than less, and they may present impact measurements on a highly visual dashboard that tracks overarching strategies, programs, and results—all to achieve a larger goal.

Figure 8.2
Millennials as Nonprofit Leaders: Five Key Takeaways

1 Connect Millennial leaders with mentors outside the organization—these may include corporate and other nonprofit executives.

2 Create at least one learning experience or professional development class for Millennial leaders to understand how each communicates, leads, and develops solutions to problems.

3 Build a board resource list to detail specific skills and qualities of each board member that are at the Millennial executives' disposal.

4 Define specific topics that must be covered with the board prior to any execution by Millennial leaders.

5 Provide an online forum for Millennial leaders to chat with stakeholders and volunteers about the future of the organization and where they see it heading.

A SPECIAL NOTE TO THE EXECUTIVE LEADER

As an executive, you must create an awareness that celebrates characteristics and values across all generations and across all stakeholders. An understanding of different work styles and communication preferences, and a vision of what a team should look like, are all valuable in helping to prevent conflict and get the job done. Millennials also enjoy creative problem solving. They want to tackle challenges head-on and develop new innovative approaches in an effort to change their environments for the better.

When we try to describe Millennial leaders, it can be difficult to summarize all the specific qualities that may embody a generation comprising more than eighty million people. But we do know that Millennial leaders tend to exhibit common characteristics that have led to the institutional changes we are beginning to see take hold in organizations throughout the country—characteristics including *proactive, focused, dynamic, resilient, self-aware, ambitious, visionary,* and *transparent.*

CONCLUSION

Every fifteen to twenty years a new generation comes of age, transitions to adulthood, and makes broad assertions about how they are the ones positioned to change the world. Millennials are no different. Coming of age at the turn of the twenty-first century doesn't make us smarter, more driven, or better problem solvers. (In fact, it may have made us more distracted, impatient, and unsure.) But it does uniquely position us to drive change in a different kind of way, with new tools and approaches for today's civic landscape.

Millennials are different because our world and cultural experiences are unique. World events and defining moments such as the September 11 attacks shaped our views and catapulted us into adulthood. We reached out to victims of Hurricane Katrina and the Haiti earthquake because we watched the story unfold right before our eyes. We signed up for programs like Teach For America and Habitat for Humanity at historic rates because our generation was programmed for instant gratification and we could see the fruits of our labor at the end of those engagements.

We build and enhance technology platforms quicker than ever before. Then, as new technology is released, we are the generation to test it, familiarize ourselves with it, train those around us in how to use it, and reinvent change with it. We discuss the latest current events, then send our friends links to our favorite blogs or videos on the subject. We know so much about so much. We read everything and anything that we think might point us in the direction of some kind of enlightenment. We believe we will find an alternative outside of government when Social Security runs dry. And we hope we can find ways to pay back our mounting student debt. It wasn't our generation that brought us to this point, but it will be our generation that has no choice but to act.

So one question remains: Are you (and your organization) ready for us?

Today's nonprofit leader focuses on donors, volunteers, and constituents with capacity, financial or otherwise. Because of this, and for good reason, Baby Boomers and the Greatest Generation have typically been the target of their outreach efforts. But Millennials are the cohort they *need* to be cultivating, and fast.

In our travels across the country, we've met with countless nonprofit and organizational leaders, and the questions are the same whether we're at a national nonprofit in New York City or a small community-based organization in Terre Haute, Indiana. Executive leaders want to *know* what motivates Millennials. They want to *know* the "secret sauce" to meaningful engagement with them. They want to *know* what it's going to take to get them to show up and stick around.

We don't claim to have all of the answers. In fact, we don't think anyone does. Understanding Millennials is an evolving process, and we are still at the beginning of seeing what our generation's larger impact on institutions will be. Many questions remain: Will institutions survive? Should they? Will the rise of free agents force organizations to relinquish more control? Will the democratization of philanthropy and government replace the command-and-control systems that have governed them for so long?

Perhaps the one thing we do know is that organizations are left with little choice but to adapt to a new reality. Millennials are wired to work differently—collaboratively, transparently, interactively, and entrepreneurially—to effect positive change in their local communities and around the world. This book is the first attempt at a blueprint to help you navigate the unknown territory that Millennials are bringing to your organization.

We wanted to leave you with the following assertions about those Millennials who are driving change and reimagining institutions in ways that resonate with their values and experiences.

- **Get over the technology.** It's easy to offer up technology as the silver bullet to solving an organization's disconnect with Millennials. But Millennials don't necessarily see technology in terms of compelling new apps or social media platforms. Rather, they see technology as an extension of relationships and a natural part of their lives.
- **Forget about work-life balance; embrace work-life blending.** Generation X introduced the mantra of work-life balance so they could spend more time away from work devoted to their families and their personal well-being. But

Millennials prefer work-life blending, a state of perpetually being in professional and personal mode at the same time. This means Millennials can become your round-the-clock evangelists *if* they feel supported and trusted.

- **Millennials have an unwavering commitment to social responsibility.** They aren't just looking at entering traditional nonprofit institutions to influence social change. They know they can "do good" by joining businesses with a double bottom line or by entering a start-up with a pro-social mission. Unless nonprofits are able to attract the entrepreneurial, technologically savvy Millennial, they may struggle to compete with their pro-social competitors across other sectors.

- **Friends—and their opinions—matter.** This generation is moved by their peers talking about the next consumer product to buy, the best place for sushi, and the most exciting organization to support. Peers help Millennials make decisions—especially when it comes to how they engage with organizations. To connect with them, organizations need to be clear, succinct, and sharable at all times.

- **Millennials are fearless—so you should be too.** This fearlessness has enabled creativity, inventiveness, and the rise of a brand-new category of professionals transforming our planet: social entrepreneurs and social innovators, many of whom we profiled throughout this book. But now it is time for yours to be a fearless organization. Let's put aside the reasons why you don't want to get started engaging Millennials. Let the negativity fall away, and instead focus on the opportunity the generation brings to your organization. Join Millennials in their quest to be fearless, and channel their energy, excitement, and ideas to your organization.

MOVING AT THE SPEED OF CHANGE

The first decade of the twenty-first century brought significant change—socially, technologically, economically—and more radical changes are likely yet to come. Change is nothing new, but the accelerated speed of change in today's society demands that nonprofits think differently in order to keep up. Indeed, to not only survive but thrive, the nonprofit sector must stay attuned to these shifts and be open to new and different approaches. It is our responsibility to reenvision and help shape a sector in need of the new wave of optimism found in the Millennial generation.

The speed of today's lifestyle is getting faster and faster. Because of the interconnectivity between us all and the tools we have at our disposal, we are running rather than walking through our everyday lives—and usually doing so while looking down at a handheld screen of one shape or another.

Some may find this frightening. We find it exhilarating.

Not because we are Millennials. Rather, because it means so many ideas, concepts, and solutions will now take less time to implement and less time to reach the people that nonprofits are serving who are truly in need. It means it will take less time to research and develop a new drug to fight cancer. It means we are steps closer to helping someone halfway around the world obtain the food, water, and livelihood that we in the West too often take for granted.

Truly, we live in a remarkable time. But though change is happening quickly, it is also an iterative process of discovery that will continue to evolve if we can reach across demographics—age, race, and others—to come together and recognize this moment.

We invite you to continue this conversation at www.causeforchangebook.com. On the website we will highlight the impressive work of Millennial leaders and organizations who are successfully engaging this generation. Equally important, we will profile individuals across all generations who are championing Cause for Change movements within their organizations. The site will contain worksheets, platform examples, and other resources for you to get the latest on Millennial activism and engagement. We hope you'll share your stories with us and with one another.

Change isn't something that is going to happen; change is happening right now. Let Millennials help you and your organization get up to speed. Let them help you create impact even faster than you have been able to without them. There's never been a more important Cause for Change.

NOTES

CHAPTER ONE

1. William Strauss and Neil Howe, *Generations: The History of America's Future 1584 to 2069* (New York: Morrow, 1991).

2. Michael Hais and Morley Winograd, "It's Official: Millennials Realigned American Politics in 2008." http://www.huffingtonpost.com/michael-hais -and-morley-winograd/its-official-millennials_b_144357.html

3. Duncan Macleod, "The Great Schlep Gets Results," The Inspiration Room Blog, November 17, 2008. http://theinspirationroom.com/daily/2008 /the-great-schlep-gets-results/

4. Beth Kanter and Allison Fine, *The Networked Nonprofit: Connecting with Social Media to Drive Change* (San Francisco: Jossey-Bass, 2010).

5. Alexis de Tocqueville, *Democracy in America* (Chicago: University of Chicago Press, 2000).

6. Dvorit Mansur, interview with Derrick Feldmann, March 20, 2012.

CHAPTER THREE

1. Dan Morrison, "The Art of Activating Slacktivism," Case Foundation's Social Citizens blog, March 23, 2010. http://www.socialcitizens.org/blog /art-activating-slacktivism

2. Georgetown University Center for Social Impact and Ogilvy Worldwide, "The Dynamics of Cause Engagement," November 2011. http://csic .georgetown.edu/research/215767.html

3. Cone Research, Cone Cause Evolution Study, Cone 2010. http://www .conecomm.com/2010-cone-cause-evolution-study

4. Pew Internet and American Life Project, "The Viral Kony 2012 Video," March 15, 2012. http://pewinternet.org/Reports/2012/Kony-2012-Video/Main-report.aspx

5. Temkin Group, "Data Snapshot: How Consumers Give Feedback, 2012," June 6, 2012. https://experiencematters.wordpress.com/2012/06/06/data-snapshot-how-consumers-give-feedback-2012/

6. Molly Katchpole, "Tell Bank of America: No $5 Debit Card Fees." http://www.change.org/petitions/tell-bank-of-america-no-5-debit-card-fees

7. Nick Kristoff, "After Recess—Change the World," *New York Times*, February 2012. http://www.nytimes.com/2012/02/05/opinion/sunday/kristof-after-recess-change-the-world.html

8. Change.org, "Victories." http://www.change.org/victories

9. "Take Back the Pink Reflection Document." https://docs.google.com/document/d/1EfWwN2O_o79bA-v6bSzf9dl4pUZUytoNIwEAY1CL7FI/edit

10. Ibid.

11. Ibid.

12. Ibid.

13. Ibid.

14. Ibid.

15. Ibid.

16. Achieve and Johnson Grossnickle and Associates, Millennial research reports: Millennial Donors Study 2010, Millennial Donors Study 2011, and the Millennial Impact Report 2012. www.themillennialimpact.com

17. Beth Kanter and Allison Fine, "The Giving Challenge: Assessment and Reflection Report," Case Foundation, June 22, 2009. http://www.casefoundation.org/case-studies/giving-challenge/key-results

CHAPTER FOUR

1. Aaron Marquez, "Don't Cut National Service, Millennials Stand Ready to Serve" *Huffington Post* blog, February 2011. http://www.huffingtonpost.com/aaron-marquez/dont-cut-national-service_b_824383.html

2. Corporation for National and Community Service, "2011 Volunteering in America Report," August 8, 2011. http://www.volunteeringinamerica.gov/

3. Ibid.

4. Ron Allsop, *The Trophy Kids Grow Up: How the Millennial Generation Is Shaking Up the Workplace* (San Francisco: Jossey-Bass, 2008).

5. Deloitte Development, LLC, "2010 Deloitte Volunteer IMPACT Study." http://www.deloitte.com/us/community

6. Net Impact, "Talent Report: What Workers Want," May 23, 2012. netimpact.org/whatworkerswant

CHAPTER FIVE

1. Kanter and Fine, *The Networked Nonprofit* (see chap. 1, n. 4).

2. Aaron Smith, "Real Time Charitable Giving," January 12, 2012, Pew Internet & American Life Project. http://pewinternet.org/Reports/2012/MobileGiving.aspx

3. Lucy Bernholz, "Shaking Up the Long Tail," Philanthropy 2173 blog. http://philanthropy.blogspot.com/2012/01/shaking-up-long-tail.html

CHAPTER SIX

1. Achieve and Johnson Grossnickle and Associates (see chap. 3, n. 16).

2. Helen Flannery and Rob Harris, 2011 donorCentrics Internet and Multichannel Giving Benchmarking Report (Blackbaud, July 2011).

CHAPTER SEVEN

1. Allison Fine, "What Does 'Professional' Look Like Today?" *HBR Network* blog. http://blogs.hbr.org/cs/2012/05/the_new_professional.html

2. Nilofer Merchant, *The New How: Building Business Solutions Through Collaborative Strategy* (Sebastopol, CA: O'Reilly Media, 2010).

3. Michelle Nunn, "Millennials to Business: Social Responsibility Isn't Optional," *Washington Post*, December 20, 2011. http://www.washingtonpost.com/national/on-innovations/millennials-to-business-social-responsibility-isnt-optional/2011/12/16/gIQA178D7O_story.html

4. Ibid.

5. Cisco, *Cisco Connected World Technology Report*, 2011. http://www.cisco
.com/en/US/netsol/ns1120/index.html

6. Alison Hillhouse, "Consumer Insights: MTV's 'No Collar Workers,'"
Blog.Viacom, October 4, 2012. http://blog.viacom.com/2012/10/consumer
-insights-mtvs-no-collar-workers/

7. Marla Cornelius and Tim Wolfred, *Next Generation Organizations: 9 Key
Traits* (San Francisco: CompassPoint Nonprofit Services, 2011).

CHAPTER EIGHT

1. Maya Enista Smith, personal communication with the authors, May 2, 2012.

2. Michael Maness, personal communication with the authors. April 10, 2012.

3. Jared Duval, *Next Generation Democracy: What the Open-Source
Revolution Means for Power, Politics, and Change* (New York: Bloomsbury
USA, 2010).

4. Cynthia Gibson and Nicholas Longo, *From Command to Community:
A New Approach to Leadership Education in Colleges and Universities*
(Medford, MA: Tufts, 2011).

INDEX

Page numbers in italics refer to figures.

A

A Billion + Change, 75
Achieve, Inc., 57, 58, 99, 103, *104*, 115
Action, call to. *See* Calls to action
Activism: low-threshold, 92; major roles of, 26–27; online, new wave of, questions arising from, 148–149; social, future of, 70, *71*
Activists: activating, online access for, 177; baby-boomer, children of, 80; described, 25–27; event-based group management and, 28; new breed of doers and, 70, 72; online, dismissal of, avoiding, 42–44; online sites for, power of, 48–49; self-organized group engagement and, 28; in the virtuous cycle, 22, *23*; young professional groups and, 29
Advertising Age magazine, 3
Affordability, 123, 136
Africa, 176
Alabama, 67
All for Good, 72
Alloy Media, 44
Alsop, Ron, *5*, 79–80
Alumni engagement: skewed view of, 20; young, 1, 2, 14–15, 118–119, 172
Ambitious leaders, 172
American Cancer Society, 85, 117, 121
American Heart Association, 117
American Red Cross, 116

AmeriCorps, 7, 68–69, *69*–70, 85, 172
Android tablets, 82
Annual giving, 118, 122
AOL, xi
Apple II, 6
Apps, 41, 59, 82, 109, 130, 192
Arab Spring, 149, 186
Arabella Advisors, 107
Armstrong, Lance, 44
Art and culture organizations, support for, 130
Asia, 176
Asian Millennial population, 4
Authentic engagement, 52
Authentic leadership role, desire for, 86
Authentic nonprofit leaders, 141
Authentic relationships, establishing, 135, 180
Authenticity, organizational, 61
Autonomy, 185

B

Baby Boomers, xv, 4, *5*, 34, 56, 78–79, 80, 108, 139, 144, 145, 151, 152, 153, 154, 161, 192
Bank of America, 48, 49, 177
BarCamp Omaha, 175
Bazaarvoice, 108
Be unified, as a guiding principle, 18, *32*, 33, *38*, *64*, *90*, *112*, *137*, *163*, *188*
Benchmarks, use of, 22, 34, 35

Berkman Center, 106

Berlin Wall, 6

Bernholz, Lucy, 50, 51, 107

Best Friends Humane Society, 58

Best practices, learning from, 62

Big Omaha conference, 175

Black Millennial population, 4

Blackbaud, 128

Blackouts, 106

Blogging, 26, 50, 51, 62, 97, 125, 161, 191

Blue State Digital, 8

Board engagement, 85–86, 92

Board meetings, access to, 155

Board members: future, 165; as mentors, 141, 162, 179; professional development for, *189*; transparency with, 155; working with Millennial leaders, 177–180, *189*

Board resource list, *189*

Boomers. *See* Baby Boomers

Boundaries, working across, need for, 187

BRAC USA, 170

Braden, Liz, 54, 55

Branding associations, 44, 98

Branding consistency, 60

Branding opportunities, 8, 44–45, 55, 109–110, 121

Brest, Paul, 165

Brinker, Michael, 182

BUILD concept, 18, *32*, 33–34, 37, *38*, *64*, *90*, *112*, *137*, *163*, *188*

Building Tomorrow (BT), 54–55

Bush, Barbara P., 77, 78

Business donations, 75

C

CalculateIt.org, 54–55

Calls to action: aspects pertaining to, 67–92; clear, importance of, 89, 100, 118; getting people to respond to, 62; special note to executive leaders about, 91–92. *See also* Activism; Activists; Volunteering

Cancer organizations, traditionally conservative, 175–176

Capital campaigns, 95–96, 118

Capital, human, capitalizing on, 185

Career advancement, having explicit paths for, 152–153

Career ladder, 142–143

Career path, nonlinear, 142, 184

Career-building opportunities, providing, 87

Case Foundation, xi–xii, xiii, 61

Cashmore, Pete, 98

Catchafire, 170

Catchafire.com, 75

Cause champions: converting Millennials into, 9; role as, 26; searching for, 108; in the workplace, 160

Cause marketing campaigns, evolution of, 44–45

Causes: compelling, importance of, 130, 131; life stage of, leader relationships with stakeholders based on the, 181–182

Causes.com, partnering with, 49, 50

CauseWired, 51

Celebrities, 99, 108, 130, 131, 175

Center for American Progress, 4

Center for Information and Research on Civic Learning and Engagement (CIRCLE), 3

Challenger disaster, 6

Challenges, facing: asking about, 166; head-on, 171

Challenging work, importance of, 144, 167

Change, rate of, 193–194. *See also* Organizational change; Social change

Change-makers, organizing and building a new generation of, 173–174

Change.org, 48, 177

charity: water, 53, 121

Chat forums, 43, 44, 157, 164, *189. See also* Instant messaging

Chicago Humanities Festival, 102–103

Children's Hospital, 109–110

Chile, 67

Chong, Rachael, 170

Cisco Connected World Technology Report, 149

Citizen Effect, 43

Citizen Engagement Lab (CEL), 170–171

Citizen Schools, 70

City Year, 69

Civic engagement, 44, 88, 92, 174

Classifying constituents, 23
Clear communication, 24
Clear systems, importance of, 152
Clickthroughs, analyzing, 56
Climate Campaign, 184
Clinton, Hillary, 48
Cohen, Yael, 174–175
Collaboration and teamwork, xvi, 10, 70, 145, 151, 155, 159, 161, 184. *See also* Partnership opportunities
Collaborative organizations, 146
Collective identity, sharing a, 50
College Explorer study, 44
Colton, Lisa, 50
Committee engagement, 85, 86, 92
Communication: clear and present, importance of, 24; direct, lessening impact of, 95; expectations for, 178; instruments needed for, questionnaire for discussing, 36; one-way, change from, 142; ongoing, encouraging, 160; preferred frequency and methods of, 125; quick, enabling, 162; in the workplace, 151, 158. *See also specific communication tools*
Community service, 7
CompassPoint, 152
Competition, xvi, 13, 116, 184
Computer games, 6
Cone Cause Evolution Study, 44
Congressional Appropriations process, 69
Connected Age, 153
Connected generation. *See* Millennials
Connectedness, importance of, 9, 14. *See also* Social connections
Conscious consumerism, 45
Consistency, 60
Constant Contact, 56
Constituents: with capacity, focus on, 192; classifying, 23; movement of, between organizations and engagement levels, 27; new, building an army of, 160, 185; next generation of, 3, 39; shifting demographics of, 13; today's Millennial, 21; tracking and identifying, 24
Consumer marketing, xi, 45

Content Consumers: described, 25; in the virtuous cycle, 22, *23*
Content creator, role as, 26
Control, illusion of, giving up the, 56, 98, 105
Convenience, 81–82
Conversation creators, 8
Conversion forms, 103, *104*
Conversion rates, high, 25, 93–94
Copycat campaigns, 48
Corporate ladder, 142, 144
Corporation for National and Community Service, 70
Coworkers: as friends, 150; fundraising targeting, *120*, 134; influence of, 126–127; networking with, in the workplace, 157; treatment by, 141. *See also Peer entries and Social media entries*
Creative Capital Pitch Sessions, 175
Creativeness, 9–10, 17, 68, 150, 151, 167, 184, 185, 189
Cross-departmental institutional involvement, 17
Cross-generation collaboration, 172
Cross-generational mentoring, 161
Cross-sector collaborations, appreciation of, 167
Cross-silo collaboration, 146
Crowd funding, 121–122
Crowdrise, 119
Crowdsourcing, 82, 83, 180, 183
Culture change. *See* Organizational change; Social change
Customer relationship management (CRM), shift from, 8
Customer-managed relationship, shift to, 8

D

Daily deal model, 97
Dashboards, 105, 157, 170
Deloitte Volunteer IMPACT study, 86, 88
Democracy in America (Tocqueville), 12
Design thinking, creativity and, 9–10, 17
Determine success, as a guiding principle, 18, *32, 34, 38, 64, 90, 112, 137, 163, 188*
Device choice, importance of, 150

Dial-up Internet, 6

Digital experience, expectations of the, 51–52

Digital media, capitalizing on, 8. *See also specific types of digital media*

"Digital natives" label, xi, 6

Digitally connected, as a trait, 9. *See also* Social media

Direct communication, lessening impact of, 95

Direct contact information, providing, *65*

Direct mail, 60, *120*, 125, 128, 129, 132, 134, 136

Disaster relief, new paradigm for, 67, 138

Discretionary spending, 14, 115

Discrimination, 80

Discussions/forums online. *See* Chat forums

"Donate Now" buttons, 49

Donating. *See* Giving

donorCentrics Internet and Multichannel Giving Benchmarking Report, 128

Donors: age of, as a factor in giving, 128; aspects pertaining to Millennials as, 115–138; aware of leaders' interests, 171; with capacity, focus on, 192; desiring specific requests, 127; as drivers of change, 109; existing, focusing resources on, 3, 115; final thoughts on, 135, *137*; first-time/entry-level, characteristics of, 130, 137; focusing on participation of, not on amount, 124; grassroots model of engaging, 169; level of engagement by, differing viewpoints on, 19–20; next generation of, 3, 39; online-acquired versus mail-acquired, 128; people influencing, 126–127, 130–131, 135; shifting demographics of, 13; slacktivists as, 43

DonorsChoose, 122

Drop-off occurrence, biggest, 25

Dunbar, Robin, 107

"Dunbar's Number," 107

Duval, Jared, 185

Dynamic leaders, 170–171

Dynamics of Cause Engagement (Georgetown University and Ogilvy Worldwide), 43

E

Earth Day, 80

Economic change, 193. *See also* U.S. economy

Education organizations, support for, 130

Egypt, 149

Election, historic, 4, 7–8

Elliot, Brian, 93–94, 100

Email, 2, 6, 8, 43, 50, 57, 58, 60, 72, 94, 119, 138; flexibility with, in the workplace, 150; frequency of, 110; giving in response to, 128, 129; preferences involving, 125, 126, 129

Email campaign management programs, 56

Emma, 56

Employee benefits, 149–151, 162

Employee recognition, 88

Employee retention, 88

Empowerment, in the workplace, 146

Encouragement, two-way, providing, 179

Energy Action Coalition, 184, 185

E-newsletters, 56, 57, 58, 60. *See also* Email

Engagement concepts: new, 19–20, 21; outdated, 19, 20

Engagement continuum, building a new, 80–85

Engagement levels: individual, defining, as a virtuous cycle, 22–27; and the one-third model, 73; peer- and group-based, defining, 27–31; of slacktivists, 43–44. *See also specific types of engagement and levels*

Engagement questionnaire, for nonprofits, 35–36

Engagement strategy, platform for an. *See* Millennial Engagement Platform

Environmental factors, affect of, 6–7

Episodic volunteering. *See* Short-term volunteering

Epstein, Daniel, 171

Event participation, 62; events with influential speakers and, 127; peer fundraising and, *120*; slacktivists and, 43; special-event fundraising and, 96, 117; types of fundraising events and, 131, 132

Event registration, 58, 117

Event-based group engagement, 28, 117, 118, 119, 131–132, 135, *137*

Events online, 43

Executive leaders: expecting to be heard by, 151; future, 165; as mentors, *189*; special note to, 39, 65, 91–92, 113, 138, 141, 164, 189;

transparency with, 155. *See also* Millennial leaders; Nonprofit leaders

Expectations: adopting high, of Millennial leadership, 186–187; specific, need for, in board-CEO relationship, 178–179

Expertise, influence of, 98

External outreach model, 159

F

F*ck Cancer, 175

Facebook, xvi, 4, 8, 11, 15, 19, 41, 51, 52, *65*, 83, 88, 97, 101; actual giving via, *129*, 130, 133; and branding consistency, 60; branding opportunities on, 109–110; call to action on, 67; censoring and, 106; counting fans on, issue of, 56–57; coworkers connected via, 150, 157; creating a page on, 61, 93–94; frequency of updating, 53; liking on, 42, 62, 109; networking in the workplace with, 157; partnering with Causes, 49, 50; and peer fundraising, *120*, 134; peer influence and, 91, 96, 134; preferences involving, 125, 126; privacy and, 58; promotion through, 72; security concerns involving, 133; survey on, 89; word-of-mouth marketing and, 46, 47, 54

Face-to-face contact, preference for, 60, 126–127, 135. *See also* Personal asks

Failing forward, as a leadership trait, 176–177

Faith-based causes, support for, 130

Family: fundraising targeting, *120*, 134; influence of, on donors, 126–127, 130–131, 135; mission-life balance involving, 159. *See also Social media entries*

Fearless organizations, becoming, 193

Feedback, 11, 27, 47, *65*, 72, 87, 89, 118–119, 153, 156

Feedback loop, 56–57

Feedback mechanisms, providing, 59, 156

Feedback sites, 46–48

Feeding America, 121

Filtering, 53

Financial reporting, importance of, 131

Financial resources, needed, questionnaire for discussing, 36

Financial supporter, role as, 26–27

Fine, Allison, 10, 50, 99, 145

First impressions, 55, 87, 104, 126

Flexibility, 68, 86, 150, 151, 154, 158, 167, 184

Focus groups, 27, 87, 102, 133, 168

Focused leaders, 169–170

Following, 14, 62, 99, 170

Follow-up, importance of, 89. *See also* Feedback

Ford Motor Company, 45

Formative years, 6–7

For-profit workplaces, 142, 143, 154, 158, 193

Free agents, 10, 94, 99, 100, 101, 103, 104, 105, 113, 192. *See also* Peer Agents and Influencers

Friendfactor, 94

Friending, 14

Friends: coworkers as, 150; fundraising targeting, *120*, 134; influence of, 126–127, 130, 131; mission-life balance involving, 158–159. *See also Peer entries and Social media entries*

Friends of the Earth, 165

From Command to Community: A New Approach to Leadership Education in Colleges and Universities (Gibson and Longo), 187

Fun events, importance of, 131–132

Fundly, 119

Fundraising practices, 10, 53, 95, 96, 117, 119–123, 131–132, 133–134; biggest pet peeves about, 134; common mistakes in, avoiding, *120*; special note to executive leaders about, 138. *See also* Donors; Giving

G

Game-related activities, 131, 132

Gap, the, 78

Gay rights, 93–94

Gen X-ers, xv, 4, *5*, 34, 56, 79, 150, 153, 161, 192

Gen Y label, 3, 170, 175

Generation C label, 41, 61

Generation Connected. *See* Millennials

Generations, described, *5*. *See also* Baby Boomers; Gen X-ers; Millennials; Traditionalists

Generations: The History of America's Future, 1584 to 2069 (Strauss and Howe), 3

Georgetown University's Center for Social Impact Communication, 43

Gibson, Cynthia, 187

Gift size, avoiding focus on, 26–27

"Give Brian Equality" page, 93–94

Giving: alumni, expectations of, 15; annual, 118, 122; basing engagement on amount of, issue of, 20; as civic engagement, 92; correlation between volunteering and, 70; ease of, importance of, 132–133; by friends, family, and coworkers, *120*; gap in amount of, 123–124; incremental, through various means, 127–128, 130, 132; key takeaways on, *138*; likeliness of, 92; and the Millennial Engagement Platform, *137*; motivations for, 99, 126, 130–131, 133; nature of Millennial, and trends, 123–134; online, 43, 44, *120*, 128, 129, 132, 133, 135; preferred channels for, 128, 129–130; preferred means of soliciting donors for, 126–127; preferred technology for, 126; special note to executive leaders about, 138; specific requests for, importance of, 127; tangible, providing opportunities for, 10; text, 57–58, 107, 116–117, 126, *129*, 130, 133, 138; trust and, 130–131. *See also* Donors; Fundraising practices; Volunteering

Giving circles, 73, 122, 123, 130

Giving habits, 116, 127–130

Giving plans: gap in, 123–124; over time, 128

Giving preferences, 129

Giving Sum, 73–74

Global Citizen Year, 70

Global citizens, 6

Global Fund to Fight AIDS, Tuberculosis and Malaria (GFATM), 44

Global Health Corps, 70, 77–78

Global society, understanding our, asking about, 166

Global warming, 80

Going-against-the-norm leaders, 176

Golden Rule, 62

Google, 4, 25, 55, 106, 125

Google+ Hangouts, 157

Gore, Al, 80

Government sector, 12, 169, 192

Grassroots engagement, 96, 106, 169, 175

Great Nonprofits, 48, 72, 110

Great Schlep, The, 8

Greatest Generation. *See* Traditionalists

Gross Domestic Product (GDP), 13

Group engagement. *See* Peer- and group-based engagement

Group volunteering, *81*

Group-based consumption, 97

Groupon, 97

H

Habitat for Humanity, 191

Hais, Michael, 7

Haiti earthquake, 6, 67, 68, 106–107, 116, 126, 176, 191

Hands Across America, 96, 117

Harvard Business Review, 145

Harvard Business School, 47, 93

Harvard University, 95, 106

Hashtags, 50, 51

Hewlett Foundation, 165

Hierarchy, xii, 13, 65, 144, 145, 151, 152, 155, 166, 177, 180

Hispanic Millennial population, 4

Historical events, key, xii, *5*, 6–7

Homepages, optimizing websites beyond, 55, 110

Honesty, 2, 52, 135, 145, 155, 180, 181

Hope Phones, 176

Howe, Neil, 3

Huffington Post, 69

Hughes, Chris, 8

Human capital, capitalizing on, 185

Human resources, needed, questionnaire for discussing, 35

Human services organizations, support for, 130

Humane Society, 108

Humanizing online interactions, 52–55

Hurricane Andrew, 117

Hurricane Katrina, 6, 191

Hurst, Aaron, 75

I

Identified.com, 150

Identify key change makers, as a guiding principle, 18, *32*, 34, *38*, *64*, *90*, *112*, *137*, *163*, *188*

"Ideocracy," 152

Images and video, use of, 26, *65*, 131

Immediacy, 51, 52

Impact: broader, with partnerships, 184, 185; long-term, testing a new approach's potential for, 176; operationalizing the, continued quest for, 146, 156, 167; perceived lack of, as a barrier, 123; seeing, from nonprofit work, 153, 164, 170; showing, importance of, 88–89, 133–134, 135

Impact studies, 86, 87–88

Impulsivity, 8, 10, 24, 116, 117, 132, 133, 135

Inconvenient Truth, An (documentary), 80

Individual engagement: defining, 22–27; levels of, 24–27; virtuous cycle of, 22, *23*

Influencers, defining, 97. *See also* Peer Agents and Influencers

Information: access to, importance of, 11; searching for, preferences in, 55, 125; sharing, in collaborative organizations, 146; specific, role of, in giving decisions, 131; substantive, desire for, 124–125

Information overload, 103

Infrastructure needs, questionnaire for discussing, 35–36

Innovation: asking about, 166; pioneering, 180

Inquisitors: described, 24; in the virtuous cycle, 22, *23*

Instant messaging, 88, 125, 150, 157

Institutional survival, issue of, 192

Interconnected society, understanding today's, 166, 193

Interest graphs: defining, 108; examples of, 108–109; leveraging, 109–110

Internal service delivery model, issue with, 159

Internet: dial-up, 6; importance of the, 149; rise of the, 11–12; searching for supporters and cause champions on the, 108; world without the, 8. *See also Online entries and Web entries*

Internet and American Life project, 106

Invisible Children, 46

Inviting engagement, 23

iPads, 82

iPhone, 57

J

Japan earthquake and tsunami, 116

Jesuits, 68

Jewish Millennials, 8

John Hopkins Nonprofit Economic Data Project, 13

Johnson Grossnickle and Associates (JGA), 57, 58, 99, 103, 115

K

KaBOOM!, 84, 122

Kanter, Beth, 10, 50, 51, 99

Katchpole, Molly, 48, 49, 51

Kennedy, Robert F., 1

Kennedy Serve America Act, 69

Key takeaways, *65*, *91*, *113*, *138*, *164*, *189*

Kickstarter, 183

Kiva, 122

Knight Foundation, 180

Knowledge barrier, 123

"Komen Kan Kiss My Mammogram" campaign, 50

"Kony 2012" video, 45–46

Kony, Joseph, 46

Kristof, Nick, 48

Kutcher, Ashton, 99

L

Latin America, 176

Lead by engagement, as a guiding principle, 18, *32*, 34, *38*, *64*, *90*, *112*, *137*, *163*, *188*

Leaderless movements, 147–148, 149

Leaders. *See* Executive leaders; Millennial leaders; Nonprofit leaders

Leadership development, 17, 152. *See also* Professional development

Leadership Inviting, as a core component, 17, *32*, 37, *38*, *64*, *90*, *112*, *137*, *163*, *188*

Leadership mentors, 140, 141

Leadership roles: authentic, 86; in a collaborative organization, 146; need to fill, as Boomers retire, 153; shared, 178, 182; in volunteering, *81*, 85–86, 92

Leadership style, asking about, 166

Leadership track, creating a, *164*

Leadership transition, planning for, 165

Legacy building, 88

Level playing field, importance of a, 155

LGBT (lesbian gay bisexual transgender) equality, 93–94

Libya, 149

Liking, 42, 62, 109

LinkedIn, 61

List building, 56, 59

Listening, importance of, 62, 119, 151–152

LIVESTRONG Foundation, 44, 108

Living Social, 97

Longo, Nicholas, 187

Long-term investment, 33

Long-term volunteering, 7, 84–85, 92

Lorax website, 48

Low-threshold activism, 92

Loyalty, concepts of, outdated, 19, 20, 100

Luca, Michael, 47

M

MailChimp, 56

Mailed letters/print communication. *See* Direct mail

Mailing-in donations, 128, 129, 132

Make a Difference Day, 83

Malawi, 176

Maness, Michael, 180

Manufacturing sector, 13

Market segmentation, 56

Marketing. *See specific marketing methods and tools*

Marketing growth, 160

Marquez, Aaron, 69

Martin Luther King, Jr. Day of Service, 83

Martin, Trayvon, 177

Mashable, 98

Matching gifts, 130, 131

Maturation, 124, 130

Maurin, Zach, 69, 172

Mausner, Dvorit, 14–15, 118, 172

McCain, John, 4, 7

Meaning, search for, in the workplace, 68, 142

Meaningful work, views on, 143–144

Media exposure, 48, 96

Medic Mobile, 176

Meetings: board, access to, 155; running, *164*

Mentor reviews, 156

Mentoring, importance of, 161, 179–180, *189*

Mentorship, types of, 161–162

Merchant, Nilofer, 146

Message content, 24, 52, 56, 60, 118, 131

Message exposure, 24

Message redundancy, *120*

Messaging, 7, 26, 28, 52, 98, 100, 103, *104*, 117, 121, 135

Met Opera, 58

mGive, 106

Michael J. Fox Foundation, 121

Microfinance, 122

Micro-volunteering, 75, 81–82, *82*–83, 85, 170

Middle East tensions, 6

Migrant Workers, 80

Millennial Branding, 150

Millennial Donors Study, 99, 123

Millennial Engagement Platform: components of the, described, 16–17; creating a strategy for the, 22–23, 34–37; in detail, *38*; donor giving and the, *137*; guiding principles for the, described, 17–18; implementing the, 33–34; institutionalizing the, 39; introduction to the, 31–33; and Millennial nonprofit leaders, 187, *188*; and the nonprofit workplace, *163*, *164*; peer influence and the, *112*; social media and the, 63, *64*; special note to executive leaders about the, 39; summary of the, 37; volunteering and the, *90*. *See also specific aspects of Millennial engagement*

Millennial Impact Report, 57, 58, 60, 70, 72, 74, 77, 85, 96, 103, 116, 123, 128, 133

Millennial leaders: aspects pertaining to, 165–189; building new partnerships, 184–186; characteristics of, 168–177, 189;

high expectations of, 186–187; key takeaways on, *189*; and the Millennial Engagement Platform, 187, *188*; special note to executive leaders about, 189; spotlight on, 182–183; and working with boards, 177–180, *189*; and working with stakeholders and funders, 180–182

Millennials: ability of, to be involved, analyzing potential challenges affecting, 36–37; characteristics of, xi, xii, xiii, xv, xvi, 4, *5*, 6, 9–11, 14, 70, 116, 184, 189, 192, 193; "coming of age" phase of, 4, 191; demands placed on, 14; environmental factors affecting, 6–7; as ethnically and racially diverse, 4; evolving world of, 17, 18; first use of, as a term, 3; formative years of, 6–7; as a generational category, years defining, 3–4, *5*; historic election involving, 4, 7–8; importance of caring about, xii, xiii, xiv, 135; intention of, xv–xvi; key historical events experienced by, xii, *5*, 6–7, 191; maturation of, 124, 130; minority population of, 6; as the next greatest generation, xiii; other labels for, xi, 3, 6, 41, 61, 170, 175; race/ethnicity of, 4; recognition of, 79–80; recruitment of, 79; retention of, 79; spending power of, 14, 115, 116; and their population size, 4, *5*, 153, 168; tracking the path of, 22; understanding, as an evolving process, 192

"Millennials by design" focus, 15–16

Minority Millennial population, 4, 6

Mission: compelling, importance of a, 130, 131; external outreach model for serving the, 159; furthering the, seeking change for, 156, 167

Mission alignment, 143, 153

Mission-life balance, understanding, 158–159

Missouri, 67

Mistakes, making, 61, 62, 145, 161, 176

Mixed race/ethnic Millennial population, 4

Mobile devices, importance of, 24, 25, 47, 57–59, 81–82, 116–117, 133, 135, 150, 159, 176. *See also* Apps

Mobilize.org, 173–174

Monetary giving: basing engagement on, issue with, 20; gap in amount of, 123–124; and gift

size, avoiding focus on, 26–27; low-threshold activism and, 92; various ways of, to many organizations, 127–130. *See also* Donors; Fundraising practices; Giving

Monterey County Rape Crisis Center, 89

Moore, Mik, 8

More Birthdays, 121

Morrison, Dan, 43

Motivations for giving, 99, 126, 130–131, 133

MTV, 151

Multichannel approach, 59–60, 128, 129, 130, 136, 142

Muscular Dystrophy Association, 96, 117

My.BarackObama.com, 8

N

National Committee for Responsive Philanthropy, 165

National Conference on Citizenship (NCoC), 174

National Council of La Raza, 165

Nesbit, Josh, 176

Net Generation label, 3

Net Impact, 87

Network for Good, 72

Networked model, 168

Networked Nonprofit, The (Kanter and Fine), 10, 99

Network-managed volunteering, 82–85

Networks: core, working with individuals outside of, 95; enabling, in the workplace, 157; leveraging, 86–87, 95. *See also* Social connections; Social media

New How, The (Merchant), 146

New Politics Institute, 4

New professional behavior, *145*

"New Professional, The" (Fine), 145

New York Times, 48

Next Generation Democracy (Duval), 185

No Collar Workers study, 151, 152

Nonprofit leaders: authentic, 141; challenges facing, 2, 15; future, 14, 18, 39, 165; joining in online chats with employees, 157; as mentors, 141, 161, 162; potential, 22, 166; questions for posing to, 166; recommended attributes of, 165–166; today's, focus of, 192. *See also* Board members; Executive leaders; Millennial leaders

Nonprofit sector: full-time employment in the, story tracing the journey to obtain, 139–141; growth of the, 12–13; keeping up with the rate of change, importance of the, 193–194; Millennial view of the, 165, 169; origins and structure of the, 12; traditional way of thinking about the, 12

Nonprofit workplace: aspects pertaining to the, 139–164; challenges and shortcomings in the, 153–154; clear systems supporting the, 152; designing a new environment for the, 164; employee benefits in the, providing new, 149–151; flexibility in the, 150, 151, 154, 158, 167; focus on the work product in the, 144, 147; goals for the, creating new, *164*; investing in new ideas in the, 140; key takeaways on the, 164, *164*; and the Millennial Engagement Platform, *163*, 164; networked, importance of a, 157; nonlinear career path in the, 142–143; physical environment in the, 151; pressures bringing changes to the, 142; senior staff encouraging a Millennial-friendly, *164*; special note to executive leaders about the, 164; status quo in the, reevaluating the, 144–145, 154; technology in the, access to, 149–150, 167; and ten qualities of a successful Millennial-friendly environment, 153–160; and why today's work environment is so different, 144–146

Nonprofits: business models of, relying on peer-based fundraising, 119, 121; changing structure of, 142, 145; competing with for-profits that do good, 143, 193; competition among, xvi, 13, 116, 184; failing at engaging Millennials, xvi, 2–3, 115; formal structure of, struggle to fit in the, 141; infrastructure needs for, questionnaire for discussing the, 35–36; internal issues of, as potential roadblocks to Millennial involvement, addressing, 37; key to successful, 142;

leadership of, meeting the, 131; learning about, preferred methods for, 60; need for, to adapt now, 13–15, 193; number of, in the United States, 60; progressive, 165; readiness of, for Millennial engagement, 16, 192; as real organizations, status of, proving, 62; small, advantage of, 60–61; as social organizations, 42; types of, that are most supported, 130. *See also Organizational entries and specific aspects of nonprofit organizations*

No-vacation policies, 150

Nunn, Michelle, 148

O

Obama, Barack, 4, 7–8

Obama for America campaign, 138

Occupy Wall Street movement, 147–148, 149

Ogilvy Worldwide, 43

Old professional behavior, *145*

One Percent Foundation, 122–123

One Percent Giving Circle (OPGC), 122, 123

One-click actions, 44, 49, 55, 103

One-hit social media campaigns, likeliness of donating to, 126

One-size-fits-all approach, 3

One-third model of engagement, 73

One-time volunteers, *81*

Online activists/activism, 42–44, 148–149

Online communities, 43. *See also* Social media

Online election campaigns, 8, 138

Online giving: actual, 128, 129, 132; common mistake involving, avoiding, *120*; ease of, importance of, 133; as an entry point, 135; preference for, 129; slacktivists and, 43; and social marketing campaigns, 44

Online opportunities, 43

Online space, reserving, 61

Online-acquired donors, 128

Open Graph, 109

Open rates, analyzing, 56

Openness and transparency, xii, xvi, 10, 11, 16, 17, 70, 89, 131, 141, 142, 150, 155, 164, 166, 175. *See also* Tangible Transparency, as a core component

Oprah, 99

Organization spotlight: on Building Tomorrow, 54–55; on Chicago Humanities Festival, 102–103; on Global Health Corps, 77–78; on One Percent Foundation, 122–123; on People for Urban Progress, 182–184; on University of Pennsylvania's Penn Fund, 118–119

Organizational adaptation, 61

Organizational authenticity, 61

Organizational change: certainty of, 162; demand for, 193; difficulty of, 39; to drive greater impact, 156, 167; first step towards, 18; necessary time for, 164; need for, 21; readiness for, 162; that detrimentally affects Millennial advancement, 153–154; trends influencing, 145

Organizational culture, positive, allowing for a, 150–151, 160

Organizational leadership, 140

Organizational role, strengthening the, in the community, 185–186

Organizational shift, 23, 94

Organizational strategic plan, ensuring an engagement strategy falls within the, 34–35

Organizational structure, 13, 141, 142, 145, 146, 152, 155, 167, 177. *See also* Hierarchy

Organizational sustainability, working toward, 153

Organizational updates, accessing, 57

Organizational values, defining and sharing, 146

Our Dream Playground, 84, 122

Outreach versus operations, issue of, 178

Overcharging, *120*

Overposting messages, *120*

Ownership, 113

P

Pakistan, 67

Paperless contact, 110

Participatory democracy model, 148

Parties, 131, 132

Partnership opportunities: allowing, 159–160; building new, approach of Millennial leaders to, 184–186; looking for, 171; visionary, 178

Payroll deductions, giving via, *129*, 130

Peace Corps, 7

Peer Agents and Influencers, 52; conversion rates of, 25; described, 27; event-based group management and, 28; identifying and interacting with, 62; importance of, 97–99; promotion through, 72; self-organized group engagement and, 28; today's, described, 99–100; in the virtuous cycle, 22, *23*; young professional groups and, 29

Peer- and group-based engagement: defining, 27–31; event-based, 28, 117, 118, 119, 131–132, 135, *137*; levels of, 28–29; self-organized, 28; young professional group, 29–31

Peer fundraising, 119–123, 134

Peer identification activity, 34

Peer influence: in action, case studies on, 105–105; aspects pertaining to, 93–113; in giving, 119, 130, 134, 135, 136; giving permission to, 104–105; key takeaways on, *113*; leveraging, 105, 134, 135; and the Millennial Engagement Platform, *112*; old school versus new school, 95–96; power of, 47, 73, 193; special note to executive leaders about, 113; in volunteering, 72; and when it doesn't work, 103–104

Peer recruiting, 172

Peer reviews, 156

Peiper, Audrey, 102, 103

Penn Foundation, 172

Penn Fund, 14–15, 118–119

People for Urban Progress (PUP), 182–184

People's Fleet program, 45

Pepsi Co., 45

Pepsi Refresh program, 45

Personal asks, 27, 128, 129, 135, 136

Personal connection, role of, in decisions to give, 126, 130, 131

Personalized approach, proximity to a, 61

Pet peeves, biggest, about fundraising, 134

Petitions, 27, 42, 44, 48, 50, 92, 106, 177

Pew Research Center, 3–4, 46, 87, 106
Philanthropy: democratizing, 27, 192; ingraining, in everyday life, goal of, 73; lifelong, empowering, 122, 123. *See also* Giving
Phone calls, receiving, issue with, 58
Phone requests, giving in response to, *129*, 130
Phones. *See* Mobile devices; Smartphones; Texting
Physical work environment, 151
Pink Ribbon Revolt, 49–51
Pinterest website, 51
Place-based model, issue with a, 159
Planned Parenthood, 48, 49, 50, 51
Planned Parenthood Saved Me (blog), 50–51
Points of Light Institute, 148
Polarization, 123–124
Political leanings, 4
Polling, 4, 27, *65*, 83, 143
Pollution, 80
Pooling resources, 27, 67, 121
Population figures, 4, 5, 6
Power shift, 49, 145
Print communication/mailed letters. *See* Direct mail
Privacy issues, 58, 151
Private sector, 12, 169. *See also* For-profit workplaces
Pro bono service, 75
Proactive leaders, 169
Professional behavior, new definition of, 145
Professional development: importance of, to Millennials, 153–154; mentorships through, 161, *162*; for Millennial leaders and board members, *189*. *See also* Leadership development
Professional groups. *See* Young professional groups
Protect Internet Piracy Act (PIPA), 106
Public Allies, 85

R
Race/ethnicity, Millennial population by, 4
Rapid adaptation, 61
Rattray, Ben, 177
Razoo, 119

Reciprocity, 101
Recognition, 78, 79–80, 88, 110
Recognition gifts, 127
Recruitment, 78–79
Red Cross, 108–109
Reddit, 106
Referrals, relying on, 94
Reich, Brian, 148–149
Relationship map, 108
Relationship stages, with stakeholders, 181–182
Relationships: authentic, establishing, 135, 180; board-CEO, 177–178; building, 62, 119, 124, 135, 177, 185; importance of, 14, 34, 41, 63, 126, 133, 171; masters of, Millennial leaders as, 173–174; peer, premium placed on, 100; stability of, 107–108; stakeholder-leader, 180–182; technology and, 63, 134, 192; vibrancy built through, 186
Relevancy, 97, 101
Religion, 4
Report on America's Giving Challenge (Case Foundation), 61
Resilient leaders, 171
Resource pooling, 27, 67, 121
Resources allocated to engaging Millennials: nonprofits failing at, 2–3; ongoing, importance of, 17, 33; questionnaire for discussing, 35–36; through technology, 150
Response rates, 110
Responsibility, taking, 176–177
Restoration Hardware, 78
Retail trade sector, 13
Retention, 78, 79, 86–87, 88
Return on investment (ROI), 3, 52, 59, 86, 88
Risk takers, leaders as, 174–175, 186
Risk taking, supporting, 157–158, 167, 174
Risk tolerance, 61
Rock the Vote, 173
Roosevelt, Franklin D., xiii–xiv
Rudat, Stephanie, 50, 51

S
Salary, importance level assigned to, 87, 142, 149, 151, 153, 167, 172
Salvi, Ameet, 78

Saudia Arabia, 48

Schleppers, 8

School-based programs, 117

School-required volunteering, 79–80

Search engines, 55. *See also* Google

Security concerns, 58, 133

Self-aware leaders, 171–172

Self-organization: interest graphs and, 109; origins of, 11–13; power of, and online movements, 48–49; supporting, 26, 48–49; as a trait of Millennials, 10–11, 169; volunteering and, 84

Self-organized group engagement, 28

September 11, 2001, 6, 191

ServeNext, 69, 172

Shift and Reset (Reich), 148–149

Short-term volunteering, 7, 26, 28, 80, 82–83, 83–84, 86, 92

Silent Generation. *See* Traditionalists

Silicon Prairie News, 175

Silos, xii, xiii, 146

Skill sets, making use of, 74–75, *76*, 77, 78, 85, 87, 88, *91*, 134, 170

Skype, 157

Slacktivists, dismissal of, avoiding, 42–44

Slobotski, Jeff, 175

Smartphones, use of, 57–58, 58–59, 133, 135. *See also* Mobile devices, importance of

Smith, David, 174

Smith, Maya Enista, 173, 179–180

Social action sites, 48–49

Social activism, future of, 70, *71*

"Social by design" mantra, 15

Social capital, building, 101

Social change: deeper, providing connections to, 91; drivers of, 6–7, 24, 109, 186, 191, 192; lines between, and business and politics, blurring of, 69; looking beyond barriers to, 171; new agents of, 100, 167, 169; new ways of bringing out about, desire for, 165; old and new approaches to, creating a bridge between, 105; and the rate of change, 193; slacktivists and, 43; social media and, 42; team-based approach to driving, 155; today's

nonprofit influencers of, 99; yearning for, 18, 168–169

"Social citizens" label, xii

Social connections: leveraging, 15, 17, 42; limits of, 107–108. *See also* Networks; Relationships; Social media

Social Connectivity, as a core component, 17, *32*, 33, 37, *38*, *64*, *90*, *112*, *137*, *163*, *164*, *188*

Social graph, 108

Social Justice Fund, 169

Social marketing campaigns, 44–45, 126, 138

Social media, 2, 8, 9, 10, 20, 136, 192; authentic conversations in, building relationships based on, 135; cause champions and, 26; contact via, preference for, 60; expanding reach with, 159; growing influence of, new breed of influencers arising from, 97; influence of, on professional behavior, 145; learning how to leverage, 161; myth about, 41; and the nonprofit workplace, 150, 160, *164*; online opportunities involving, 43, 177; openness and transparency in, 11; optimizing, for peer influence, 104; peer agents and, 27; peer fundraising and, 119, 121; peer influence and developments in, 95; privacy and, 58; providing educational sessions through, *164*; rethinking, as a giving medium, 130; and slacktivism, 42–43; value of, 41, 63, 110, 111; word-of-mouth marketing and, 46–47; young professional groups and, 29. *See also specific social media platforms and tools*

Social media strategy: aspects pertaining to, 42–65; importance of developing a, 42; key takeaways on, *65*; and the Millennial Engagement Platform, 63, *64*; practical tips for building a, 61–62; self-organized, movements and campaigns demonstrating, 48–51, 177; special note to executive leaders about, 65

Social organizations, 42, 63

Social responsibility, unwavering commitment to, 193

Social review sites, 46–48

Social Security, 191

Soliciting preferences, 126–127

Solution-centered, xii, xiii, 10, 17, 147, 155, 171

Solution-Inspired, as a core component, 17, *32*, *33*, 37, *38*, *64*, *90*, *112*, *137*, *163*, *188*

Space shuttle disaster, 6

Sparked.com, 75, 77, 81, 82

Special-event fundraising, 96, 117

Spending power, 14, 115, 116

Spier, Zeke, 169

Sports activities, 131, 132

Spotify, 109

Stakeholder-Millennial leader relationship, 180–182

Starbucks, 109

State of Young America, The (poll), 143

Status quo, reevaluating/challenging the, 144–145, 154, 167, 176

Stereotyping, xv, 9, 125

Stewardship, 118, 119

Stop Internet Piracy Act legislation, 48

Stop Online Piracy Act (SOPA), 106

Strangers, trusting, 108

Strauss, William, 3

Student Sierra Coalition, 185

Study-abroad programs, 166–167

Sudan, 67

Super Bowl, the, 45, 51

Susan G. Komen for the Cure foundation, 48, 49–51

Sustainable organizations, working toward, 153

Sustainable solutions, need for, 15–16

T

Take Back the Pink campaign, 50–51, 101

Talent Report: What Workers Want (Net Impact), 87

Tangible gifting opportunities, providing, 10

Tangible impact, showing, 133, 134

Tangible Transparency, as a core component, 17, *32*, 33, 37, *38*, *64*, *90*, *112*, 135, *137*, *163*, *188*

Taproot Foundation, 75, 85

Tapscott, Don, 3

Teach for America, 70, 191

Team Fox, 121

Team Rubicon, 67, 68

Team-based approach. *See* Collaboration and teamwork

Technological environment, understanding the, 34

Technology: access to, importance of, in the workplace, 149–150, 167; adaptation to, 6; adoption of, paradox of, 41; advancements in, xiii, 6; appeal of, limits to the, 58; comfort level with, asking about, 166; mind-set behind, 63; needed, questionnaire for discussing, 36; and the rate of change, 193, 194; and relationships, 63, 134, 192; significant change in, 193; usage of, 6, 7, 10, 24, 191. *See also specific types of technology*

Temkin Group, 46

Terrorist attacks, 6, 191

Texas, 67

Text giving, 57–58, 107, 116–117, 126, *129*, 130, 133, 138

Text polls, 27

Texting, 4, 8, 9, 14, 41, 43, 57, 58, 125, 150, 176

Thai-Burma border, 67

Thank-yous, 62, 119

Three-sector structure, blending of the, 12

Ticket sales, mobile, 117

Time, donating. *See* Volunteering

Time spent engaging Millennials: nonprofits failing at, 2–3; ongoing, importance of, 17, 33

Tocqueville, Alexis de, 12

Tolerance level, 6

TOMS Shoes, 24

Tracking, 22, 24

Traditional career ladder, 142

Traditional employee benefits, 149

Traditional nonprofit institutions, possibilities for, with Millennial leadership, 187

Traditional organizational structure, 142, 145. *See also* Hierarchy

Traditionalists: described, 5; as the Greatest Generation, xiii, 192; as the Silent Generation, 153; in the workplace, 5, 153

Transparency. *See* Openness and transparency

Traveling abroad, 166

Trend setters, xi

TripAdvisor, 47

Trophy Kids Grow Up, The (Alsop), 5, 80

Trust, 4, 11, 47, 98, 99, 101, 110, 130–131, 135, 138, 156, 180, 181, 186, 187, 193

Tumblr, 50

Tunisia, 149

Tupperware parties, 95

Tweeting, 4, 8, 9, 14, 43, 51, 57, 62, 106, 116

Twitter, xvi, 8, 41, 44, 51, 52, 88; censoring and, 106; counting followers on, issue of, 56–57; creating an account on, 61; and peer fundraising, *120*; peer influence and, 96; preferences involving, 125; reciprocity in action via, 101; word-of-mouth marketing and, 46, 47

2008 election, 4, 7–8

U

Uganda, 46, 54, 55

Understand their environment, as a guiding principle, 18, *32*, 33–34, *38*, *64*, *90*, *112*, *137*, *163*, *188*

United Way, 100

Universal Studios, 48

University of Pennsylvania, 14–15, 118–119, 172

Unreasonable Institute, 171

U.S. Army Reserves, 69

U.S. Congress, 69, 106, 172

U.S. economy: current, effect of, on Millennials, xiii, 142, 143; growing up in a fragile, effect of, xii; largest sectors of, 13; significant change in, 193

U.S. Postal Service, 43

User-generated content (UGC): expansion of, 110; influence of, 108

V

Valued, importance of feeling, 144

Vaynerchuk, Gary, 98

Veterans, skills of, leveraging, xiii, 67

Vietnam War, 80

Viewing trends, analyzing, 56

VIP experience, providing a, 118, 119

Viral marketing, 45–46

Virtual Food Drive program, 121

Virtual workdays, 151

Visionary leaders, 174

Visionary partnership, 178

Volunteer advisory committee, *91*

Volunteer Match, 72

Volunteer resources, needed, questionnaire for discussing, 36

Volunteering: on boards, 85–86, 92, 124; continuum of, *81*, 92; convenience in, 81–82; crowdsourcing and, 82, 83; gap in amount of, 124; group, *81*; guidelines for engaging Millennials in, 88–91; impact from, showing, importance of, 88–89; leadership roles in, *81*; long-term, 7, 84–85, 92; micro-, 75, 81–82, 82–83, 85, 170; and the Millennial Engagement Platform, *90*; network-managed, 82–85; online, 43, 44; opportunities for, 72; percentage of Millennials that are, 70, 72; preferences for, 74–75, *76*; preferred means of soliciting donors for, 126–127; return on investment in, 86; school-required, 79–80; short-term, 7, 26, 28, 80, 82–83, 83–84, 86, 92; specific requests for, importance of, 127; in the workplace, 87–88. *See also* Calls to action; Giving

Volunteering in America Report, 70

Volunteering plans, gap in, 124

Volunteers: with capacity, focus on, 192; as drivers of change, 109; next generation of, 39; one-time, *81*; online forum for chatting with, *189*; recognition of, 78, 79–80, 88; recruitment of, 78–79; retention of, 78, 79, 86–87; role as, 26; skilled, access to, 170; slacktivists as, 43; structures for, 7

Voter turnout, 4, 7, 8

Voting online, 43

W

Wales, Jimmy, 106

Wallach, Ari, 8

Ward, Amy Sample, 50, 51, 105

Washington Post, 148

WaterForward campaign, 53
Watson, Tom, 51
Wealth transfer, 14
Web-based giving. *See* Online giving
Web-enabled/wireless devices. *See* Mobile devices, importance of
Website contact, preference for, 60
Websites: branded, for peer fundraising, 121; looking to, for volunteering, 72; optimization of, 24, 25, 55, 58–59, 104, 110; what to avoid with, *120. See also specific online platforms and campaigns*
Welcome guides, *91*
White Millennial population, 4
Wiki campaign, 50
Wikipedia, 4, 106
William and Flora Hewlett Foundation, 165
Williams, Erica, 170–171
Winograd, Morley, 7
Wireless devices. *See* Mobile devices, importance of
Wood, Jake, 67, 68
Word-of-mouth marketing (WOMM), 46–47, 54, 102
Work product, focus on the, versus work processes, 144, 147
Work-life balance, 150, 154, 158, 172, 192
Work-life blending, embracing, 143, 192–193

Workplace: four generations in the, *5*; fundraising in the, 131; generations in the, *5*, 153; older generations in the, 142, 144, 153, 155, 158, 159, 160; reshaping of the, 151; searching for meaning in the, 68, 142, 143; successfully entering the, as a factor in giving, 124; traditional, delaying entry into the, 68; volunteering in the, 87–88. *See also* Nonprofit workplace
World Wildlife Fund, 109

Y

Yelp, 47
Yemen, 149
Young Alumni Participation, 172
Young Invincibles, 143
Young professional groups: as an engagement strategy, pros and cons of, 29–31; as a group engagement level, 29; spotlight on, 102–103
Younger generation. *See* Millennials
YouTube, 4, 49, 61, 97
YPenn program, 118
YPulse, 97

Z

Zandt, Deanna, 50
Zanzibar, 78
Zipcar, 24